Medieval Germany, 500–1300
A Political Interpretation

D0609687

European History in Perspective
General Editor: Jeremy Black

Published
Benjamin Arnold   *Medieval Germany, 500–1300*
Ronald Asch   *The Thirty Years War*
Christopher Bartlett   *Peace, War and the European Powers, 1814–1914*
Mark Galeotti   *Gorbachev and his Revolution*
Peter Waldron   *The End of Imperial Russia, 1855–1917*

Forthcoming
Nigel Aston   *The French Revolution*
N. J. Atkin   *The Fifth French Republic*
Ross Balzaretti   *Medieval Italy: A Cultural History*
Robert Bireley   *The Counter Reformation*
Donna Bohanan   *Crown and Nobility in Early Modern France*
Robin Brown   *Warfare in Twentieth-Century Europe*
Patricia Clavin   *The Great Depression, 1929–39*
Roger Collins   *Charlemagne*
Geoff Cubitt   *Politics in France, 1814–1876*
John Foot   *The Creation of Modern Italy*
Alexander Grab   *Napoleon and the Transformation of Europe*
O. P. Grell   *The European Reformation*
Nicholas Henshall   *The Zenith of Absolute Monarchy, 1650–1750*
Colin Imber   *The Ottoman Empire, 1300 1481*
Martin Johnson   *The Dreyfus Affair*
Timothy Kirk   *Germany and the Third Reich*
Peter Linehan   *Medieval Spain, 589–1492*
Marisa Linton   *The Causes of the French Revolution*
Simon Lloyd   *The Crusading Movement*
William S. Maltby   *The Reign of Charles V*
David Moon   *Peter the Great's Russia*
Peter Musgrave   *The Early Modern European Economy*
Kevin Passmore   *The French Third Republic, 1870–1940*
J. L. Price   *The Dutch Republic in the Seventeenth Century*
Roger Price   *1848: A Year of Revolution*
A. W. Purdue   *The Second World War*
Maria Quine   *A Social History of Fascist Italy*
Martyn Rady   *The Habsburg Monarchy, 1848–1918*
Francisco J. Romero-Salvado   *A History of Contemporary Spain*
Richard Sakwa   *Twentieth-Century Russia*
Thomas J. Schaeper   *The Enlightenment*
Brenda Simms   *A History of Germany, 1779–1850*
Graeme Small   *Later Medieval France*
David Sturdy   *Louis XIV*
Hunt Tooley   *The Western Front*
Peter G. Wallace   *The Long European Reformation*
Patrick Williams   *Philip II*
Peter Wilson   *From Reich to Revolution: Germany, 1600–1806*

Medieval Germany 500–1300

A Political Interpretation

BENJAMIN ARNOLD

First published 1997 by
MACMILLAN PRESS LTD
Houndmills, Basingstoke, Hampshire RG21 6XS
and London
Companies and representatives
throughout the world

ISBN 0–333–61091–1 hardcover
ISBN 0–333–61092–X paperback

A catalogue record for this book is available
from the British Library.

This book is printed on paper suitable for recycling and
made from fully manged and sustained forest sources.

10   9   8   7   6   5   4   3   2   1
06 05 04 03 02 01 00 99 98 97

Copy-edited and typeset by Povey–Edmondson
Tavistock and Rochdale, England

Printed in Hong Kong

To the memory of my teachers of medieval history
Karl Leyser
Bruce McFarlane
Beryl Smalley
Michael Wallace-Hadrill

Contents

vii

Preface and Acknowledgements

The purpose of this book is to promote a clearer understanding of politics in medieval Germany, which is so often remarked upon as different in its political structure from the other kingdoms in medieval Europe. There is no continuous narrative of political history, but guidance on three central features which were politically interactive: the peoples or *gentes* of medieval Germany and their enduring diversity; the neo-Roman western Empire adopted by the Franks and the Germans, and its impact; and the consequences of German kingship with its various institutional arrangements.

The notes and bibliography are deliberately short, and represent only a fraction of works and sources consulted over the years.

BENJAMIN ARNOLD

Reading, England
March 1996

The author and publishers are grateful to the following authors and to their publishers for permission to reproduce copyright material: Alan Sutton for R. Vaughan, *Chronicles of Matthew Paris* (1984); Addison Wesley Longman for T. Reuter, *Germany in the Early Middle Ages* (1991), J. Sayers, *Innocent III. Leader of Europe* (1993), I. Wood, *The Merovingian Kingdoms* (1994); Columbia University Press for E. Emerton, *The Correspondence of Pope Gregory VII* (1932, 1969), B. McGinn, *Visions of the End* (1979), C. C. Mierow, *The Deeds of Frederick Barbarossa* (1953), T. E. Mommsen and K. F. Morrison, *Imperial Lives and Letters* (1962); Edward Arnold for R. Folz, *The Concept of Empire in Western Europe* (1969), H. R. Loyn and J. Percival, *The Reign of Charlemagne* (1975); George Allen & Unwin for B. H. Hill, *Medieval Monarchy in Action* (1972); Hambledon Press for K. J. Leyser, *Medieval Germany and its Neighbours* (1982); Leuven University Press for W. Verbeke, D. Verhelst and A. Welkenhuysen, *The Use and Abuse of Eschatology in the Middle Ages* (1988); Manchester University Press for T. Reuter, *The Annals of Fulda* (1992); Notre Dame University Press for F. J. Tschan, *Saint Bernward of Hildesheim*, vol.1 (1942); Oxford University Press for H. E. Mayer, *A History of the Crusades* (1972, 1988); Penguin Books for L. Thorpe, *Einhard and Notker. Two Lives of Charlemagne* (1969); Routledge for G. P. Fehring, *The Archaeology of Medieval Germany* (1991), F. A. Wright, *The Works of Liudprand of Cremona* (1930); University of California Press for J. Bumke, *Courtly Culture: Literature and Society in the High Middle Ages* (1991); University of Pennsylvania Press for H. Turtledove, *The Chronicle of Theophanes* (1982).

Every effort has been made to contact all the copyright-holders, but if any have been inadvertently omitted the publishers will be pleased to make the necessary arrangement at the earliest opportunity.

Introduction: German Political Identity in the Middle Ages

In the art of historiography as practised in Germany in the Middle Ages as well as in the diplomatic language used by the royal chancery there, it proved well nigh impossible for a precise definition of the German polity to be established. This is partly to be explained by the fact that the diverse provinces of which medieval Germany was made up were at first incorporated into the much larger empire of the Franks, a process virtually completed during the reign of Charlemagne (768–814), except for the Slavic regions assimilated later on. This empire took the name of 'Roman' soon after 800. When it was finally divided into three kingdoms by Charlmagne's grandsons in 842 and 843, the German part was quite naturally designated the 'kingdom of the eastern Franks' and the label endured as late as the twelfth century.[1] In the tenth century this East Frankish kingdom, united since 961 with the Lombard kingdom consisting of northern Italy and Tuscany and combined with the Slav conquests made by the Saxons since the 920s, was consigned to a new West Roman Empire symbolised by the Saxon ruler Otto the Great's imperial coronation in Rome in February 962. The kingdom of Burgundy, mostly French- or Provençal-speaking, was added by inheritance and military force between 1032 and 1034.

Thus far we have Franks, Romans, Lombards, Slavs, Saxons, Burgundians, Provençals — so where are the Germans? Their identity by language, or more correctly, by languages, long preceded any realistic national or racial category. In 788 Charlemagne as Frankish ruler summoned a council to Ingelheim on the Rhine, not far from Mainz. According to the source he persuaded 'the Franks and

1

Bavarians, Lombards and Saxons' to agree to the deposition of Duke Tassilo III of Bavaria for treason. The report is in Latin, but the proceedings appear to have taken place *theodisca lingua*, 'in the language of the people', the Latin invention of phrase being based upon the Old High German word *thiot* meaning people.[2] But which people? It is not likely that separate Germanic tongues such as Frankish, Bavarian, Lombard and Saxon would have been mutually comprehensible, and in any case the vernacular employed by the Lombards was, by this date, in all probability the form of sub-Latin current in northern Italy. So the one vernacular word given in the text, *harisliz* or 'desertion from the army', may have needed elaboration to the assembly at Ingelheim. Duke Tassilo III was convicted of refusing military support to Charlemagne's father, King Pepin the Short, for the campaign against Aquitaine in 763. This was more or less a trumped-up charge. The motive was to confiscate Bavaria in order to secure the frontiers and communications in the East, in preparation for the onslaught upon the Avar khanate undertaken by the Franks between 791 and 803.

It is not possible to ascertain whether *harisliz* as preserved in the *Annales regni Francorum* is nearer to the Frankish, Bavarian or Saxon tongues, although Frankish is more likely. As far as we know, the Frankish language was in decline in the eighth century as Romance or Old French took over in the Gallic provinces actually settled by the Franks, except for a broad strip of territory immediately west of the Rhine. Writing in 817 shortly after Charlemagne's death, his friend and biographer Einhard claimed that the emperor was interested in reviving the Frankish tongue, giving as his example the names of the months and the winds which were standardised according to the theory of the court.[3] Some of these names were used unchanged in medieval German and survived even into modern times. The relation of Frankish to Middle High German was therefore close, but this does little to enlighten the linguistic problem posed by the council at Ingelheim: that the Franks, Saxons, Bavarians and Lombards spoke different dialects.

Looking at the puzzle another way, it transpires that the medieval Germans were not one people but several: Saxons, Franconians, Lotharingians, Swabians (or Alemanni as an alternative description) and Bavarians. The Raetians and Carinthians inhabiting the Alpine valleys usually counted as separate peoples into the bargain. So did the coastal Frisians and, inland, the Thuringians, the neighbours of the Saxons to the north-west and south-east respectively, their history often influenced by Saxon domination. These divisions into *gentes* or peoples are essential for understanding the social, legal and political structure of medieval Germany, as well as its economic and linguistic variety. But it proved by no means impossible to create a *regnum* or kingdom out of them.[4] The first time this was attempted was during the 830s as Charlemagne's grandsons quarrelled amongst themselves and with their own father, Emperor Louis the Pious, to secure individual inheritances of their own. Just as the *Annales regni Francorum* for 788 imply mutual comprehension for a political purpose, so does Nithard's significant narrative about the deal struck in 842 for the partition of the Frankish Empire into autonomous kingdoms. But Nithard sets about it by emphasising linguistic differences.

Charles the Bald, king of West Francia, and Louis, king of East Francia, met at Strasbourg in February 842 and again agreed to set upon their elder brother, Emperor Lothar I, king of Italy. Having already defeated him at the Battle of Fontenoy in 841, they were successful in their enterprise, and the Empire was divided into three parts, one for each brother, by the Treaty of Verdun in 843. Nithard reports that at Strasbourg, Charles and Louis had sworn oaths of mutual support, Charles 'in the German tongue', *teudisca lingua*, and Louis 'in the Romance tongue', *romana lingua*,[5] so that the officers in the armies which they had brought with them would comprehend the obligations mutually undertaken. It is sometimes claimed that the story is a confection by Nithard, an illegitimate grandson of Charlemagne, in order to tidy up the dynasty's history. Yet the general implication is that the peoples whom King Louis then ruled, the Saxons, Franconians, Swabians and Bavarians, ought to have understood something put to them in what philologists call Old High German.

But we are still a long way from a German kingdom or a German people, although Louis has later been called, quite erroneously, 'Louis the German' to suit historiographical fashion. Louis was a Frank and his descendants were kings of East Francia, and for the sake of legitimacy the title persisted into the next century. When the first king from the Saxon dynasty, Henry I, met his western colleague Charles the Simple at Bonn in 921, they were duly recorded in their treaty as *rex Francorum orientalium*, 'king of the eastern Franks', and *rex Francorum occidentalium*, 'king of the western Franks', respectively.[6] But the literary culture of the tenth and eleventh centuries turned the eastern Franks into Germans all the same, employing a model from classical Latin which was, as we shall see, quite inappropriate; the name of Teuton.

As he wrote up his report about his recent but unsuccessful embassy to Constantinople in 969, Bishop Liudprand of Cremona complained that both the Latin and the Teutonic peoples had been insulted in his hearing at the Byzantine court.[7] 'Latin' and 'Teutonic' were stylish labels for the Italians and Germans, the subjects of Liudprand's employer, Emperor Otto the Great. A bit later than this, the Saxon bishop Thietmar of Merseburg, who died in 1018, also used Teuton and Teutonic for the Germans in order to distinguish them from the Lombards and the Slavs.[8] The imperial chaplain Wipo, biographer of Emperor Conrad II (1024–39), similarly used Teuton to describe imperial subjects north of the Alps as opposed to Italians.[9]

A generation later the annalist Lampert of Hersfeld was making greater use of *teutonicus* for the people and region north of the Alps, but often in a sense actually hostile to rule by the king.[10] In narrating the confrontations between Henry IV (1056–1106) and the Saxons which began in 1073 and between the king and Pope Gregory VII (1073–85) which broke out in 1076, Lampert was extremely antipathetic to the king and may well have adopted from papal letters the idea of using Teutonic for German in order to confine the authority of Henry IV to one kingdom as opposed to the more formidable and universal power which the German rulers normally claimed as Roman emperors.[11] Although the king's father, Emperor Henry III, had rationally been entitled *rex Teutonicorum* or 'king of the Teutons' in an imperial diploma drawn up in 1049,[12] this quite new accolade had rather blown up in the face of Henry IV when it was used by his enemies.

The lesson was rubbed in at Canossa Castle in January 1077 when one of the most dramatic meetings in diplomatic history was played out, the submission of Henry IV to Gregory VII as a penitent excommunicate. The king's oath to the pope drawn up by the papal scribe entitles him *rex Teutonicorum* and his opponents in Germany, the archbishops, bishops, dukes, counts and other princes in the *regnum Teutonicorum*.[13] Under such circumstances it is hardly surprising that this 'Teutonic' label was not adopted by the German royal chancery until the dust had settled, in the twelfth century. It is also prudent to regard the report for 920 in the Salzburg Annals that the Bavarians elected their duke Arnulf to the *regnum Teutonicorum* – the discovery of this in 1921 obviously excited scholarly debate – as a twelfth-century interpolation, exactly when one might expect it on cultural and linguistic grounds.[14]

The quest for a post-Frankish political identity for the Germans runs into difficulties because the word 'Teutonic' was an elitist literary adjective not well fitted to the diverse group of peoples north of the Alps and east of the Rhine. Its adoption derived not from popular parlance but from the classical Roman heritage enjoyed by a small clerical minority in the medieval West. Latin authors in antique times had quite often employed Teuton as a synonym for German, ironically in that the tribe of the Teutons which had invaded Gaul was annihilated by the Roman general Marius in 103 BCE. But the primitive ferocity of the Teutons was long remembered by the Romans, and was applied by a forced analogy to the Germans as a whole, simply because their bellicosity was much feared in the classical Roman Empire. Yet Tacitus in his treatise *Germania* did not even mention the Teutons, while Pliny identified them merely as a clan of the Ingaevones, themselves supposedly a subdivision of the ancient Germans.[15]

It is likely that medieval German authors were struck by the philological similarity between the first syllable of Latin *teutonicus* and Middle High German *diutsch*, the forerunner of the modern word *deutsch* meaning German. This is borne out by a chancery diploma for the archbishop of Salzburg in 977 which mentions a mountain *qui Diutisce vocatur* (called in German) Wassenberg, but other diploma writers preferred the phrase *Teutonica lingua*, 'in the German tongue', at this time.[16]

According to Thangmar's biography of Bishop Bernward of Hildesheim, Otto III referred in a speech delivered in 1001 to *mei Saxones et cuncti Theotisci, sanguis meus*, 'my Saxons and all Germans, my blood'.[17] At the end of the eleventh century, Abbot Norbert of Iburg wrote that by the time Charlemagne had conquered the Saxons, he had united *universa gens Teutonica*, 'the whole German race', under one rule.[18] The analogy was carried forward by the authors of the twelfth century. Well-informed chroniclers such as Frutolf of Michelsberg and Ekkehard of Aura used it often. Ekkehard pointed out that the *populus Theutonicus* did not respond to the First Crusade because Empire and Papacy were at loggerheads: 'This trumpet call hardly resounded amongst the Franconians, the Saxons and Thuringians, the Bavarians and Alemannians . . . .'.[19] Provost Gerhoh of Reichersberg, a learned Bavarian churchman, used *teutonicus* in a charter he drew up for King Conrad III to authenticate in 1142. Abbot Wibald of Corvey employed *Theotonicus* in the letter he wrote to Pope Eugenius III in 1152 to announce Frederick Barbarossa's election as German king.[20] In their account of the early years of this reign, Bishop Otto of Freising and his continuator Rahewin were quite liberal with the adjective *teutonicus* as well.[21]

As early as 1030 the verb *teutonizare* had been invented in dog-Latin to mean 'naming something in German'. Meginfrid of Magdeburg applied it to the city-name of Regensburg in his biography of St Emmeram, and in 1079 Berthold of Reichenau wrote of ballistic siege engines being used in the current civil war that they were called mangonels in German, *theutonizant*.[22] And since an autonomous kingdom east of the Rhine had persisted for more than three centuries by the time that Otto and Rahewin were composing the *Gesta Frederici*, one might have been permitted to think that the description Teutonic in succession to Frankish would by then have prevailed. But this was not so. Towards the end of the eleventh century the adjective *aleman* was adopted into Old French to designate Teutonic or German speakers. This is difficult to explain, because the medieval language line between French and German ran through the province of Lotharingia, not Alemannia (i.e. Swabia) at all. Nevertheless, *aleman* was at once rendered back into literary Latin as the description for Germans and Germany, and was rapidly taken up in the German kingdom as well. For example, when Helmold of Bosau mentioned the leaders of the Second Crusade in his *Chronicle of the Slavs*, he called Conrad III king of Alemannia and Louis VII king of Francia. Shortly before this, when the royal chancery drew up a letter to send to Emperor Manuel I at Constantinople, Conrad III's subjects were described as *Alemanni* in one sentence and *Teutonici* in the next.[23] Bishop Otto of Freising disapproved of such novelties:

> Some think that the whole Teutonic land is called Alemannia and that all Teutons should be called Alemannians, but only that province which is Swabia . . . should be called Alemannia and solely the people inhabiting it can rightly be called Alemannians.[24]

As we shall see, the bishop's ethnographic observation was correct, but his secretary Rahewin took no notice of it. In the new mode he was keen to use Alemannia and Alemannians for Germany and Germans. Bishop Otto had tried to preserve the old-fashioned equation of Teutonic and Frankish; for 1154 he recorded a custom 'of the kings of the Franks who are also kings of the Teutons', to set up camp at Roncaglia on the way to Rome for the imperial coronation. This is what Frederick Barbarossa was doing at the time of Otto's report, but the fact is that the use of Roncaglia as a meeting place for the court and army in the Lombard kingdom cannot be traced before the eleventh century, long after Frankish power had crumbled. For 1155 the bishop then credits Barbarossa with a long speech denouncing the Roman Commune in which he employed a biblical turn of phrase to assert that 'the hand of the Franks or Teutons is not yet waxed short.' When the Germans then attacked the Romans, Otto referred to the 'Teutonic iron' with which the Franks secure the Roman Empire which is their right.[25]

In spite of Otto of Freising's rearguard action to preserve Frank as the correct synonym for Teuton in these passages, the fashion for Alemannia won the day and successfully invaded the royal chancery.[26] There were of course many literary practices from France which were imported into twelfth-century Germany, and this may be enough to explain the diffusion of *aleman*. But much later Alexander of Roes came up with an explanation which might have something in it. Writing in 1281, he suggested that ever since a duke of Swabia was elected king, that is, Frederick Barbarossa in 1152, the dynasty had relied so heavily upon their own people, Alemannians synonymous with Swabians, that the practice of calling the whole kingdom Alemannia became fully entrenched.[27]

We can observe the need perceived in Germany's medieval historiography and other literate endeavour for adjectives suitable to describe the western Roman Empire's subjects north of the Alps. But Frankish, Teutonic, and Alemannic were more the property of elitist literary traditions than popular established usage, and the same can be shown for the most obvious classical name of all, Germania and its adjective Germanic. In Roman geography the Rhine marked the boundary between Gaul and Germany and the distinction was preserved in medieval sources as well, although the actual language frontier between the Germanic tongues and the Romance which evolved into French lay well to the west of the river. This reverence for classical learning meant that Carolingian sources such as Einhard's *Life of Charlemagne* and the *Annals of Fulda* often use Gaul and Germany in this geographical sense of their division at the Rhine. The *Annals of Fulda* even speak of the German people, *populus Germanicus*,[28] but this turns out not to signify a community of language or politics, but simply the inhabitants of the Germanic as opposed to the Gallic regions of the Frankish Empire. So when the source records Emperor Charles III the Fat coming back from Italy in 882 to hold court at Worms on the Rhine for raising an army against the Northmen, the author accurately lists his East Frankish subjects as Franks (i.e. Franconians), Bavarians, Alemans, Thuringians and Saxons,[29] not as Germans.

In the Latin historiography of medieval Germany, Germania did have its place as a widely understood designation for the kingdom north of the Alps. Generally the distinction with Gaul was preserved, and the left-bank province of Lotharingia which had finally been incorporated into the East Frankish realm in 925 was often referred to as Gallia or Gaul in the sources. Widukind of Corvey, Thietmar of Merseburg and Adam of Bremen all use Germania in the geographical sense,[30] and in his biography of Conrad II, Wipo earnestly reminds his readers or hearers of the proper distinctions. For the king's election in 1024 the magnates of the realm camped beside the Rhine. Wipo quotes Caesar on the river as the frontier between Gaul and Germany and then lists the peoples in the manner of the *Annals of Fulda* for 882. From Gaul, the lower Lotharingians and upper Lotharingians (the duchy had been divided in 959) and the left-bank Franconians arrived. From Germany came the Saxons with their Slav allies, the eastern (i.e. right-bank) Franconians, the Bavarians and the Swabians.[31] Nothing could exceed such technical correctness.

Although Germania was often used in the same geographical sense in the twelfth-century chronicles as well, it was, as we might by now expect, only rarely called a *regnum* or kingdom. Ekkehard of Aura provided an example when he reported Henry V's veiled threat in 1110 to bring Italy back into association with the *regnum Germanicum* from which it had escaped during the long disturbances of the War of Investitures ever since 1076.[32] Having tried to educate his readers about the correct use of Alemannia, it is not surprising that Bishop Otto of Freising was a stickler for the punctilious distinction between Germany and Gaul. Referring to Duke Frederick II's siege of Mainz in 1117, the bishop mentioned that towards Gaul there are hills behind the town and towards Germany there lies the Rhine in front. The same point was elaborated for Frederick Barbarossa's visit to Worms for Christmas in 1155. As another town on the Rhine, Otto of Freising referred to its rich resources in the Gallic hinterland to the west as well as in the forested German region to the east. Such exactness had already come up in reporting Abbot Bernard of Clairvaux's tour of duty in launching the Second Crusade in 1146. After exciting innumerable hearts 'in occidental Gaul' (i.e. France; oriental Gaul is Lotharingia), the abbot came to 'the kingdom of the East Franks' – thus the *orientale Francorum regnum* of Otto's text takes us straight back to the literary world of the Carolingians – to stir up the Germans as crusaders.[33]

It would be easy to carp at such pedantry, but Otto of Freising knew what he was about. Germany meant geography and politics meant

Rome, both papal and imperial. In other words, the political dimension of the twelfth century was the Roman Empire, which contained the Teutonic, Burgundian and Italian kingdoms, and the religious dimension was the Roman Church governed by the Papacy. In the text of Otto and Rahewin about Frederick Barbarossa the words German, Frank, Teuton, Aleman and Roman are deployed with such generosity and diversity that any hope of deducing a political terminology from them is defied. The chroniclers and commentators, the chancery scribes and other writers of charters thus possessed a variety of expression which could be applied to medieval Germans, but the categories cannot be strained too hard for an exactitude which did not exist. As late as the 1280s Alexander of Roes still thought he had to explain to his readers that the kings of the Franks or the Germans were also called kings or emperors of the Romans, and that the Teutonic or German peoples were one and the same.[34] Perception and terminology had not shifted all that far from the era of Otto of Freising.

From the written record provided by the latinate elite, it is not difficult to discern that *teutonicus* was used more often for language and people and Germania for geography, while Alemannia and Alemannic as novelties enjoyed a sudden ascent in the twelfth century. None of this really explains the persistent use of Frankish and Francia or the much more prevalent and consistent use of the Roman name until one accepts the significance of the Roman Empire taking precedence over any imaginable configuration of a 'German state' in the Middle Ages, even after *regnum Teutonicum* was cautiously adopted into chancery practice in the twelfth century.[35]

A further point revealed by so many of the chroniclers is the parallel political weight of the provinces alongside the kingdom itself. At the height of Henry IV's confrontation with the princes, for example, Lampert of Hersfeld has the king attempting to defend the honour of the German realm, *regnum Teutonicum*, while his enemies, who have Lampert's every sympathy, are paraded in the text as the princes of Swabia, Bavaria, Saxony, Lotharingia and Franconia in their true constitutional diversity. But they certainly act as a body, *universi in commune*, to defend what they regard as the welfare of the realm against the excommunicated king.[36]

If the search for a realistic political definition for medieval Germany through the Teutonic, Germanic and Alemannic usages proves negative, then it is by no means fruitless. After all, the words were quite often applied to the people, the languages, and the land. As we can see, their conjunction with *regnum* meaning realm or kingdom sometimes occurs even in royal chancery practice, but its relative rarity is mystifying until the true structure of the polity is taken into account: the autonomous provinces into which the kingdom was divided, and the neo-Roman western Empire of which they all constituted parts.

Even though Lampert of Hersfeld was inclined to be carried away by his political prejudices, he was certainly not the only author to conceive of German politics in terms of the provinces standing on a par with the kingdom. The sources considered so far have, apart from the Strasbourg oaths of 842 and Einhard's list of the Frankish months and winds, been in Latin. But we are fortunate in possessing a short vernacular text from the early twelfth century which also comments directly upon the problem of the German polity and its tripartite structure; provinces, kingdom and Empire. The German scholar Heinz Thomas has recently redirected attention to the *Annolied* in its function as a foundation story for the medieval German realm.[37] In spite of its brevity (878 lines), the *Annolied* fulfils a variety of literary and ideological functions and is of great significance in using the formulation *Diutschi* or 'German', the modern German word *deutsch*, in a consistent way for the first time.[38]

Etymologically the word *deutsch* derives from the Old High German *thiot* meaning 'the people', which the anonymous author takes to the next stage almost without tautology; *Diutischiu liute* (line 474), 'the German people' and *Diutschiu lant* (line 274), 'the German land', like the modern name Deutschland. The author also knew of the correct classical distinction between Gaul and Germany which we have encountered before, *Gallia unti Germânia* (line 417), but neglects it in a modernising tendency when describing Cologne, strictly speaking in Gaul, as the finest town *in Diutischemi lande* (line 112), 'in German lands'. Apart from a fantastic claim that German was spoken in Armenia (lines 315–17), the country from which the Bavarians were supposed to have emigrated, this is virtually the limit of the author's interest in things *deutsch* because the foundation legends as developed in the text concern the Roman Empire as the polity and its transalpine inhabitants as the peoples we have already met: the Swabians, Bavarians, Saxons and Franconians (lines 281–398) each with a myth sustaining ancient far-off origins in Armenia (Bavarians), from Alexander the Great's army (Saxons), somewhere unspecified overseas (Swabians) and at Priam's Troy (Franconians).

In the *Annolied* such fancies were part of an enormously inventive German cultural tradition culminating in the humanist scholarship of the Renaissance era which sought for Germany's origin and identity in the classical past. For example, the idea that the Saxons originated from Alexander the Great's army dispersed from Babylon after his early death was an old tale known to Widukind of Corvey in the tenth century and repeated by Eike von Repgow in the thirteenth.[39] The dignity of classical learning, even where it was fundamentally erroneous and then misapplied, sustained what was the case in twelfth-century politics, the actual division of the *Diutschiu lant* into its constituent peoples, although they also knew very well how to function under the headings of the German *regnum* and the Roman *imperium*.

This the author of the *Annolied* explains by means of the following legend. Having with difficulty defeated the four German peoples, Julius Caesar returned to a sour reception at Rome. So he summoned the Germans to assist him in outfacing the ungrateful Senate. German military might thus becomes the foundation for the new imperial regime of the Caesars. This is, of course, divorced from any kind of historical reality, yet it provided a convincing explanatory myth for the German polity of the eleventh and twelfth centuries, the time when the author of the *Annolied* lived. It is actually the post-962 neo-Roman Empire of Otto the Great and his successors, and in it the Saxons, Franconians, Swabians, Lotharingians and Franconians are rightly identified as the powerful peoples who support the crown or, *inter alia*, come to oppose it, as in Henry IV's bad years. But since it was Caesar, according to the author of the *Annolied*, who actually founded this Empire, one can see why he or she mentions that 'even today the kings are called *keisere*, Caesars' (line 272) in Germany.

The *Annolied*, which was supposed to be the *vita* of a saint, Archbishop Anno II of Cologne who reigned from 1056 to 1075, thus provided a powerful political explanation for current German kingship and above all, for its command of the western Roman Empire provided *ab initio* to Caesar by the German peoples and then descending directly to the eleventh and twelfth centuries, whereas we know that this configuration was put together in the tenth century under Otto the Great. The other message, that the German lands were ruled by one king but were inhabited by several peoples, was adaptable because it was realistic. In his private legal treatise, the *Sachsenspiegel*, which Eike von Repgow was writing in the third decade of the thirteenth century, he took for granted that the 'German lands' were Bavaria, Swabia, Franconia and Saxony and adds another belief which is a myth, that they had all been kingdoms in origin.[40] There is not much foundation for that idea, although the Carolingian dynasty had sometimes maintained Bavaria as a sub-kingdom in the ninth century. But the explanation was persistent. At about the same time as the *Annolied* was composed, Ekkehard of Aura referred to the *regna Germaniae*, 'the realms of Germany'.[41]

Time and again the chronicle literature reflects what the author of the *Annolied* and Eike von Repgow have to say about the peoples and provinces of medieval German politics. In a well-known case, the *Narratio de electione Lotharii*, probably composed by an Austrian abbot about Lothar III's election to the Empire in 1125, the author explained how it was the *provinciae principes*, the magnates of the provinces, that is, Bavaria, Saxony, Swabia and Franconia (here including the Lotharingians), who met at Mainz to elect the next king.[42] Their host and the senior elector of the Empire, Archbishop Adalbert I of Mainz, organised them for his own purposes into a college of forty, ten from each province. The motive was to exclude the duke of Swabia's claim, and Duke Lothar of Saxony was duly elected in spite of the descent of the proceedings into some disorder. The rights of the several provincial aristocracies are the same as Wipo reported of Conrad II's election in 1024. That event was then followed up with an *iter* or royal perambulation to visit the peoples on the spot and to impose royal peace and protection, *tuitio*, on what are once more called the *regna* or realms in the plural; first Lotharingia, then Saxony, eastern Franconia and Bavaria, and finally Swabia.[43]

In his formidable work on the *Regnum Teutonicum* published in 1970, the German historian Eckhard Müller-Mertens indicated that any definition of medieval Germany in more than the geographical sense will always prove elusive.[44] The source material reviewed in this introduction seems to me to support this view strongly. There was not yet a German political or popular consciousness to pitch against the grand inherited conception of a neo-Roman Empire as expounded in the ideology of the court with the support of the Church. The German royal dynasties which reigned in the Empire were elected by the magnates, secular and ecclesiastical, of separate provinces, sometimes called *regna*, with distinct political traditions of their own. Even before considering the political weight of the actual orders (or classes, in modern parlance) of society, medieval Germany laboured at the least under a tripartite political structure of Empire, kingdom and provinces. But how did they originate, and what was their effect?

Part I: The Peoples and Provinces of Medieval Germany

In considering the problem of the peoples, the *gentes* living in their regions which, as we have seen, were also called *regna* and *provinciae* as well as duchies, we arrive at one of the basic dimensions of medieval German politics. When Otto the Great, crowned emperor in 962, and his successors re-established the western Roman Empire as the official political structure for their possessions in the last four decades of the tenth century, this created no real challenge to the identities of the various subject peoples. In 983, for example, Otto II held an imperial assembly at Verona consisting of 'Saxons, Swabians and Lotharingians, Bavarians, Italians and others (probably the Slavs or Franconians are indicated here), dissimilar in race, language and custom'. This dissimilarity was typical of medieval society and culture, and was not perceived as a source of political weakness. When his son Otto III arrived in Rome for his imperial coronation in 996, his entourage consisted of Romans, Franks, Bavarians, Saxons, Alsatians, Swabians and Lotharingians.[1] The individual identities of the diverse peoples within the imperial realm, consisting at that time of Germany and Italy, was thus a living political reality which needs to be explained.

The Foundation of Bavaria

When Jordanes, historian of the Goths, writing in the mid-sixth century, mentioned in his *Getica* that the Bavarians lived to the east of the Swabians, he landed us with one of the more intractable puzzles of early medieval ethnogenesis.[2] The name Bavarian appears for the first time. It has been asserted that the Bavarians were essentially a Germanic people or group of peoples arriving from the north-east of present-day Bavaria, who were able to take advantage of the collapse of Roman Noricum and Raetia II in the later fifth century, and settled amongst the remnant of the sub-Roman population.[3] But archaeological, toponymic and linguistic evidence have not been able to provide a convincing foundation for this theory. It is suggested that the vigour of sub-Roman demographic survival may have been underestimated and that the very name 'Bavarian' may be based upon the Latin *in Pago Iuvauum*, 'in the district of Salzburg', rather than upon some tribal name.[4] A proposal linked to this is that early Bavarian was a 'fusion-creole' of Alemannic and proto-Ladin dialects, so that the principal Germanic contribution to Bavarian settlement would have come from the west, not from the north-east at all.

So the actual derivation of the Bavarians will exercise the archaeologists and historians of ethnogenesis for a long time to come. Politically the Gothic king of Italy, Theoderic the Great, exercised a species of protectorate north of the Alps as far as the Danube in the first quarter of the sixth century. In the second half of the century, when Frankish power was on the increase east of the Rhine, a ducal dynasty was established by Garibald I of Bavaria, undoubtedly with Frankish assistance. His family usually goes by the name of the Agilolfings, as given in the Latin version of the laws of the Bavarians, the *Lex Baiwariorum*, which was probably codified between 739 and 743.[5] Such dynastic names usually refer to a founding ancestor, but there is controversy about which Agilolf was relevant to this case. Was he a Bavarian, a Frank, a Burgundian or a Lombard? And if he was not Bavarian, why was he acceptable?[6] To these conundrums there are no clear answers.

The transmission of the Latin title *dux* or duke into Germanic society has also aroused some difficulties of interpretation. Its military character in the Roman Empire was confirmed during the reorganisation of the army under Diocletian (284–305) and its rendering into Old High German as *heritogo* or *herizogo*, 'leader of an army', also betokens the needs of military command. But it appears that the Germanic dukes of the sixth and seventh centuries, and the dukes appointed by the Merovingian kings of Francia inside their realm, had taken up substantial judicial and administrative responsibilities as well.[7] So the projection of *dux* into the early medieval political vocabulary needed to explain the Germanic world is a reasonable enough reflection of high

status plus military command, without excluding other important
governing functions. The Agilolfing dynasty was to endure in Bavaria
until it was toppled by Charlemagne in 788, as we have seen.

Toponymic and archaeological study reveals a Bavarian programme of settlement in which the River Lech effectively marked
the western boundary with the Swabians. The Bavarians also opposed
the western advance of the Avars and the Slavs into the Alpine regions
to the south and east of their own settlement areas. The Lombards who
had migrated into Italy since 568 represented another threat. Each
side fought for control of the Alpine command post at Brixen, because
it dominated access to the Brenner Pass to the north, the Lombard
plain to the south, and the Drave valley to the east, a valuable
warpath against the Slavs. But Brixen did not finally pass under
Bavarian hegemony until as late as 765. In the east, the River Enns
had originally marked another boundary of settlement which the
Bavarians were later able to cross in order to colonise an eastern
march now know as Lower Austria. The leading place in the whole
duchy was the Roman town of Regensburg on the Danube, which also
indicates the significance of the Danube plain for Bavarian settlement.
Regensburg was the principal residence of the Agilolfing dukes, and
retained something of its character as a Bavarian capital as late as the
thirteenth century. Some of the wooded country to the north, known
appropriately as the *Nordgau* or northern region,[8] was also gradually
assarted and settled by the Bavarians, but it was a long process
stretching away, rather like the colonisation of the Alpine valleys, into
the thirteenth century.

If agrarian settlement, Regensburg's central position and the installation of the Agilolfing ducal dynasty provided some practical basis
for a Bavarian identity between the sixth and the eighth centuries,
then further cultural focus was provided by the institutions of the
Christian Church and by the codification of the duchy's law. Roman
Noricum was converted before the Bavarian period, and there survives
the dramatic account by Eugippius of the difficulties into which the
faith was then driven by the barbarian migrations, contained in the
Commemoration of the Life of St Severin, the Norican teacher and abbot
who died in 482. His pupil Eugippius described how the monastery
had to be abandoned as the last vestiges of Roman rule disappeared,
and the monks fled to Italy. However, the German scholar Friedrich
Lotter has pointed out the tendentious nature of this text, and it has to
be used with caution as an account of actual events. In effect, the new

Bavaria which succeeded Noricum had to be missionised afresh, and the recent archaeology of seventh-century rural churches in the duchy confirms the vigour of this missionary effort.[9]

To some extent this was achieved by Irish monks from Luxeuil in Burgundy, who founded the monastery of Weltenburg on the Danube above Regensburg, as the tradition relates. Of the Frankish missionaries who arrived later, the work of Emmeram at Regensburg, Corbinian at Freising and Rupert at Salzburg turned them into saints popularly revered throughout the Middle Ages in Bavaria and beyond. Since the Roman bishopric at Lorch on the Danube had long since disappeared, it is perhaps surprising that it was not until 716 that Duke Theodo received licence from Pope Gregory II to set up bishoprics in Bavaria. These plans came to fruition under Duke Odilo at the behest of Pope Gregory III in 739. In order to facilitate their endowment, the sees were established at four ducal residences: Salzburg, Regensburg, Passau and Freising.[10] It would also be legitimate to infer from the spate of rich monastic foundation undertaken by the Bavarian dukes and magnates of the eighth century that the economy had become much more prosperous than in the seventh, and this may also have been decisive for permitting the successful establishment of the bishoprics as well.

The long and wearisome controversies about the origins, content and dating of the *Lex Baiwariorum*[11] do not make it an easy text to interpret. The honourable status of the Church, the protection of clerics and pilgrims, and the correct administration of ecclesiastical property were, as one might expect in a recently missionised society, strongly emphasised. The person and rights of the duke were protected, and a concise phrase about ducal powers in the personal and official senses warns against an heir attempting to dispossess his parent while he can still 'exercise jurisdiction, march with the army, judge the people, leap upon his horse and carry arms effectively'.[12] This conveys a vivid impression of the political values most appreciated by the barbarian nobility.

Naturally the duke and his family were protected by the highest fiscal compensations for injury, and after them were ranked five prominent noble lineages with their own names. It is known that there was a broader Bavarian aristocracy than just six families, but how their rights differed from those of the Bavarian free men, the *liberi*, is not easy to determine. Between the free men and the unfree, the *servi*, stood 'those set free', the *frilaz*; and all the variations in penalties incurred for delicts committed by these social groups are set out. The provision for a great scale and variety of wrongdoing and violence in an early medieval society makes for depressing reading, but the code was in essence attempting to purvey a comprehensive standard of protection for persons and property. In certain respects such codes may have projected wishful thinking, but the *Lex Baiwariorum* was by no means moribund. At synods held in 770 and 772 by Duke Tassilo III, new or reformulated rules were added to the code.[13] Quite frequently the *Lex Baiwariorum* mentions the rights of the king, indicating the political protectorate exercised over the Bavarian duchy by the Merovingian and Carolingian rulers of Francia, a state of affairs which eventually led to the downfall of the Agilolfing dynasty in 788.

Carolingian Bavaria

The *Lex Baiwariorum* records that the Agilolfing dynasty was installed in Bavaria by the Merovingian kings of Francia. Whatever the truth, it is certain that King Clovis had subjected Bavaria's neighbours to the west, the Alemannians, to Frankish rule by the end of the fifth century, and that the succession of Alemannic dukes which the Merovingians installed and deposed in the first half of the sixth century was designed to support Frankish rule. Clovis's sons also put an end to the old Thuringian kingdom in central Germany in 531, and all these events greatly changed the political balance north of the Alps in favour of the Merovingians once Theoderic the Great had died in 526. Even if Garibald I of Bavaria was not in fact a Merovingian nominee, Bavaria did operate within the long shadow of the Franks, although the rising authority of the Lombards in Italy after 568 paradoxically gave the Bavarians some scope for manoeuvre in playing them off against the Franks. But normally the Lombards and Bavarians had their own territorial rivalries with which to contend. Source material is thin for the sixth century, but it appears that the Bavarians like the Alemannians were gradually able to free themselves from Frankish influence after the death of Dagobert I in 638 or 639, which was followed by another partition of the Merovingian realm.[14]

With the rise to power by the end of the seventh century of the Austrasian mayors of the palace who later went by the name of Carolingian, the Franks revived a more aggressive approach to what they considered their rightful hegemony over neighbouring peoples. Charles Martel, who established himself as mayor of the palace by 718, launched expeditions against Bavaria in 725 and 728, taking advantage of debilitating rivalries within the Agilolfing dynasty. But as the reasonably vigorous ecclesiastical and legal history of eighth-century Bavaria may indicate, the inner cohesion of Bavarian society was not easy to overthrow. Charles Martel's sons attacked Bavaria with some success in 743 and 749, yet the accession of the young Duke Tassilo III, who was in any case their nephew, was permitted to go ahead in 748. For the time being the Carolingians were satisfied with the revival of the Frankish protectorate over Bavaria, and once Pepin the Short had proclaimed himself king in 751 he was able to entangle Tassilo III, hardly more than a child, into the Carolingian political and military orbit. The decisive act was the oath of submission taken by Tassilo III and other Bavarian magnates to the Carolingian ruling house at Compiègne in 757, but as the German historian Johannes Fried has pointed out, the main sources for such events, the *Annales regni Francorum*, were confected from the 790s onwards to justify the successes of the Carolingian dynasty, and may not therefore be very reliable about its enemies such as Tassilo III.[15] Within a few years of 757, the duke had switched to a policy of independence for Bavaria. As we have seen, he withdrew his military resources from King Pepin's campaign against Aquitaine organised for 763, later used as the basis for the treason charge against him levelled in 788. Duke Tassilo III took another but always uncertain line in Bavarian foreign policy, alliance with the Lombards, and in 765 he married a daughter of the Lombard king. For the time being, Bavarian autonomy was vindicated.

It may well be in recognition of the relative strength of Bavaria in the eighth century that Charlemagne, who succeeded his father Pepin the Short in 768, did not at first seek a solution to Bavaria's virtual defection from the Frankish alliance. The conqueror was concerned with his projects against Saxony and Lombardy; his annexation of the Lombard kingdom in 774 in any case removed Tassilo III's erstwhile ally. But in the 780s Charlemagne did decide, as we have seen, to incorporate Bavaria into his realm in order to facilitate his projected conquest of the Avar khanate centred in Pannonia to the east of Bavaria. The principal motive for this act of aggression, in which nearly all the Avars were exterminated, was to seize the fabled treasure hoard of the Avar khans, which possibly turned Charlemagne into the richest barbarian warlord since Alaric had looted the wealth of Rome in 410. In 787 a renewed combination of military force and diplomatic negotiation reminiscent of the 740s and 750s reduced Duke Tassilo III once more to a creature of the Frankish court. Charlemagne then insisted upon his cousin's deposition, and after the trial at Ingelheim in 788, Tassilo III and the rest of his family disappeared as prisoners into Frankish monasteries. In his *Life of Charlemagne*, Einhard dishonestly blames everything on Tassilo himself, supposedly nagged by his wife to defy the Frankish ruler in revenge for her father's defeat in 774.[16]

With the Avar war in prospect, it was in Charlemagne's interest to conciliate the Bavarian Church and aristocracy, and no attempt was made to partition the duchy or to put down its legal and social integrity. Holding court in 788 in Regensburg, which he called 'our town', the Frankish king claimed that the Bavarian duchy had returned to its rightful jurisdiction within the wider realm.[17] This explanation and the lack of reprisals appear to have been acceptable. Einhard reports that the king installed a number of Frankish counts to replace ducal authority, although one of them, Gerold, known as *praefectus* of Bavaria, seems to have operated more like a Frankish version of Bavarian duke. The unity of Bavaria was also underlined by the promotion of Salzburg in 798 into the metropolitan see, not only for Bavaria but also for the lands being wrested from the Avars. Above all, the *Lex Baiwariorum* was confirmed and extended by an imperial capitulary at the beginning of the ninth century.[18]

Although Charlemagne had already arranged in 806 for the division of the various provinces of his realm among his sons, in the event only Louis I the Pious survived him. So, in the first realistic partition of the Frankish Empire in the ninth century, the *Ordinatio Imperii* of 817,[19] Bavaria was awarded to Louis the Pious's younger son Louis, later known as 'Louis the German'. The ordinance is revealing in that it correctly identifies Bavaria's role within the East Frankish world of the ninth and tenth centuries, a role which was the direct consequence of the overthrow of the Avar khanate by Charlemagne in the 790s. Emperor Louis asserted that 'we wish Louis to have Bavaria and the Carentani (Carinthians) and the Bohemians (the Franks claimed a protectorate over the Czechs) and the Avars (a remnant after 796) and the Slavs who inhabit the eastern part of Bavaria. . .'. In other words, the ruler of Bavaria was to watch over a vast region to the east and south of the old duchy, and to exercise Frankish hegemony over all the Slavic peoples who occupied a circuit of what were claimed to be Frankish marches stretching from Bohemia to Carinthia. Bavaria sustained this watchdog function for a long time. In the ninth century the principal threat to Frankish power was represented by the rise of the Moravian principality, and in the tenth by the occupation of

Pannonia by the Magyars, known to the West as Hungarians.[20] As we shall see, this essential defensive task was taken away from Bavaria in 976 with the creation of Austria as an autonomous march, and with the severance of Carinthia from Bavaria as a new duchy complete with its own complex of marches.

In 817 Louis the German was still a child. He was sent to Bavaria as king in 826, and his chief residence was established at Regensburg in traditional style. With a chancery of his own from 829, he was recorded as 'king of the Bavarians by divine generosity'. He also issued charters from his palaces at Ötting, Ranshofen and Osterhofen, all known as residences of the Agilolfing dukes as well.[21] So the regime was careful to sustain memories of Bavarian continuity from duchy into kingdom. But Louis the German was ambitious. He extorted a much larger East Frankish kingdom from his father in the 830s and Frankfurt on the River Main, much closer to the centre of Frankish imperial politics, became his chief residence. Towards the end of his reign, Louis the Pious sought to deprive Louis the German of his share of the Empire except for the original grant of Bavaria made in 817.[22] But the younger Louis's hold upon all of East Francia was eventually confirmed by the Treaty of Verdun in 843, as we have seen.

The most important source for the politics of the eastern Frankish lands in the ninth century, the *Annals of Fulda*, reveal that Bavaria remained the essential centre of support provided to Louis the German and his descendants. Although it is difficult to draw structural inferences from the text, it appears that the transfer from Agilolfing to Carolingian rule had been judiciously managed. From the Bavarian point of view the most significant of Louis the German's descendants was Arnulf of Carinthia, who carried through a coup against Emperor Charles III in 887 and was elected king of East Francia. The new ruler relied upon Bavaria as the mainstay of his authority, symbolised by rebuilding the palace at Regensburg as his principal residence. About a third of his charters were issued from the chancery in Regensburg,[23] a remarkable percentage considering the peripatetic character of Carolingian kingship. Arnulf's ambitions in Frankish politics culminated in his imperial coronation at Rome in 896, but his place in Bavarian history was to conserve the tradition of Bavaria's authentic identity as an autonomous society which could then be transferred to the Liutpolding margraves and dukes of the tenth century. The emperor died in 899 and was buried in the monastery of St Emmeram in Regensburg.

The Age of the Liutpolding and Saxon Dukes

At the beginning of the tenth century the Bavarians were facing a major crisis as victims of the Magyars, the nomadic group of peoples deriving ultimately from central Asia who had seized the Pannonian plain in the 890s. At this stage of their history, the Magyars made horseborne pillage of their neighbours on a large scale a frequent if not annual event. In 900 Emperor Arnulf was succeeded by a minor, and the Bavarian aristocracy was obliged to take its own measures for defence. Even in its dissolution, the Frankish Empire was capable of using its military institutions in reaction to new needs. Ever since the fall of the Avar realm in 796, Bavaria had gradually been endowed with new military marches to the south and east of the duchy, to defend the Frankish Empire from the Slavs and Bulgarians. It was therefore natural that the Bavarian margraves should respond to the Magyar menace.

Until the arrival of the Magyars, the Slavic realm of Moravia was the most threatening of Bavaria's rivals, but that polity was already falling apart under Magyar attack before Emperor Arnulf's death. Since his son and successor Louis the Child generally resided in the Rhineland with his regents, notably Archbishop Hatto of Mainz, a capable Bavarian magnate, Margrave Liutpold, who had already risen high in Arnulf of Carinthia's time, was entrusted with the defence of Bavaria. At first the Bavarians scored some successes, but this was reversed in 907 at Bratislava (Pressburg) on the Danube when the Magyars destroyed a large Bavarian army, killing Margrave Liutpold, several bishops and many counts. More than one source emphasises the magnitude of this disaster for Bavaria.[24]

Margrave Liutpold appears to have been the most eminent Bavarian aristocrat of his time. He was related to the Carolingian house,[25] and so great was his political authority that, in spite of the Battle of Bratislava, his son Arnulf was able to succeed him. Arnulf was a vigorous ruler. Not only was he able to come to terms temporarily with the Magyars, but he also tried to restore the shaken status of Bavaria by having himself declared duke. He did his best to defend the independence of Bavaria from the kings who succeeded Louis the Child, the last of the Carolingian line in East Francia, who died in 911. As we have seen, there is even a report that after the election of the Saxon king Henry I in 919, Arnulf had himself proclaimed a king, but the transmission of the text makes it hard to interpret. In any case it is not known whether Arnulf intended himself as a rival king for the whole of East Francia, or was simply underlining the independence of the Bavarian *regnum* in defiance of the royal election of 919, in which only Franconians and Saxons had taken part.[26] In 911 the Lotharingians had already indicated something similar in seceding to join West Francia. Whatever was meant by Arnulf's royal title, it did not stick. By 921 the duke had recognised Henry I as king, and in 936 permitted the marriage of his daughter Judith to Henry's younger son, also called Henry.

Arnulf's use of the ducal title and his flirtation with a royal one can be taken to indicate that in spite of the collapse of Carolingian rule and the rise of the Magyars, the Bavarians' social, legal and political identity as an autonomous people was to be maintained. It does not seem very likely that the Liutpolding duchy was conceived as a national revival or successor to the Agilolfing duchy once Carolingian dominion imposed in 788 had, for all intents and purposes, vanished in 899. The chronological gap is too wide for a reactivated Agilolfing past to have overturned the Carolingian settlement from which the current Bavarian aristocracy and Church had in any case inherited their wealth and authority.[27] All that Duke Arnulf and his circle needed to emphasise were Bavaria's integrity and continuity as a Carolingian-type province of the ninth century, particularly in recuperating after 907. In this they were successful, yet the Liutpolding dynasty was not to last for very long. Upon the duke's death in 937, the new Saxon king Otto I was already in a strong enough position to object to Arnulf's sons, and appointed his brother Berthold as duke in 938 instead. The reasons for this are not clear, but the drift of Otto's policy is known. He desired to establish royal authority over duchies without disturbing their institutions and also permitting a great degree of autonomy. Upon Duke Berthold's death in 947, he tried a variation in removing the Liutpolding dynasty altogether and appointing his brother Henry, married to a Liutpolding, instead. A concerted royal policy of appointing candidates who were thought to favour the court had begun in earnest, and was to last into the twelfth century when ducal titles were multiplied and reformulated.

The new Bavarian duchy founded by Arnulf was to undergo one more revolution before the end of the tenth century, and this concerns its role as the defensive bastion for the south-east of the whole kingdom. Just as Arnulf of Carinthia and Margrave Liutpold had first learned their business in the marches of Bavaria, so the new Saxon duke Henry was enabled to make his mark in the military sense by

taking the offensive against the Magyars. He invaded Hungary with
some success in 950, greatly raising his prestige in the eyes of the
Bavarians. In recognition of Bavaria's contribution to the defence of
the whole realm, Otto I rewarded his brother with the old Lombard
duchy of Friuli in 952, thus extending Bavarian hegemony as far south
as the Adriatic. With the evaporation of the Magyar menace after
Otto's victory at the River Lech in 955, further restoration of the
marches lost in the 890s could proceed. Not only was the eastern
march along the Danube between its tributaries, the Enns and the
Leitha, beginning to be re-established by about 970,[28] but four other
marches based upon the accessible and productive valleys of the Mur,
the Drave, the Save and the Sann rivers restored the previous
Carolingian scheme of defensive territorial outposts. Behind Bavarian
armour came new settlers and the revived institutions of the Church.

But the first Saxon duke of Bavaria was followed by his son, likewise
called Henry (955–76, 985–95), an obstreperous character (in later
historiography he became known as 'the Wrangler') whose enmity with
Otto II (973–83) was to cost Bavaria the permanent loss of some of the
marches in 976. For reasons which are not well understood, Duke
Henry II hatched a plot against Otto II at the beginning of the reign.
After many twists to a scenario which included the emperor's campaign
to Bavaria and Henry's deposition and imprisonment, the duchy's
potential was reduced by removing the eastern march on the Danube,
the margraviate of Austria, and the large Carinthian march to the
south, which was promoted into a separate duchy.[29] Both Austria and
Carinthia were entrusted to surviving members of the previous ducal
dynasty in Bavaria, the Liutpoldings. Bavaria itself was conferred upon
the emperor's Saxon nephew, Duke Otto of Swabia. Although the
deposed duke was eventually restored to Bavaria during the next reign,
the decisive changes made by Otto II to the geopolitical structure of
Bavaria were to be maintained. In any case the creation or restoration
of Carinthia as a separate duchy made political sense once the Magyar
threat had receded, because the demographic basis of Carinthia was
now gradually shifting from Slav to German through new settlement.
So the old Carantania came to be perceived as the outpost of the
Empire with its own marches in the Mur and Save valleys.

Carinthia to 976

The first surviving testimony to the name Carantania or Carinthia is
to be found in the compilation of the seventh-century 'Geographer of

Ravenna', applied to the small central plain of modern Carinthia, which had originally been Romanised and converted to the Christian faith. Settled by the Slavs in the wake of the Lombard migration from Pannonia to Italy in 568, Carantania belonged to the shadowy Slav realm of the Frankish adventurer Samo, whose hegemony in eastern Europe in the seventh century is outlined in the *Fourth Book of the Chronicle of Fredegar*. But the main source for early Carinthian history remains the *Conversio Bagoariorum et Carantanorum*, composed at Salzburg about 870.[30] Again we are faced with the disadvantages of such texts. The *Conversio* is far removed chronologically from the supposed conditions which it reports. And it was put together for a specific purpose, to justify the ninth-century claims made by the archdiocese of Salzburg, created in 798, over the Carinthian province. Nevertheless, it is likely, as the text reports, that the Slavs of Carinthia did live under dukes of their own. One of them appealed in the 740s, according to the *Conversio*, to the dukes of Bavaria for protection against the Avars. This is what presented the see of Salzburg with the opportunity for its missionary activities, and also testifies to the increased power of Bavaria in the eighth century.

The alignment of the Carinthian dukes, the church of Salzburg, and the rulers of Bavaria does not appear to have been modified by the revolution of 788 by which Charlemagne had deposed Tassilo III. As elsewhere in his realm, the Frankish king was concerned to preserve the integrity of provinces as traditional units within the new, large Carolingian structure of conquest.[31] Nevertheless, Carinthia was being settled by immigrants from German-speaking lands, and in addition to the institutions of the Church, the appearance of counties there testifies to the Frankish political protectorate.[32] The original Slav dukedom seems to have evaporated in the third decade of the ninth century, but during this era of growing military pressures within and beyond the Frankish Empire, the military significance of Carinthia as a march also increased. It was here that the East Frankish king Arnulf received his political training, as we have seen. The Magyar menace in the tenth century meant that the strategic significance of Carinthia was enhanced. As we have seen, this important area of mixed Slav and German settlement was detached from Bavaria by Otto II in 976; the ducal title was revived; and a series of German magnates was appointed to the ducal office at the behest of the imperial court.

Alemannia (Swabia) and Alpine Raetia

As the name itself probably indicates, the Alemannians are thought to
have been a confederation of smaller Germanic groups who had
already coalesced by the third century, perhaps for the purpose of
occupying the *Agri Decumates* evacuated by Roman power about 250
CE, although their area of settlement was broader.[33] A significant
element in their composition consisted of Suevi or Swabians from the
Elbe basin, and the association of the two names – also testified by
Jordanes in his *Getica* – was never forgotten. From the tenth century
the name Swabia gradually ousted that of Alemannia, just as the name
'Angle' prevailed over 'Saxon' in giving the territorial name for
occupied Britain. But the two descriptions, Swabian and Alemannic,
were still known as alternatives for the provincial name as late as the
thirteenth century,[34] in spite of the adoption of the latter for all
Germans in the twelfth century, as we discovered in the Introduction.

In contrast with the large-scale movement of other Germanic
peoples in the fourth and fifth centuries, the Alemannians stuck to
their central settlement area east of the Rhine southwards from its
confluence with the Main, and eastwards to the upper reaches of the
Danube. Whether Roman sites, *castra* and *villae*, were used by the
Alemannians remains a matter of controversy, but on their own
account they founded large fortified settlements on high ground,
probably in fear of Roman raids. So when the Romans abandoned
their German *limes* or fortified frontier in the third century and
withdrew to the line drawn by the upper Rhine, the Alemannians
took the opportunity to become the first of the Germanic peoples to
occupy a portion of the classical Roman Empire for themselves, apart
from the Goths in Dacia. Surprisingly this seems to have isolated them
from Latin influence, and the Alemannians were among the last of the
migratory peoples to be converted to Christianity.

In the fifth century the Alemannians again sought to extend their
area of settlement, and at the same time the *gens* or nation is thought to
have set up a sole king, at least in name. This era of expansion
eventually brought them into conflict with the Franks. The Merovingian king Clovis I defeated them not far from Cologne during their
invasion of the lower Rhineland in 496 or 497, and the subsequent
invasion of Alemannia in 506 brought the province under Frankish
domination if not rule. At the same period, Alemannic settlement was

extending east towards the River Lech, south into Alpine Raetia, and west into Alsace.

The Merovingian conquerors of Alemannia set up dukes with the intention of sustaining Frankish political influence. We know that the Franks imposed and deposed dukes at those times when Merovingian royal authority was strong, but it is not known whether the dukes were Franks or Alemannians. The sixth-century Byzantine author Agathias observed that though the Alemannians lived under Frankish suzerainty, they preserved their own customs and law. This certainly fits the evidence for Chlothar II's (584–629) confirmation of the *Pactus legis Alamannorum* or law-code of the Alemannians, preserved only in later fragments. If it is remarkable that the Alemannians appear for the most part to have remained pagan until the early seventh century, then King Dagobert I (623/9–38/9) reactivated episcopal authority in the see of Constance partly to facilitate Christian missionary work. The Irish mission in Burgundy also extended to neighbouring Alemannia in the person of Columbanus' pupil Gallus, in whose name the foundation at St Gallen had a great future as one of the most prominent of all German monasteries. Another significant foundation was Pirmin's monastery at Reichenau from 724, but there remains a controversy about the relative importance of Carolingian and Alemannic ducal patronage in this case.

In spite of their defeat in 506, political pressures from the Franks were not designed to erode the integrity of the Alemannians as a distinct people, and in this respect the Alemannic experience resembled Frankish policy towards conquered nations both in the Merovingian and Carolingian eras, as we saw in the case of the Bavarians. A politically loyal aristocracy, Church and people living under their own law was the state of affairs instinctively favoured by the Franks. In the second half of the seventh century, however, the marked decline of Merovingian royal authority played into the hands of the Alemannians and a much stronger hereditary dukedom emerged. The Alemannic dukes themselves supported the rise to power of the Austrasian mayors of the palace, the later Carolingian dynasty, in the interests of the autonomy they hoped to preserve. But this policy backfired. From 709 Pepin II sponsored military expeditions against the Alemannians, but Duke Lantfrid was able to defend the independence of Alemannia until his death in 730. This was the last era of Alemannic autonomy. When Charles Martel, mayor of the palace of Austrasia, died in 741, he had assigned Alemannia to his elder son

Carloman, who put paid to Alemannic independence in 744 and dealt with the recalcitrant aristocracy at Cannstadt in 746. The sources about what happened at Cannstadt are obscure,[35] ranging from a full-scale massacre to capital sentences carried out after a trial. The Franks then took further measures to secure their rule. The ducal fisc and much of the property of the Alemannic nobility passed into the control of the Carolingians; Frankish counts were appointed; and new monasteries were founded with Frankish support.

As in the case of the Bavarians and, as we shall observe later, the Saxons, the survival of their law-code, the *Lex Alamannorum*, almost certainly testifies to the integration of a single society built out of tribal fragments and given a unifying name.[36] There are two intriguing reports about its codification. The fragmentary *Pactus* version ascribes this to an assembly summoned from all parts of the Frankish realm in the time of Chlothar II, consisting of many bishops, counts and dukes. This raises interesting prospects about co-operation between the peoples whom the Merovingians had brought under their control. But the *Lex* itself refers to the time of Duke Lantfrid (710–30) when a meeting of nobles called *maiores* saw to it that the law was restored under the guidance of the duke. Naturally the difficulties of reconciling such divergent traditions and general problems in analysing the texts have resulted in unresolved scholarly controversy.[37] If the longer text, the *Lex*, can be dated to the period 712–25, the preferred choice of the majority in legal scholarship, then it arises as an act of solidarity in the last days of Alemannic independence before the second subjection of the duchy to the Franks, consummated in blood in 746.

Rather like the *Lex Baiwariorum*, Alemannic law is much concerned with a privileged position for the Church. It also ascribes formidable powers to the duke: in peace keeping, the administration of justice and in the conduct of war. In dealing with the law as it affected the people, the code is essentially a catalogue of appropriate compositions. Both in the *Pactus* and the later *Lex* the divisions and subdivisions of nobles, free men and the servile groups are more complicated than in the equivalent Saxon and Bavarian codes. In the Alemannic versions, however, the traditions and content indicate considerable influence both of Frankish custom and of the rules of the Church, without excluding the theory of a direct relation with the *Lex Baiwariorum*.[38]

The assimilation of Alemannia into the Frankish Empire was a long and painful experience, and the levels of violence render comparison with Saxony more fruitful than with Bavaria. But the Frankish ruling elite showed once again that behind the ruthlessness of its use of force against the Alemannians from the 490s to the 740s, it knew how to deploy a repertoire of institutions which did provide a conquered nation with a stable situation in the greater Frankish realm: the preservation of the people's law; an administration of justice largely through the organisation of counties; the reconciliation of local aristocracies to Frankish authority; and, above all, a share in the religious and literate culture of the Christian Church through the foundation or restoration or improved funding of bishoprics and monasteries. It is clear that the Franks were unprincipled warmongers, but in terms of their time, they knew how to patronise a Christian culture with which nearly all their victims could then identify. The day of judgement at Cannstadt may have ended Alemannic autonomy for good, but Alemannia retained its identity and its Christian culture flourished.[39]

During the political tergiversations of Louis the Pious's reign (814–40) and its aftermath down to the Treaty of Verdun in 843, Alemannia was assigned to Louis the German's East Frankish kingdom. For a time the province was given as a separate realm to one of Louis the German's sons, the later emperor Charles the Fat, but the main shift in Alemannic political history, after well over a century of Carolingian rule, was the emergence of a new ducal regime out of the power struggles between the Church and aristocracy in the late ninth and early tenth centuries. Whereas in Saxony and Bavaria the emergence of new dukes at that time is associated, at least in current historiographical theory, with the needs of defence against the Slavs, the Danes and the Magyars, in Franconia and Alemannia the new dukes were the victors of vicious internal feuds which were one consequence of the disintegration of Carolingian regnal authority in East Francia in the 880s, accelerated after Emperor Arnulf's death in 899. This emperor's mainstay in Alemannia was one of the ablest and most ambitious churchmen in the Carolingian establishment, Bishop Salomo III of Constance (890–919), who was at the same time abbot of St Gallen, and therefore disposed of formidable material resources for underlining his local authority in Alemannia.

It is difficult to discern whether the late ninth-century power struggle in Alemannia was simply timed to fit the eclipse of the Carolingians, or if there were deeper structural rivalries between churchmen and nobles, and amongst aristocrats themselves, with a much longer political ancestry. There is something to be said for the latter argument. We know that the principal resources of the

Alemannic dukes were situated around Lake Constance, and this prosperous complex was taken over by the Carolingians in the 740s. But during the first Frankish conquest, in the sixth century, the Merovingian king Theudebert I (534–48) had deliberately severed from Alemannia a portion of the Roman province Raetia I which then had Chur on the upper Rhine for its administrative centre, in order to secure the Franks their passage from Burgundy to the relevant Alpine passes into Italy, since confrontations between the Lombard and Frankish realms were at that time of the greatest moment. This Alpine Raetia was settled by the Alemannians, but the Franks stuck to their domination of the region. It was called *ducatus Curiensis*, the 'duchy of Chur', and its status separate from lowland Alemannia was underlined by the promulgation for its inhabitants of a law-code put together from several Roman, Frankish and even Visigothic sources, appearing as the *Lex Romana Curiensis*.[40] The record of this which has survived is in fact a private work of the eighth century, but scholars have had little reason to carp at its reality as an effective *lex*, its provisions still appearing to have been valid in the tenth century.

The bishop of Chur was a figure of some authority in Alpine Raetia, but by the ninth century at the latest the Franks had introduced a reasonably effective comital administration.[41] In this respect, of course, the history of the Chur *ducatus* resembles that of Alemannia after 744 and of Bavaria after 788: the consolidation of Frankish comital authority in conquered areas as a method of political assimilation, although the nature of the sources makes the detail difficult to discern.[42] One of the counts in early ninth-century Alpine Raetia was called Hunfrid, and his descendants, who are variously described as counts or margraves or dukes, built up a political domination over Alpine Raetia down to the time of Bishop Salomo III.

In the emergency represented by the end of effective Carolingian rule added to the Magyar invasion of Alemannia in 910, Margrave Burchard I of Raetia, the leading descendant of Hunfrid, had himself proclaimed duke of Alemannia. Confronted by Bishop Salomo III in alliance with Burchard's chief rival among the Alemannic nobility, Count Palatine Erchanger, the margrave was captured in 911 and put to death. In order to legitimise this local coup, the bishop invited the new king of East Francia, Conrad I (911–18) to his abbey of St Gallen and arranged for him to marry the count palatine's sister, widow of Margrave Liutpold of Bavaria who had fallen at Bratislava in 907. But for reasons which remain obscure, the rationale for this alliance in Alemannia of the crown, the Church and the group represented by the count palatine soon broke down. After intense feuds Erchanger was captured, and the king had his brother-in-law executed in 917. These lurid events in Alemannic history simply illustrate the crises experienced everywhere in East Francia early in the tenth century: the evaporation of practical Carolingian rule after 899; the relative inability of trained churchmen to fill the gap; and the almost limitless ambitions of secular magnates to seize regional authority underlined by ducal titles where possible. Now it was the margrave's son Burchard II who had his revenge, and the Hunfrid family temporarily achieved its aim of recognition as dukes of Swabia[43] from 917.

When Duke Henry of Saxony was elected East Frankish king in 919 by the Franconians and the Saxons, the Swabians, like the Bavarians, were not initially inclined to accept his title. But the new king proved powerful enough to invade Swabia and Burchard II prudently submitted. The duke pursued a foreign policy of his own, which proved his undoing. He was killed in Italy in 926. The Swabians then accepted King Henry's offer of a Franconian cousin of King Conrad I's as duke, Hermann I, who married Burchard II's widow. The thrust of this shrewd move was to extend to the Swabians an alliance with Franconians and Saxons, the peoples who had made Henry I a king in the first place. Now the Swabians – as well as the Lotharingians who had returned to their East Frankish allegiance in 925 – were being reconciled to the Saxon regime which had succeeded to the Carolingian legacy of Louis the German.

The end-result of the Swabian experience shows that the authority of the Church, represented principally by the see of Constance in this case, and the local power of dynasties, in this case the Hunfrid family from Alpine Raetia being the most prominent, were not a true match for ascendant royal rights as devolved to Henry I. More successful in Swabia and Lotharingia than in Bavaria, Henry I showed at least from 926 that Swabian politics might be supervised from a distance. But it was his son Otto the Great who was enabled to use the dukedoms almost in the manner of appanages, with his brother Henry installed in Bavaria, as we have seen; his son-in-law Conrad the Red in Lotharingia; and his son Liudolf in Swabia. In 947 Liudolf married Hermann I of Swabia's daughter Ida and succeeded as duke in 949. But as so often in the history of medieval Europe's ruling dynasties, Duke Liudolf thought he had reasons for chafing at parental restriction. Making trouble for his father in Germany as well as Italy, he was eventually deposed from the Swabian dukedom in 954. After attempting to regain his status by force, he died in 957. Otto I felt so secure in his relationship with Swabia that in a gesture of reconciliation he appointed the representative of the Hunfrid dynasty, Burchard III, as duke (954–73) to replace Liudolf.[44] Just as Franconia and Saxony had managed to agree upon a new royal candidate in 919, so the other provinces and peoples of the East Frankish realm put together by the Carolingians came to accept the exposition of royal authority by the Saxon dynasty: Lotharingia from 925 onwards, Swabia from 926 and Bavaria from 936.

Franconia Until the Tenth Century

The Germanic tribal name of 'Franci', the Franks, is known in Latin sources from as early as the third century, applied to one or more of the many ethnic groups which the Romans perceived as a threat to the Rhine frontier. It was not until the disintegration of Roman authority in Gaul in the fifth century and the rise to power of the Merovingian king Childeric I (circa 460–82) in the north-east of the country that the establishment of the Franks as a major force becomes less obscure in the historical record.[45] But fundamental problems about the ethnogenesis of the Franks and the nature of their armed migration into Gaul have long been matters of learned debate,[46] with some of the information from surviving sources verging on the mythical.[47] Once established under Childeric's descendants, it becomes clear that under Merovingian command the Franks of Gaul could launch military expeditions of frightening efficacy, defeating the Alemannians (506), the Visigoths (507), the Thuringians (531) and the Burgundians (534) in turn.[48]

The Frankish kingdom thus expanded rapidly, and became the leading power in western Europe following the death in 526 of the Gothic king of Italy, Theoderic the Great. In the wake of conquest the Franks extended their colonising activities more for political advantage than from a real demographic need for new areas. In any case the whole of central Germany between Saxony to the north and Swabia and Bavaria to the south was settled by the Franks between the sixth and the ninth centuries. This testifies to the vigour of the rulers of Austrasian Francia, both Merovingian and Carolingian, in their desire to dominate the region east of the Rhine.[49] The settlement would hardly have been possible without the defeat of the Alemannians in 506, themselves on the lookout for new settlement areas, and their expulsion from the region of the lower Main and the lower Neckar rivers. The destruction of the Thuringian kingdom in 531 was crucial because it opened the whole of the Main basin to Frankish domination.

Although the territorial name Franconia does not reach the surviving sources until as late as 1053,[50] the patient work of settlement in the river valleys and forested uplands of Franconia testifies to the tenacity of the demographic expansion of the Franks, which also took them as far afield as the Loire basin. As the Frankish *Lex Salica* put it, this law was valid from the River Loire to the Hercynian Forest, a classical name ascribed, probably incorrectly, to the woodlands of Germany. Much of the Frankish settlement area in Franconia, often identifiable through the place-name ending -*heim*, was dominated by the Thuringian *ducatus*, which the Franks themselves set up in the seventh century. But as the German scholar Franz-Josef Schmale has pointed out, we lack any written sources about the initial settlement across the Rhine, and the charters only begin to record place-names in the eighth century.[51] This is the time when a more forward policy of Frankish domination and integration was being established by Charles Martel and his successors, and this fits with the picture of renewed ecclesiastical and administrative organisation throughout the Frankish world. As a bishop entrusted with a roving commission from Pope Gregory II in 722, the Anglo-Saxon missionary Boniface and his circle concentrated their efforts upon Franconia and Thuringia, at the same time offering assistance in founding the Bavarian bishoprics.[52] Monasteries were founded by Boniface and his friends, the most significant in Franconia being Fulda. Between 741 and 743 the see of Würzburg was founded for central Franconia, on the site associated with the seventh-century Irish missionary and martyr Kilian, about whom very little reliable information has survived.

The obscurity of the sources about political and ecclesiastical power in Franconia is alleviated by the record of a gift of twenty-five royal manors to Würzburg in the 740s as part of its endowment,[53] and the standing of the see's first incumbent, Bishop Burchard, was much enhanced when he was sent to Rome with Abbot Fulrad of St Denis to ask Pope Zacharias the great question of whether the Carolingian mayors of the palace ought to take over from the Merovingians as Frankish kings. The answer was affirmative, and Pepin the Short was consecrated in 751. In Franconia the development of manors, parishes and villages went forward under the patronage of the crown, the Church, and the secular landowners,[54] although modern scholarly

analysis of information about the settlement is divided on the toponymic and topographical evidence available. As the incorporation of
Saxony and Bavaria became ever more important issues in Charlemagne's reign, so the central geographical significance of Franconia
increased. The roads saw the frequent passage of armies and public
works were undertaken, including a great wooden bridge over the
Rhine at Mainz which eventually burned down in 813 and the failed
attempt to link the Main and Danube basins with a canal between
their tributaries near Weissenburg im Sand.[55] Saxons deported
during Charlemagne's occupation of the north were settled in Franconia.

Although the Franks knew how to impose their will by force, the
codification of law as a necessary dimension to political life brought
them into line with the other barbarian nations. The British scholar
Ian Wood claims that 'the great law-books of the Merovingian kingdom, the *Pactus Legis Salicae* and the *Lex Ribvaria*, were only one part of
the legal output of the period, and they suggest that the Merovingian
kings legislated often'.[56] Such activity influenced the many versions of
Frankish law, *Lex Salica* being a hold-all term for what appears to have
comprised the customs of the majority of the Franks.[57] The shorter
version of its prologue is interesting in ascribing law-finding to four
named individuals who came from three *villae* or manors east of the
Rhine called 'Bothem, Salehem, Widohem'. There is now little likelihood of identifying the persons or places. Were they Franks from the
original Frankish settlement area east of the lower Rhine or are they,
as the place-name endings may suggest, from the 'new' Franconia
across the middle Rhine?

There is no clear way of telling which of the Frankish codes or,
rather, which of the various recensions of the Salic and Ripuarian
material, were relevant to the Franks of Franconia. As the complicated
histories of the Alemannian and Bavarian codes have also shown, they
were in any case related to the Frankish law. If the prologue of the *Lex
Baiwariorum* can be believed, the Frankish king Theuderic

> chose wise men who were well-versed in the ancient laws in his
> kingdom. In his own words he ordered them to write down the law
> of the Franks and the Alamans and Bavarians, for each people
> which was in his power, according to their custom, and he added
> what needed to be added, and he removed what was unsuitable and
> not properly arranged. And he altered those things which followed
> pagan custom to follow Christian law.[58]

Such statements are likely to reflect the continuous activity of revising the codes as each of the peoples consolidated its settlement areas between the sixth and the eighth centuries. One effect of the colonisation of Franconia was therefore to extend 'the law of the Franks' from Gaul right into the centre of Germany.

In Charlemagne's time Franconia was still the eastward salient of the great Gallic province of Austrasia. Then the conflicts amongst Louis the Pious's sons and the definitive division of the Carolingian Empire at Verdun in 843 assigned Franconia to its East Frankish destiny. What made the acquisition of Franconia particularly advantageous to Louis the German was the inclusion of Mainz, Worms and Speyer on the Rhine, with the rich west-bank portions of their dioceses. This central portion of the Rhineland was the core area from which the settlement of Franconia had begun, and contained substantial royal fisc. The incorporation of Franconia was essential to the viability of the East Frankish kingdom. Its geographical position and its economic and ecclesiastical prominence assisted in the evolution of greater unity for East Francia in the ninth and tenth centuries. The metropolitan see of Mainz, the leading church in Germany, normally supported the royal court; there were important royal residences at Frankfurt am Main and at Ingelheim; and like Bavaria and Saxony, Franconia shared in the strategic tasks of confrontation with the pagan Slavs to the east.

Stemmed to some extent by Emperor Arnulf, the gradual disintegration of Carolingian royal authority pointed in Franconia to the same result as in the other East Frankish provinces: the emergence of a new *ducatus* as a kind of rescue-package. Somewhat reminiscent of the scenario in Alemannia, Franconia's experience involved dynastic rivalries as well as the machinations of churchmen. To start with the main protagonists were Bishop Arn of Würzburg (855–92) and two rival comital families in which Poppo and Conrad were the respective dynastic leading names. As early as 866 one of the Poppo family, Count Henry, was commander of Louis the Younger's army, at that time in revolt against Louis the German, and by the time of his death in 886, Henry was entitled margrave of the Franks.[59] In 892 his successor Margrave Poppo in league with Bishop Arn engineered against the Slavs an expedition which had not been sanctioned by King Arnulf, but the plan went wrong, the army was mauled and the bishop killed, and Margrave Poppo was punished by the loss of his offices and much of his property.[60] So the rival Conradines found themselves in the ascendant. One of the Conradines, the cleric Rudolf, became bishop of Würzburg and another, Count Conrad, stepped into the leading political position in Franconia. The result was a fierce feud between the Conradines and the Poppo dynasty, who were also known as the Babenbergs, at least in later historiography, after their castle at Bamberg.

In a series of campaigns, the Conradines got the better of the Babenbergs. Widukind of Corvey records the grim tale, several times repeated in the sources, of how Adalbert of Babenberg, both of whose brothers had already been killed in the feud, was besieged in 906 in his castle at Theres and was then tricked into giving himself up, only to be executed by orders of the royal court.[61] Having secured the support of the king's tutor, Archbishop Hatto of Mainz, the Conradines set him the problem of breaking the Babenbergs' power. The archbishop rode to Theres for a parley and was admitted to the castle. He swore to Adalbert that either he would secure his peace with the royal court, and *a fortiori* the Conradines, or deliver him back in safety to Theres.

Taken in by the archbishop, Adalbert offered him some refreshment before they left. Hatto declined, urging them to be on their way. After a short while the archbishop pretended to change his mind and recommended a swift return to the castle for a snack as a precaution against the long journey and the late hour. Thus refreshed, they journeyed to the court where Adalbert was arrested and executed. The archbishop held that he had indeed conducted Adalbert back to his castle in safety, the obligation being at an end when they left for the second time. The details may carry the flavour of a folk-tale, but the essential ferocity of politics at this time and the actual fact of Adalbert's execution are authentic. Widukind asks if anything could be more wicked than such treachery, but admitted that many lives were saved because the cause of the Babenbergs collapsed and the feud came to an end.

Adalbert of Babenberg's death did not bring his dynasty to an end, but this and the Magyar threat permitted the assumption of ducal powers and title by his rival, Count Conrad. The new duke retained great influence at the Carolingian court, and when the Saxon duke Otto renounced any bid for the vacant throne on Louis the Child's death, it was Conrad who was elected king at Forchheim in 911. His rise through comital and ducal to regal status shows not only the volatility of East Frankish politics at the time, but also the tendency of the Carolingian sub-kingdoms to fall into the hands of new dynasties. This had already been experienced in West Francia, Burgundy, Provence, and Italy. So Conrad I's election was not a revolutionary act but another response to the emergency posed by the Magyars and a testimony to the ascent of ducal power after the death of Emperor Arnulf in 899. As king, Conrad conferred his ducal status upon his brother Eberhard. But the grounding of the Franconian *ducatus* upon the Conradine counties rendered Eberhard a less powerful or secure figure than Henry of Saxony or Arnulf of Bavaria, who were much better endowed with lands. The sources hardly ever credit Eberhard with the title *dux*, preferring 'count' as more realistic in his case.[62]

Taken together, the central geographical position of Franconia in the kingdom of East Francia, the recent Conradine victory over the Babenbergs, and the election of 911 seemed to prophesy a Franconian royal regime for the tenth century. But in spite of Conrad I's traditional Carolingian-style political alliance with the Church, his reign was not a success. When he died in 918, he in any case left no son as a possible successor. In some interesting passages Widukind of Corvey described how the dying king realised that Duke Henry of Saxony was the most capable magnate in the kingdom, and that since the Conradines had less luck, he advised Eberhard to hand over the insignia and to offer Henry the throne. The election duly took place at Fritzlar in Franconia in 919.[63] Events may not have unfolded so smoothly as Widukind suggests. After all, he was writing the success story of the Saxons and their leaders in the 970s, long after the events reported. However, Eberhard did stick to the bargain with Henry I and in 936 attended the coronation of his successor, Otto the Great, at Aachen as the representative of Franconia.

Then, as so often in East Francia, the mutual political relationship suddenly turned sour as the result of a local feud from which aristocratic pride with its built-in demand for fitting revenges could only back down with great difficulty to avoid losing face. In this case it resulted in Eberhard's violent end. In 937 he punished a Saxon vassal of his own called Bruning by burning down his castle at Helmern and killing the garrison. The new king was irritated by this intrusion into his own duchy, although Bruning was at fault for refusing service due to Eberhard, and imposed a stiff penalty.[64] Eberhard took offence, and in revenge against the king was soon caught up in the power struggle over the throne which unfolded from 937 to 941 between Otto I and his brothers, at the same time as pursuing Bruning with fire and sword. This is a good example of how a local but violent dispute could bubble up to the highest level of politics, involving rivalries between duchies and even the crown itself. After many twists in the story,[65] Eberhard eventually backed Otto's younger brother Henry for the throne, but lost his life at the Battle of Andernach in 939.

One significant consequence of this victory was Otto I's suppression of the Franconian *ducatus* altogether. Like his brother, Eberhard left no direct heir, so that a balance between the comital dynasties as well as the churches of Franconia could the more easily be manipulated by the Saxons. Frankfurt, Mainz and Worms were restored to their central position as residences of the itinerant royal court. Since there was no hostile reaction to the subordination of Franconia to Saxony, it can again be inferred that it had not proved possible to establish ducal authority to the same degree as in Bavaria, Swabia and Saxony itself, due to the relatively restricted territorial basis of the Conradine family. But the abolition of the *ducatus*, at least until its partial resuscitation under the bishops of Würzburg in the eleventh and twelfth centuries, was by no means designed to upset the socio-legal identity, originally forged under *Lex Salica* and *Lex Ribvaria*, of the Franconian people, which matched that of the other medieval German national groups.

The Establishment of Lotharingia

In 843 the Treaty of Verdun partitioned the Frankish province of Austrasia between Emperor Lothar I and Louis the German.[66] As we have seen, Louis's portion consisted of the colonial province of Franconia which had been added to Austrasia by settlement between the sixth and the eighth centuries. The decisions of 843 were creative in the political sense of laying the foundation for another Frankish duchy. For upon Emperor Lothar's death in 855 his portion of Austrasia was assigned to his second son Lothar II, and it is to him that the new province owed its historical name: *Lotharii regnum*, 'the realm of Lothar', that is, Lotharingia. The two parts of old Austrasia, Lotharingia and Franconia, thus had acquired new names, and shared the same Frankish ancestry and the use of *Lex Ribvaria* and *Lex Salica*. This is why so many of the sources continued to subsume them under the heading of one *gens*, the Franks, as late as the twelfth century.

When Lothar II died without legitimate offspring in 869 his uncles, Charles the Bald and Louis the German, partitioned the new Lotharingia between them by the Treaty of Meersen in 870. This is the first in a series of contradictory political decisions made about Lotharingia during the next fifty-five years, so it is remarkable that its integrity as a novel political construction survived.[67] Probably this is attributable to the strong ties of the aristocracy and the Church to the political traditions of the Carolingian past from which they had enormously benefited, situated as they were at the very heart of the Carolingian Empire. This would certainly explain why Lotharingia seceded from Conrad I's kingdom in 911, and joined West Francia where a Carolingian still reigned. The Meersen agreement was overturned in 880 when the whole of Lotharingia passed to East Francia by the Treaty of Ribémont, and in 895 King Arnulf set up his illegitimate son Zwentibold as king of Lotharingia. This was typical of the multiplication of Carolingian sub-kingdoms towards the end of the ninth century.

This arrangement did not last long. King Zwentibold was killed in a feud in 900, so the government of Louis the Child sent the Conradine count Gebhard from Franconia as their representative. It was characteristic of the fragmented nature of politics at this time that the new duke was obliged to share what authority he could muster with the indigenous Count Reginar and his supporters. So the history of Lotharingia, in spite of its novel delineation, came to reflect the political condition of all the East Frankish provinces during the dissolution of the Carolingian Empire: the rise of aristocrats to greater regional autonomy.

Lotharingia may have transferred itself to West Francia in 911, but in spite of his visits to the province, King Charles the Simple's authority was hampered by the aristocracy, which put forward Giselbert from the Reginar dynasty as duke some time after 915.[68] The death of King Charles in 923 made it easier for Henry I of East Francia to attract Lotharingia back to his suzerainty by confirming Duke Giselbert's authority in 925. But Giselbert was then caught up in those wrangles about the royal inheritance which broke out early in Otto I's reign. The duke had married Otto's sister Gerberga in 929, and this closeness to the Saxon house may explain why he decided to back Otto's brother Henry when trouble broke out in 937 and 938. It appears that Queen Matilda, mother of Otto and Henry, inclined to Henry's cause, so Gerberga and Giselbert were, in all likelihood, motivated into joining what looked like the dynastic majority against Otto I. It did them no good. As Otto regained the upper hand, Giselbert was drowned in the Rhine at the Battle of Andernach while his colleague Eberhard of Franconia expired on the bank. Gerberga was conveniently kidnapped, and married King Louis IV of West Francia.

During three generations of the most disturbed history of their province since the initial Frankish occupation, the Austrasian nobility of Lotharingia had nevertheless forged a new identity since 855. This was not only in response to the harmful ambitions of the west and east Frankish rulers, but also to the constant raids of the Northmen and to a lesser extent, of the Magyars. Nobles and churchmen, as in all provinces of the disintegrating Carolingian Empire, responded ingeniously to the irruptions of violence and tried to augment their local authority, although paradoxically this so often resulted in further devastation caused by their own feuds.

The Frisians

The Treaty of Verdun assigned the North Sea coastlands populated by the Frisians to what was to become Lotharingia after 855. The Frisians had evolved a strong sense of identity under their own rulers long before the Frankish military and ecclesiastical onslaught of the eighth century put paid to their independence.[69] From the 690s onwards the Frisians came under pressure to submit to the hegemony of the Carolingians and to their faith, with the see of Utrecht planned as the missionary machine aimed at the vast lowland countryside. As elsewhere the Franks pursued their policy with great tenacity for several decades. After the death of a capable leader, the Frisian king Radbod in 719, the superior resources of the Franks showed up to better effect. Again, the goal was the assimilation of Frisia as a piece under Frankish dominion rather than the suppression of a separate identity. This is why the *Lex Frisionum* was recorded at the beginning of the ninth century[70] after a long struggle from the 730s to the 790s, which had resulted in the end of Frisian political independence. But the communal structures of Frisian society in relatively isolated marshlands worked in their favour. It may not have proved possible to resist the expanding power of the Franks, but it was certainly possible to retain social autonomy in an association of self-directing regions. The author of the *Vita Bonifatii*, composed after the bishop's ill-timed visit to Frisia in 754 which ended in his assassination, shrewdly remarked of these districts that 'from the diversity of their names the peculiar quality of a single people is nevertheless indicated'.[71] The associative structure of Frisian communities was not an obstacle to Frankish royal policy of accepting social diversity as long as the cultural ligament, the Christian faith, was respected and the essential terms of political loyalty to the court were faithfully observed.

Saxony and the Franks

In the sources the Frankish and Alemannian names are first attested in the third century, the Bavarian in the sixth. Recorded by the Alexandrian geographer Claudius Ptolemy in the second century, the Saxon name thus appears to precede them all. The source is surprisingly credible about their homeland: where the Cimbrian peninsula adjoins the continent – in today's terms, where southern Jutland and *Land* Schleswig-Holstein meet. The rise of the Saxons to domination of almost the whole of what is now north-west Germany by the beginning of the eighth century invites a contrast with the other powerful Germanic peoples. The Goths, Vandals, Suevi, Burgundians and Lombards migrated long distances from their original settlement areas, but the Saxons never lost their ethnic grip upon the region of the lower Elbe as they extended their occupation of the land southwards into the Weser basin, south-east to the River Saale, and south-west towards the Rhine. A significant proportion of Saxons made the sea crossing to Britain in the fifth century, and set up the extensive areas of settlement there which are testified, amongst other ways, in the modern '-sex' ending in British regional names.

In later times the continental Saxons developed foundation stories about their origins from overseas, ranging from the imaginary (Babylonia) to the possible (Scandinavia). The idea behind such myths appears to have been to establish Saxon credentials as a single conquering force, but the reality may well have been quite at odds with this. If the name and identity of 'Saxon' does go back to the second century CE, then the ethnogenesis of a much larger Saxon people over the next centuries points to something different from an outright conquest: the gradual assimilation of several smaller groups under one leading name, that of Saxon. Such integrative processes, involving the extension of one national name over diverse ethnic elements, have been investigated for the Franks and the Goths. If the Saxons did evolve through such an ethnic confederation, then demographically it seems to have been a success. By the fourth century the Saxons also represented a major seaborne menace to the Roman Empire, and the fifth witnessed migrations to Britain which were decisive in establishing a new Germanic language and a revised racial structure there.[73]

It has been suggested by the German scholars Karl Jordan and Walther Lammers that for the continental history of the early Saxons, the stories of conquest based upon tribal traditions and the theory of a confederation based upon comparative ethnology, archaeology and topographical studies can be reconciled:[74]

> This 'theory of conquest' stands in contrast to the 'theory of confederation', following which the tribe arose upon the peaceful union of several different peoples. There is much to be said for both factors having played a decisive role in the rise, whereby a ruling class arriving from the north dominated the original population.

One problem is that the most coherent written evidence about the early integration and subsequent expansion of the Saxons is based upon traditions recorded by ecclesiastics the ninth and tenth centuries, notably Rudolf of Fulda in his *Translatio sancti Alexandri*, Hucbald in his *Vita Lebuini* and Widukind of Corvey in his *Rerum gestarum Saxonicarum*. So we are landed with a difficulty already experienced with the *Conversio Bagoariorum et Carantanorum* – a long time-lag between event and report clouded by the ideological needs of authors. Taken with other sources, notably the *Lex Saxonum* from the first decade of the ninth century,[75] the reports about the Saxons are nevertheless valuable for recording a tripartite division of society into noble, free and semi-servile, thus reflecting what was recorded elsewhere for the early Germanic nations.

The material in the ninth- and tenth-century authors is enticing, but its chronological separation from events and its inner contradictions have aroused unresolved controversies about its real worth for interpreting the history of the Saxons before the beginnings of the Frankish conquest in 772.[76] No doubt Hucbald, Rudolf and Widukind relied upon tradition in good faith. But we probably have here another case where national memory was an imaginative construction more misleading than enlightening about actual historical evolution, rather like the polemics of Gildas and the triumphalism of Bede in 'explaining' the Anglo-Saxon occupation of Britain. The new generation of archaeological investigation in Saxony will in any case shed more light upon the issues.

The portrait of the pre-conquest Saxons presented in the later tradition is of a pagan and bellicose people who knew neither royal nor ducal rule. The tribal area was divided into four parts: Eastphalia, Westphalia, the northern region, and Engern in the centre, where an annual assembly of Saxons was said to have been held at Marklo on the Weser.[77] Under their aristocracy the Saxons were divided into as many as sixty or eighty sub-regions, and rather like the small *Sclaviniae* upon which the Slav colonisation of the Balkans seems to have depended, this type of contemporary sub-structure may well have secured the spread of Saxon control far to the south and west of the River Elbe.

From the sixth century there is hard evidence about Saxon interaction with the Franks, their eventual conquerors. This was stimulated by the collapse of the Thuringian kingdom in central Germany, overthrown by the Franks in 531 and 532. The Saxons co-operated in this exercise and thereby increased their own territory as far south as the River Unstrut. From this time the Franks regarded the Saxons as another of their tributary peoples living east of the Rhine, a relationship repudiated by the Saxons during the decline of Merovingian kingship. Even Dagobert I, credited as a strong ruler, remitted tribute in exchange for defensive measures against the Slavs because this was of use to Franks and Saxons alike.

As the Carolingian dynasty began to patronise the reorganisation of the Church in central and southern Germany under the auspices of the papal mission headed by Boniface, so the pagan societies of Saxony and Frisia stood out in greater relief. Just as the Saxons were taking an interest in the lower Rhineland as a possible settlement area, so the Carolingian mayors of the palace sporadically attacked Saxony in the first half of the eighth century, a foretaste of the great onslaught from 772 to 804. It appears to have been one of Charlemagne's earliest ambitions as ruthless warlord and pious Christian to take over Saxony and its souls in their entirety. Einhard claims that no other war undertaken by the Franks, probably the most bellicose of all the barbarian peoples, was so protracted, savage, and laborious. He does not hide the sufferings of the Saxons either, with reports of slaughter, devastation and incendiarism continually inflicted by both sides.[78] Thus the Saxons proved an unexpected match for the dreaded Frankish war machine, which had vanquished the Lombards in a single campaign in 774. More than one source gropes for an explanation which encompasses the ideal of ascendant Christian faith putting out the demonic embers of paganism in Saxony. What is extraordinary is that their victimisation by bloodthirsty Franks did not deter the Saxons from embracing Christianity in the end.

From the start the Franks realised that the effective incorporation of the Saxons into their realm depended upon the Christian mission as well as military conquest. That is why massacre and deportation paralleled by enforced baptism could be undertaken without questions of conscience at the Carolingian court. The modest material advantages of conquering an economically underdeveloped province were set against the need to fund the foundation of bishoprics, which provided the most efficacious method, even more so than counties, for extending Frankish cultural and political domination over Saxony.

One explanation proffered for the nature of Saxon resistance to the rule and religion of the Franks depends not at all upon the unity of pagan Saxon society but upon its divisions. It is thought that the Saxon nobility may have acquiesced in Frankish conquest in their own interest, because it enabled them to solve a problem of their own in establishing their authority over disaffected freemen and *liti*, half-free, whose reaction is testified by the Stellinga uprising of 841 to 842.[79] This theory is somewhat supported by the fact that when Charlemagne introduced comital jurisdiction in the Frankish mode in 782, Saxon nobles received the commissions. On the other hand the resistance was undertaken chiefly by the Westphalian aristocrat Widukind, who must therefore have put himself at the head of the anti-noble faction or force, rather like Caesar leading the populist movement against the Senate in the last days of the Roman Republic.

Such speculations are a useful way of reconciling fragmentary sources, but we can be more certain about the legal and ecclesiastical institutions with which Charlemagne sought to bend the Saxons to the new Frankish order. One of the most important bishoprics in the Frankish realm, Cologne, was promoted to metropolitan status by 800 and was assigned a huge Saxon archdiocese including suffragans at Münster, Osnabrück, Bremen and Minden. The basic work undertaken from Mainz into central Germany in the 730s and 740s, the Franconian and Thuringian missions of Boniface and his circle, was also extended into Saxony at the beginning of the ninth century with the foundation of Paderborn, Hildesheim, Verden and Halberstadt as suffragan bishoprics of Mainz.

In spite of the ferocity of the Frankish conquest of Saxony, Charlemagne was single-minded about what needed to be done to reconcile the Saxons to Frankish rule. Once the structure of the Church had been imposed and a revival of Saxon resistance upon the basis of paganism rendered less likely by massacres, mass baptism and deportation, the ruler was concerned to sustain or perhaps to exploit the inclination of Germanic peoples to make use of inherited codes of law. The Franks did not abandon the concept of Saxony as a province whose integrity would best serve the needs of so wide an *imperium*. In this sense Charlemagne treated Saxony in the same manner as Aquitaine, Lombardy, Alemannia and Bavaria. The collation and revision of the *Lex Saxonum* at the beginning of the ninth century reflects this attitude. A disciplinary capitulary for Saxony had been issued at Paderborn, probably in 785, in order to protect the newly introduced institutions and personnel of the Church. Then in 797 Charlemagne invited to his new capital at Aachen an assembly of Saxons from three of the traditional quarters, Westphalia, Engern and Eastphalia.

It appears that considerable trouble was taken in 797 to reconcile the Saxons to Frankish notions of legal administration by confirming the traditional tripartite structure into noble, free and half-free, and at the same time to make some concessions to the Saxons.[80] The edition of the *Lex Saxonum* produced a few years later had to include the alterations to Saxon custom which were caused by Frankish conquest and modes of judicial administration, as well as the forcible or voluntary conversion to the new faith insisted upon by the conquerors. For example, chapter 36 of the *Lex Saxonum* reflects the capitularies of 785 and 797 in relating the tariff of fines to Saxon social status.[81] As recorded early in the ninth century, the *Lex Saxonum* was influenced by Charlemagne's own additions to the Merovingian *Lex Ribvaria*,[82] and the structure of the text may well have been borrowed from the *Lex Ribvaria* as well.

In spite of its relatively late date as a record of Saxon law and the refraction of its material through political events since 772 and the legal enactments since 785, it is usually agreed that much of the detail in *Lex Saxonum* is descended from custom dating to the pagan era. But many problems remain in interpreting the relationship between the Saxon social groups. For example, does the *Lex Saxonum* reflect a deterioration in the status of the free and half-free which may then have turned into a cause for the Stellinga revolt in Saxony in 841? There could be no realistic retreat from Frankish institutions. Just as in Bavaria, where the establishment of bishops since 739 and the introduction of counts after 788 changed the ruling structure, so the nobility of Saxony came round as a governing elite in the Frankish mode, as 'bishops, abbots, counts, magistrates and all in high position and born of the *maiores*, greater men, in the Saxon regions'.[83]

The Emergence of the Saxon Duchy

When Saxony was incorporated into Louis the German's kingdom, one of its military functions was to hold the line against the Danish threat from the north and the Slav threat from the east. In these circumstances it was likely that the counts most enterprising in military affairs would emerge as the leaders in Saxon politics. Much of the detail is lost to us, but it appears that the richest and most successful was the Eastphalian count Liudolf (d. 866) whose sons Bruno (d. 880) and Otto (d. 912) were recorded as dukes in Saxony. This would signify their military accomplishments as well as their commanding status among the Saxon magnates. The sources for the emergence of the Saxon *ducatus* are exiguous.[84] Widukind of Corvey gives the early Liudolfings surprisingly little room in his account of Saxon history, and chiefly to point up the illustrious ancestry of Duke Otto's son Henry, whom we have already met as elected king of East Francia from 919.[85] As the German historian Walther Kienast pointed out, the Saxon ducal title of the Liudolfings was in all probability local and informal, even an outright usurpation.[86] Nevertheless, it exhibits reasonable congruence with the other provinces and peoples of East Francia towards the end of the ninth and at the beginning of the tenth centuries: a perceived need for strong, even ruthless hands to undertake the defence of the province, especially from external enemies.

The origins of the Liudolfing house in Eastphalia are obscure. Widukind was a bit better informed about the Westphalian antecedents of Henry I's second wife Matilda (with whom the author was distantly related), as an illustrious heiress and mother of Otto the Great.[87] In uniting his *ducatus* with the throne, Henry I's reign was, according to Widukind, dominated by the necessity of defending Saxony from the Magyars and the Slavs. So it was the king's prudence and prowess, particularly in the military sphere, which established the dynasty as the acceptable ruling house in East Francia. As we shall see later, Widukind's approach to the material is suspiciously tidy, but no one could deny that Henry I was a military success.[88] This had significant consequences for the structure of the Saxon duchy. From the 920s and 930s it proved possible to enforce the protectorate over the Slavs to the east of the Saale and Elbe rivers claimed by the Carolingians since the conquest of Saxony. Now the Saxons were able to restore six separate marches stretching from the Baltic – the march of the Billungs being situated opposite their dynastic base at

Lüneburg near the lower Elbe – to the marches of Zeitz and Meissen as far as the Bohemian frontier, with the North March and the marches of Lusatia and Merseburg in between. This vast region, known as Sclavinia or 'land of the Slavs' in some sources, was potentially as important as any eastern Frankish province, but the ruthlessness of Saxon rule and the crass mishandling of issues such as tribute payments and forced conversion resulted in the loss of the northern half of Sclavinia in the Slav insurgency of 983.

In 975 a diploma from Otto II's chancery divided his realm at the River Elbe into 'Christian' and 'barbarian' regions, the latter inhabited by the Slav *gentes* who, according to Thietmar of Merseburg, 'having taken up Christianity, were paying tribute to our kings and emperors'. Tendentiously, he blames the revolt upon the *superbia* or arrogance of Margrave Dietrich of the North March (965–85), an enemy of his own family. He also records the inadequacies of the conversion programme. When Bishop Boso of Merseburg (968–70) translated the *Kyrie eleison* into Slavonic, the Slavs laughed at his phrasing, claiming that it sounded like 'The alder stands in the thicket.'[89]

An immediate consequence of Otto I's succession was the promotion of his ally Hermann Billung to the second rank in Saxony after the Liudolfing house. It has been usual to count the Billung dynasty as dukes of Saxony from 936 to 1106, but Widukind of Corvey shied away from this and called Hermann Billung by an equivalent, *princeps militiae*, which could be rendered 'commander of the army', a suitable circumlocution for a duke.[90] Hermann was not unequivocally called *dux* before 968, and from 975 his descendants certainly counted as dukes.[91] The promotion of the Billung family to ducal status in the homeland of the Liudolfings or Ottonians indicates two results of the tenth-century political experience in East Francia: the acceptance after the elections of 919 and 936 of the Liudolfings as the rightful royal dynasty for the whole country, and the association of the new dukedoms in their military aspect with the needs of the crown, in organising armed contingents for the general defence of the realm which reached fruition on the battlefield of the Lechfeld in 955.[92]

Thuringia down to the Tenth Century

From another exercise in Germanic ethnogenesis we learn that by the end of the fourth century, peoples labelled Hermunduri, Angli and

Warni had coalesced as the Thuringians.[93] This is of particular interest to English speakers, because another group of Angli had joined the Germanic migration to Britain, ultimately bequeathing their name as 'England'. In Thuringia the Anglian name was also translated geographically into the small region known as Engilin.[94] Almost nothing is known in detail of the fifth-century Thuringians, a serious gap in our knowledge of European history because it was during this period that the Thuringians formed a substantial kingdom of their own, which stretched from the middle Elbe as far south as the Danube. About 510 there emerges the name of the Thuringian king Herminafrid as an ally of Theoderic the Great. By 532 Herminafrid and his kingdom were added to the list of victims of Merovingian expansion. The king was deported and the Franks subsequently murdered him. The details of Frankish dispositions in Thuringia remain obscure, but there is evidence for the two institutions which the Franks normally maintained in their conquered provinces: ducal office and a code of law.

The Thuringians remained capable of staging revolts against Frankish domination, the most significant being that of 639 by which one of the dukes installed by the Franks, Radulf, made himself into a king.[95] Important for their future was the rise of Slav power east of the River Saale, and here the Thuringians were obliged to defend the frontier in their own and the Franks' interest. In the opposite direction, the Franks themselves became the Thuringians' most formidable neighbours through the colonisation of later-named Franconia which we considered earlier. Franconia covered much of the ground previously occupied by the Thuringian kingdom. Thuringia remained rather a wild frontier region, only intermittently recognising Frankish hegemony and almost untouched by the Christian faith. The descendants of Radulf were able to maintain their autonomy until the dynasty was expelled by the Carolingians before 740.[96] The revival of Frankish power in the eighth century also touched Thuringia in the form of the Christian mission backed by the Papacy and the Carolingians. In association with the foundation of Würzburg as a bishopric by Boniface of Mainz, a see for Thuringia was established at Erfurt between 741 and 743. Although it did not survive as a separate bishopric later than 754,[97] Erfurt's incorporation into the diocese of Mainz linked almost all of Thuringia in the ecclesiastical and cultural senses to the more advanced Rhineland for the rest of the Middle Ages. Much of the missionary work in Thuringia was undertaken by monks from Hersfeld, the important Franconian abbey founded by Boniface's successor, Bishop Lul of Mainz (754–86).

Ever since the sixth century the Thuringians had been associated with the Saxons of Eastphalia, not always on good terms. But they forged a political relationship on the basis of their common need to confront the Slavs. Once Saxony had been conquered by the Franks and converted to Christianity, the relationship was strengthened by the rise of the aristocracy, some of whom were counts,[98] although most of the detail about the participation of Saxons, Franks and Thuringians is lost. Nevertheless, the dynasty of Liudolf had come to possess significant lands and jurisdictions in Thuringia, and we know that under Henry I the crown possessed Thuringian residences at Nordhausen, Tilleda and Memleben. It is also from the tenth century that a version of the Thuringian law-code survived,[99] and, like the *Lex Frisionum* and the *Lex Romana Curiensis*, the *Lex Thuringorum* is a significant testimony to the social identity of a small national group which was able, in this case, to survive the downfall of royal leadership in the sixth century and again in the eighth.

The Crown and the Dukedoms in the Tenth Century

In his history of the Saxons whose independence had been ended by Frankish conquest, Widukind of Corvey artfully turns the tables by his brilliant account of the Saxons' triumph within the wider eastern Frankish sphere of the tenth century. He begins by presenting the Saxons and Franks of the ninth century as 'now moulded by the Christian faith into brothers and almost the same people, as we now see'.[100] This made it easier for Widukind to introduce the dukes as the natural heirs of royal authority when the Carolingian line failed in 911: first Duke Otto of Saxony who refused the crown, then Duke Conrad of Franconia elected in 911, and finally the lord by his nature of all the regal virtues, Duke Henry of Saxony, the founder of the new dynasty and by the time of his death *regum maximus Europae*, 'greatest of the kings of Europe'.[101]

The question remains whether the definitive emergence of ducal power in East Francia by the first decade of the tenth century meant a revival, in difficult times, of the type of authority exercised east of the Rhine in the eighth century and subsequently put down by the Carolingians or, as seems more likely, a political and military response to crisis: the minority of Louis the Child coinciding with the first onrush of the Magyars. Continuity from the eighth century had been preserved by the Carolingians in the interests of stability: the customs, social structures and identities of the *gentes*. The military usefulness of the *ducatus* had never died out of the Carolingian political repertoire, so that its renewed prominence, coinciding with the end of the Carolingian line in East Francia, was a natural if rather sudden evolution within Frankish politics. The new dukedoms erected over the peoples and provinces represented a rational response to crisis in East Francia.

As we have seen, the *ducatus* was not at first of much assistance to Henry I, who was obliged to spend much of his reign outfacing the autonomy of Swabia, Lotharingia and Bavaria. According to Widukind, the effort was well spent. In a famous set-piece, the monk describes the installation of Henry's heir Otto I at Aachen in 936, one point being that all the dukes attended to help out with the ceremonies:[102] Giselbert of Lotharingia as organiser of the coronation feast, Eberhard of Franconia as its seneschal, Hermann of Swabia regulating the wine and beer, and Arnulf of Bavaria supervising the encampment of the visitors. Of course one must imagine the detail being delegated, since the dukes really represent the ceremonial officials of a royal court: chamberlain, seneschal, butler and marshal.

The Aachen court of 936 achieved Otto I's recognition as king, but it did little to remove the incubus of countervailing ducal power upon the realistic exercise of regnal authority in East Francia. The work of Karl Leyser has demonstrated how Otto I largely overcame this problem in several interrelated exercises.[103] The first was to confirm the demotion of his brothers from any share in royal power and status, a novel conception in all probability inflicted upon the family by Henry I in 929.[104] This marks a decisive break with Frankish tradition whereby all surviving sons of a king were entitled to royal status and a territorial share of the inheritance, the method by which Louis the German had received East Francia in the first place. Henry I pioneered not regnal primogeniture – Thangmar was his eldest son – but succession of the most suitable son. The scheme did not wash well with Otto's brothers. They and their ducal allies had to be broken by force between 937 and 941. The second exercise was to promote members of his family by appointing them as dukes when opportunity arose in Lotharingia, Swabia and Bavaria, as we have seen.

This dynastic approach to ducal politics was not successful in dissolving the autonomy of duchies in favour of royal authority, and possibly that was not Otto I's intention. In control of Franconia as well as Saxony after 939, what he asked for elsewhere in East Francia was the restoration of the Carolingian fisc to his control, and normally for the appointment of bishops to remain within the choice of the court. The third element in the king's policy presented no problem for dukes, that is, the deployment of their military potential for the necessary tasks of the time, because the very meaning of *ducatus* contained the tradition of military service to the court. Again it is Widukind of Corvey who supplies us with the images of how that worked out, in his account of the Lechfeld campaign of 955 in which the Magyars were annihilated. In spite of classicising rhetoric, Widukind preserved a convincing account of the composition of the East Frankish field army assembled from the duchies:[105] three divisions of Bavarians, whose province had just been invaded by the Magyars; one division of Franconians and Lotharingians; the military retinue of the king himself – certainly Saxons, although the main force of Saxons stayed at home engaged in the ongoing conflicts with the Slavs; two divisions of Swabians, whose province was now the most under threat from the Magyars; and one division of Czechs, 'a thousand chosen warriors' who turned up as part of East Francia's alliance with Bohemia initiated in 929.

Perhaps it was not Widukind's conscious intention in a work dedicated to the greatness of the Saxons to reveal the military prowess of the other *gentes* to quite such advantage as the Lechfeld victory obviously conferred on them. But there is no doubt that his political equation of *ducatus* with military power was correct, and this is why Otto the Great was keen to supervise it to his own advantage. This is shown up many times in the sources. One of the most remarkable is the administrative instrument sent from Italy in 981 by Otto's son Otto II to summon reinforcements from Germany for the campaign he was preparing against Islamic, and possibly Lombard and Byzantine, authority in southern Italy, which he claimed for the Empire. The German scholar Karl Ferdinand Werner has demonstrated how the inner shape of the document reflects the duchies in the geographical sense.[106] The content shows how the imperial court relied upon the duchies as the units which provided military resources although it was up to the individual lords, ecclesiastical and secular, within each duchy to bring or send the specified numbers of *loricati*, heavily armoured warriors, demanded by the emperor.

Widukind of Corvey's account of the Battle of the Lech and Otto II's list of reinforcements are extremely revealing about why the ducal structure based upon the Carolingian tradition was so useful to the Ottonian dynasty. Dukes might from time to time present political challenges to the king,[107] but in the long run the *ducatus* was essential for providing resources to the crown until the military revolution of the later eleventh century. As we shall see, the systematic reliance upon duchies broke down during the War of Investitures (1076–1122) when the magnates of Germany built up large new military retinues based upon fiefs and castles. Although the resulting multiplicity of aristo-cratic military agents somewhat resembles the list of names presented in 981, the collapse of ducal authority during the War of Investitures meant that the crown was then able to rearrange its local military support without the previous formal relationship to dukedoms as military offices. The political importance of their peace-keeping func-tion then came to overtake the military definition of *dux*.

The modern study of the eastern Frankish duchies in their relation-ship to the Ottonian and Salian ruling dynasties began with the classic analysis by Gerd Tellenbach of the successive families which were installed in the duchies since the beginning of the tenth century.[108] His work was a reminder that the duchies were not simply political institutions or military command structures over the German pro-vinces, but an integral part of the complicated world of dynastic interaction by which medieval Germany was made to tick. His findings have been developed in several directions. It has been shown that the rise and fall of ducal dynasties could not be orchestrated by the crown in its own interest without taking into account the heredi-tary claims and rights of families with ducal ancestry.[109] In other words, *ducatus* was more than an office at the disposal of the court, and rights of heredity and descent had to be weighed up when assigning new figures to the office of duke.

This type of investigation runs parallel to the question of older tribal identity. It is known that the legal homogeneity of a *gens* based upon custom and dialect went on. But it is not now widely held that the new tenth-century duchies had an institutional connexion with the auton-omous duchies suppressed by the Carolingians.[110] The new dukes shared in a structure of local power radically revised by the introduc-tion and promotion of bishops, margraves, abbots and counts during the Carolingian political settlement east of the Rhine. Before the eighth century there were, for example, no bishops or counts in Bavaria, though some process of political consultation between the dukes and the landowners must be assumed. By the tenth, assemblies of counts and bishops at Bavarian ducal courts are attested. About 990 Duke Henry II met 'all the leading men, both bishops and counts' at Ranshofen and issued a series of regulations about their current concerns.[111]

Saxon Ducal Power in the Eleventh Century

Between its revival in the late ninth and early tenth centuries and its gradual disintegration during and after the War of Investitures, the German duchy thus served a threefold purpose. The duchies were recruitment areas for armies nominally under ducal leadership and served the crown or, exceptionally, marched against it in troubled times. Secondly, the duchy enjoyed a legal dimension in which the duke took responsibility for keeping the peace. But except in a few cases he was not the lord over the comital jurisdictions. They were part of the crown's fiscal apparatus of power. Thirdly, the ruling group in the duchy was not that of an eighth-century *gens* resurgent but one of landowning magnates and churchmen with familial and dynastic connexions among the entire aristocracy of East Francia, a process encouraged by the royal court and the Church through the continual grant or enfeoffment of land and other resources and jurisdictions which took little notice of the traditional borders of the duchies recognised by legal custom. Ecclesiastical and royal service, and the lottery of marriage and inheritance, assisted in affiliating the aristocratic families of East Francia across the provincial divide. The dukes themselves were, of course, part of this far-flung aristocracy. One consequence was that their fund of authority within the duchy could not outstrip by very much the power of the leading churchmen and magnates who were their neighbours.

Such a structure did, however, encourage a struggle for parity or precedence, and the effect of this can be demonstrated relatively securely from Adam of Bremen's account of the archbishopric of Hamburg–Bremen in Saxony.[112] Of all the ducal dynasties the Saxon Billungs were perhaps the most securely established (936/68–1106) and, as a Saxon noble family, disposed of very large resources.[113] Archbishop Adalbert of Magdeburg, soon after the beginning of his pontificate in 968, tacitly recognised this when he unwisely gave Duke Hermann Billung a reception at Magdeburg according to royal protocol – procession into the fully illuminated cathedral with every bell ringing, and use of the imperial table and bedroom – much to the annoyance of Otto the Great.[114] But what Adam of Bremen shows quite clearly is that during the time of Archbishop Adalbert of Bremen (1043–72) a ruthless churchman could, with the connivance of the royal court, easily match the power of a duke and even overreach it. This the Billung family took to arms to prevent. As a regent of the Empire from 1062 to 1066, the archbishop was at last in a position to outface the Billungs, but he was suddenly deprived of his new authority soon after King Henry IV's majority was declared in 1065. Now the Billungs could turn the tables in the ongoing feud. Magnus Billung, son of the reigning duke Ordulf, was commissioned to attack the archbishopric. He seized about a third of Bremen's lands, and forced Archbishop Adalbert to concede them to him under the pretext of fief. The transaction reveals, of course, the equation of land with military and economic power, and how the Billungs turned it to their advantage against their most serious competitor. Archbishop Adalbert thereafter went into a decline, and Adam of Bremen sketches a pitiful picture of the archbishop's last years, partly in exile from Saxony and deprived of health, authority and peace of mind.

Swabia: Crown, Duke and Counts

If the Saxon case shows how ducal and archiepiscopal power could come into conflict, Wipo's biography of Emperor Conrad II reveals another aspect of the political reality with which dukes had to reckon; that the comital aristocracy in their province represented another source of power which it would be hard for any single ducal dynasty to outmatch. [115] In 1027 Duke Ernest of Swabia launched a series of feuds against his enemies which inevitably came to involve the new Salian ruler because the duke attacked the emperor's cousin, Count Hugo of Egisheim, as well as devastating imperial property and some of the Swabian churches under imperial protection. Brought to book by the emperor at a court held in Augsburg, the duke hoped to intimidate everyone by the strength of the military retinue accompanying him, and he attempted to rally the chief men in it by appealing to the traditional loyalty of the Swabians to their dukes, underlined by their actual oaths of fealty.

This was too much for the Swabian lords to swallow, and Wipo records the supposed reply of Counts Frederick and Anselm,[116] long recognised as one of the most instructive set-piece statements about aristocratic mentality from medieval Germany:[117]

We do not wish to deny that we promised fealty to you firmly against all except him who gave us to you. If we were slaves of our king and emperor, subjected by him to your jurisdiction, it would not be permissible for us to separate ourselves from you. But now, since we are free, and hold our king and emperor the supreme defender of our liberty on earth, as soon as we desert him, we lose our liberty, which no good man, as someone says, loses save with his life. Since this is so, we are willing to obey whatever honorable and just requirement you make of us. If, however, you will something which is contrary to this, we shall return freely into that position whence we came under certain conditions to you.

In other words, German counts were king's men before they were dukes' subjects. Ernest of Swabia realised at once that the counts were about to abandon him in favour of their superior loyalty to the emperor. The duke surrendered at once, and was temporarily imprisoned in Saxony.

As a duke of Swabia Ernest had counts as his followers and probably as vassals, but they also enjoyed *esprit de corps* as part of an imperial aristocracy whose highest sense of responsibility was to king and emperor, a relationship restored by Otto the Great. This was not the end of the problem, because Duke Ernest was eventually released and returned to Swabia to make more trouble. Wipo reports that the emperor had his own vassals of comital rank in the duchy, and it was one of them, Count Manegold, who eventually defeated and killed Duke Ernest in 1030. Wipo ascribes much of the trouble to yet another count, Werner of Kyburg, a close associate of Ernest of Swabia but so violent and unscrupulous in his feuds that he was outlawed as an enemy of the realm. The fact that Ernest was quite unable to restrain his own vassals of this kind prompted Conrad II to depose the duke finally in 1030.[118] Hunted down by Count Manegold, Werner and Ernest lost their lives in the battle, which also cost Manegold his life.

What the Swabian example shows is a stout sense of independence among the comital aristocracy, who owned most of the land which was not in the hands of the Church, the dukes and the crown, while in any case holding much church land in benefice. So counts were powerful. One like Werner of Kyburg proved much too dangerous an ally for the duke himself. Counts Frederick and Anselm paid much more regard to their duty towards a king than a duke, and thought it right to do so. Count Manegold was the king's man and protector of Reichenau Abbey and the see of Constance, and proved a match for the duke in the final confrontation.

Saxony and Swabia were not alone in exhibiting complicated lines of fracture between ducal, royal, ecclesiastical and comital authorities. The alliances and feuds amongst them could change literally year by year. Within the provinces the armed struggle for precedence among nobles and churchmen was a harsh but normal manifestation of local political ambition. As the German historian Hagen Keller has perceptively pointed out, such confrontations did not necessarily enjoy a political rationale which we can discern, but were motivated as much as anything by aristocratic feelings of 'hatred and anger, of arrogance or being held in disregard, of humiliation and insult',[119] effects of that touchy pride which was taken to be an aristocratic virtue. Kings themselves had interests to defend in every province, and aimed to steady local support by networks of *amicitia* or friendship with the royal court. But it was not easy for rulers to avoid involvement in feuds, especially when, as Conrad II put it, the principal troublemaker was a mad dog, in this case Ernest of Swabia.

Lotharingia and the Prevalence of Feud

The violent death of Duke Giselbert of Lotharingia in 939 during his feud with the king permitted to Otto I the disposal of the ducal title. More successful from the crown's point of view than Otto's Franconian son-in-law Conrad the Red, who reigned in Lotharingia from 944 to 953 was the king's brother Archbishop Bruno of Cologne, who doubled as duke of Lotharingia from 953 to 965. In 953 Conrad the Red backed Liudolf of Swabia's rising against Otto I. Both men felt threatened by the king's recent marriage to Adelheid of Italy and the subsequent arrangements in court and foreign policy which this implied.[120] Writing in 968 or 969, Archbishop Bruno's biographer Ruotger shows that his subject's appointment to Cologne had something to do with this, because the conspirators had planned to seize Cologne and to dominate Lotharingia from there. According to Ruotger the installation of the new archbishop came just in time to circumvent the plot and his authority was consolidated when, a little later, Otto I appointed him duke to replace Conrad the Red. Alert to the opportunity, the archbishop hurried to Aachen to meet the Lotharingian magnates and to rally them successfully to the royal cause.[121]

The collapse of the conspiracy by 954 greatly strengthened Bruno's position as duke and archbishop, and the sources generally credit his reign as a success. But in spite of his undoubted political capacity, Lotharingia was in fact becoming too varied in its aristocratic and ecclesiastical complexity of landowning and rivalry to continue much longer as a coherent duchy and province. Probably this is why upper

Lotharingia, that is, the basin of the Mosel covered by the archdiocese of Trier, was split off in 959 and placed under Count Frederick of Bar.[122] Married to a niece of Archbishop Bruno and Otto I, the connection obviously underlined his political alignment to the court, a method tried out with mixed results in the case of Conrad the Red. At the height of his power in 965, Archbishop Bruno hosted the meeting in Cologne between Otto the Great, just returned from Italy as emperor, and King Lothar of France with several other members of their closely related dynasties.[123] But then the archbishop suddenly died aged only forty, and thereafter it proved difficult to rein in the feuds of the Lotharingian aristocracy.

In some respects Lotharingia was a more advanced economic and cultural landscape than the other provinces of East Francia. During the eleventh century Cologne expanded into one of the largest and richest towns in northern Europe. The Lotharingian monastic reform programmes were, along with the Cluniac, in the vanguard of the Latin Church, and the careers of Abbot Richard of St Vannes (1004–46) and of the German court's ecclesiastical adviser, Abbot Poppo of Stablo and Malmedy (1020–48), had great influence upon the advance of monasticism. But the armed rivalries amongst the Lotharingian magnates went on, inflamed to some extent by the arrogance of the counts of Luxemburg, taking advantage of the fact that Cunegunde of Luxemburg was Henry II's (1002–24) empress. To complicate matters the houses of Bar, which held the upper Lotharingian duchy (959–1033), and Verdun, which held lower Lotharingia (1012–46, 1065–76), stemmed, like the Luxemburgs themselves, from a single magnate family of the tenth century.[124] So extensive were the holdings of the aristocracy that the creation of new and stable dynasties out of a single family was a process accelerating everywhere in Germany during the eleventh century, chiefly based upon demographic and agrarian expansion which enormously increased the resources available to the nobility. But none of this encouraged political restraint. For example, the leading representative of the house of Verdun, Godfrey III the Bearded, claimed both Lotharingias for himself after 1044 and made continual trouble for the courts of Henry III and of Henry IV's regents until his recognition in 1065. In 1047 he and his allies even managed to reduce one of the principal royal palaces, Nijmegen, to ashes. It was only rebuilt by the Staufen rulers a hundred years later.[125]

After all these destructive confrontations, the fate of the two Lotharingias as viable political constructions followed the same pattern as in the other German provinces. The rise of comital dynasties favoured by economic expansion in the eleventh century and the decline of ducal military authority during the War of Investitures eroded the status and prestige of the dukedoms. But this also paved the way for the multiplication of ducal titles and functions among the magnates, secular and ecclesiastical. From 1106 there were three ducal lines in Lotharingia: the house of Châtenois in the upper duchy, based upon Nancy; and the rival houses of Limburg and Louvain in the lower duchy.[126] From 1151 at the latest, there were then four ducal powers. Much to the disgust of the secular nobles, Conrad III wisely confirmed *ducatus* between the Rhine and the Meuse to the foremost of all lower Lotharingian magnates, the archbishop of Cologne.[127]

Franconia and the Rise of the Salian Dynasty

In his classic study of Franconia published as long ago as 1925, Bernhard Schmeidler asserted the central significance of Franconia to the ruling dynasties of medieval Germany.[128] This may come as something of a surprise, since the Franconian house of the Conradines had been unable to establish itself as a royal dynasty, and its power was broken during the revolt of 937–41 with Eberhard of Franconia's violent death in 939, as we have seen. But as a glance at the map makes plain, Franconia was central to the communications network of medieval Germany. In addition, Franconia probably ranked second after Saxony as the province where the crown was most richly endowed, even ahead of Lotharingia with the valuable royal assets around Aachen and elsewhere. Of Bavaria it was said, inaccurately, that the crown owned not a foot of land there, but the contrast with Franconia was plain. Otto the Great frequently resided at Frankfurt and Ingelheim, underlining continuity with Carolingian rule, and another legacy upon which the Ottonians and their successors relied was the prominence of the Church in Franconia in support of imperial rule. The Carolingians had promoted Mainz, with a huge archdiocese stretching from Saxony to Swabia, over all other churches in East Francia.[129] In eastern Franconia, Henry II founded a new bishopric at Bamberg in 1007, and swiftly endowed it through an extraordinary series of privileges as one of the richest ecclesiastical establishments in Germany. Then when the Salians came to the throne in 1024, Speyer was promoted as the ideological centrepiece of their regal and theocratic power.[130] The rebuilding programme for Speyer Cathedral was designed to make it the largest and most imposing church in Christendom, a truly imperial gesture outclassed in the event by the abbots of Cluny who, enriched unexpectedly by their Spanish patrons, were able to put up Cluny III by the end of the eleventh century.

In the tenth century the Salians of Worms emerged as the most significant comital dynasty in Franconia, following the disintegration of Babenberg and Conradine authority. As we have seen, Conrad the Red's appointment as duke of Lotharingia and his marriage to Otto I's daughter Liutgard brought the Salians into the limelight. The duke's fall in 953 was a setback, but he was still given the responsibility for conducting the Franconian, and probably Lotharingian, contingents to the Lechfeld campaign of 955. Widukind of Corvey gives him a fine epitaph. *Fortiter pugnans* he grew tired of the heat, and loosening his covering, fell victim to a Magyar arrow through the neck.[131] His descendants were able to construct a formidable collection of estates and jurisdictions on the middle Rhine. But in the Main valley and in the forested uplands of eastern Franconia, it was the Church which prevailed as principal landowner endowed with the sees of Mainz, Würzburg and Bamberg, and the abbeys of Fulda and Hersfeld. But as in Lotharingia, the comital dynasties were set upon a vigorous upward trajectory everywhere in Franconia from the eleventh century as well.[132] The economic revival of the Rhineland in the eleventh century was also of immense advantage to the Salian dynasty as a great landowner there. This had political consequences. When Henry IV was rejected by the Saxons in 1073, the Rhineland backed him with manpower and money and the charter with which the king rewarded the town of Worms with commercial privileges in 1074 goes so far as to recognise the political significance of townsmen's loyalty as opposed to the treachery of the magnates.[133] The rise of the towns was of the utmost significance for Franconia's and Germany's future.

Bavaria and the Crown's Authority

Bavaria was not exceptional in suffering from the ongoing violence of the tenth and eleventh centuries. For 954, for example, Widukind of Corvey recorded that 'the Bavarians were worn down by armed forces from home and abroad'. He was referring not only to the serious Magyar raid which sacked Bavaria, Swabia, Franconia and Lotharingia in turn, but also to Otto I's expeditions to Bavaria in pursuit of his rebellious son Liudolf of Swabia together with the party of Bavarian magnates that supported him. They had expelled Duke

Henry I of Bavaria, the king's brother, and had seized Regensburg itself. Here the king besieged them, and though the city was not actually stormed, Widukind circumstantially reports hard fighting here and in other parts of Bavaria.[134] Duke Henry was able to return to his duchy, but not before most of Regensburg was burned to the ground. There were further military operations in 955, and, to crown it all, another invasion by the Magyars. It is this predatory army which met annihilation at the Battle of the Lech, a confrontation in which the harassed Bavarians still undertook a vigorous part. Widukind's *fatigati* applied to the Bavarians sounds like an understatement.

We have already seen how the ducal title to Bavaria passed from the Liutpolding dynasty to the royal house of the Saxons in 947. Although this arrangement had not worked very harmoniously to the political advantage of the royal court, it eventually had the effect of turning Bavaria for the greater part of the eleventh century into an appanage of the German kingdom.[135] This came about as a consequence of Henry II's election to the throne in 1002. Since his father's death in 995 he had been duke of Bavaria and was crucially involved in the conversion of Hungary and its creation as a Christian kingdom, already a forecast of his broad vision of imperial rule as the guardian of the Christian faith. His sister Gisela was sent to marry King Stephen of Hungary (1001–38) and her retinue brought German legal and liturgical material with them to the Magyar court. Henry's education in Saxony was unusual and indicates that he was destined for the Church, like his brother Bruno,who was bishop of Augsburg from 1006 to 1029, the last male Ottonian. But in 995 Henry was sent back to Bavaria to be elected duke,[136] Thietmar of Merseburg's report constituting valuable testimony to the consensus which the royal court needed to gather in order to get the right dukes installed.

As king and emperor Henry II relied heavily upon Bavarian support, and as practical head of the German Church, he chose Bavarians as archbishops for Magdeburg, Cologne and Mainz. Between 1004 and 1009 and again between 1017 and 1026, Henry II's unreliable brother-in-law Henry of Luxemburg reigned as duke of Bavaria, but between 1009 and 1017 the duchy was under the direct control of the ruler, reminiscent of the arrangement for Franconia since 939. This experiment set a pattern for the rest of the eleventh century in Bavaria. When Henry of Luxemburg died in 1026, the new Salian king Conrad II virtually took the duchy into commission by appointing his young son Henry as Bavarian duke from 1027 to 1042, consigning him for his education to his cousin, Bishop Bruno of

Augsburg. When Henry ascended the throne in 1039 as Henry III, Bavaria was restored to the Luxemburg line from 1042 to 1047 as part of the Empire's military needs in a major confrontation with Hungary. After this the emperor reverted to the idea of Bavaria as an appanage of the dynasty, installing two of his infant sons, and then giving the province to Empress Agnes in 1055.

During her regency of the Empire (1056–62), German relations with Hungary deteriorated once more, so a competent military figure was again needed as Bavarian duke. The empress therefore chose the Saxon count Otto of Nordheim in 1061. The campaign of 1063 was a success, but not much more is known of Otto's tenancy as duke. His rebellion and removal in 1070 appear to hang together with King Henry IV's policy, adopted on achieving his majority late in 1065, of putting down the excessive authority of the churchmen and secular magnates who had risen too high in the Empire during the regency. Bavaria was then entrusted to the heir of the Swabian lands and jurisdictions of the Welf family, Margrave Azzo II of Este's son Welf IV. When Henry IV fell out with Pope Gregory VII in 1076, the new duke decided to align himself with the papally inclined dukes of Swabia, Carinthia and Saxony against the king. But the close links forged between the Bavarian duchy, several of its rich churches, a formidable selection of comital families and the royal court – a relationship going back as far as 995 – were durable enough for the king to depose Welf IV in 1077, to expel the Gregorian bishops and to take back the administration of the duchy until 1096.

The eleventh century in Bavaria therefore offers a contrast to the other provinces of the German kingdom. They retained their inherited ducal identities but also served the purposes of a unifying kingship, at least in the court's intention.[137] In Saxony the crown was not threatened by the *ducatus* of the Billung dynasty, since it was able to control its massive inheritances in Engern, Eastphalia, Thuringia and the marches directly, at least down to the Saxon revolts of 1073 and 1076. In Franconia there was no *ducatus* until the partial revival of the jurisdiction for the bishops of Würzburg in the eleventh and twelfth centuries. In any case the royal fisc in Rhenish Franconia was so substantially enriched by the Salian inheritance after 1024 that after the catastrophes of the 1070s the crown came to rely more heavily for resources on this part of Germany. In lower Lotharingia the inherited resources of the crown were certainly endangered when dukes were in opposition to the crown, as we have seen. But the actual possession of rich clusters of estates around Aachen, Duisburg, Nijmegen and elsewhere was not under threat. In Bavaria, where crown possessions were less abundant than in Saxony or the Rhineland, it appeared rational to retain control of the ducal resources in a kind of *de facto* union with the crown except when circumstances seemed to favour the appointment of a new duke such as Henry of Luxemburg or Otto of Nordheim.

Carinthia 976–1122

Like Swabia and Bavaria, the Carinthia restored as a duchy in 976 was subjected to several changes of ducal dynasty,[138] mainly to suit the interests of the royal court and to calm the rivalries of the secular magnates. In 985, for example, when Henry II of Bavaria was restored to his duchy in exchange for recognising the infant king Otto III's right to the throne, the incumbent duke of Bavaria, also called Henry, was granted Carinthia in compensation. Its duke since 978, the Salian prince Otto of Worms agreed to leave in exchange for large grants on his home ground, the Rhineland.[139] He was restored to Carinthia in 995. It was his son Bruno who became the first German pope under the reign-name of Gregory V (996–99) and two of his grandsons, both called Conrad, contested the royal election of 1024, which brought the Salians to the throne. According to Thietmar of Merseburg, Duke Henry IV of Bavaria actually offered Emperor Otto III's vacant throne to Otto of Carinthia in 1002 on account of his virtues and royal consanguinity. Both men were great-grandsons of King Henry I. When Otto declined the honour, Henry made good his own claim as King Henry II (1002–24).[140]

Carinthia was not a rich duchy at all. Much of the crown land had been given away to the Church, notably the bishoprics of Bamberg and Aquileia, or was enfeoffed to local counts.[141] This may have had something to do with Duke Adalbero's quarrel with Conrad II, which resulted in his removal in 1035. Adalbero of Eppenstein was a Bavarian margrave and had been appointed duke of Carinthia by Henry II in 1011. Conrad II took against him and accused him of treason, a charge which the court, including the emperor's own son Henry, at first refused to accept. After the emperor had fallen into a fainting fit, and then into tears at his son's feet, and then into a frightening rage, the deposition of Duke Adalbero had to be accepted. Not much about this strange business can be explained.[142] In any case Adalbero's grandsons Liutold (1077–90) and Henry (1090–1122) were restored to the Carinthian dukedom as supporters of the crown during the War of Investitures.

The duke appointed in 1061 by Empress Agnes during her regency for Henry IV was the powerful Swabian nobleman Berthold of Zähringen, possibly in compensation for the reversion of Swabia for which he had hoped in 1057 and had failed to secure. Berthold of Zähringen belonged to that privileged group of high-ranking aristocrats and churchmen who, during the regency, had enjoyed a free hand which Henry IV intended to curtail after achieving his majority in 1065. One result was the backlash early in 1076 when it became known that Pope Gregory VII had gone so far as to excommunicate the king and to suspend him from office. Berthold joined the opposition to Henry IV, which was in any case strong in his Swabian homeland, perhaps persuaded by the arguments of the papal legates. However, he could not maintain his papalist stance in Carinthia against the Eppensteins, and when Henry IV sacked him, he returned to Swabia to join the anti-Salian cause under arms there. All this hastened the disintegration of the Swabian *ducatus* by the end of the eleventh century, as we shall see.

The Provinces in the Saxon War and the War of Investitures

The military operations during the regency for Henry IV and in the early years of his personal rule showed that the ancient provinces under their dukes still provided the resources for the German kingdom in the manner demonstrated for the Lechfeld campaign of 955 and the Calabrian expedition of 982. But when the Empire was cast into decades of turmoil which began with the Saxon War of 1073–5,[143] then social, economic and military change accelerated and tended to dislocate such political unity as existed in the provinces. Although *ducatus* survived and dukedoms multiplied, Germany's structure became much more complex as counts, margraves and bishops established more viable territorial jurisdictions as well. But at first it was the tide of violence which struck contemporaries as the great conflict between Church and Empire broke out in Germany and Italy in the 1070s and 1080s. As the anonymous author of the *Annolied* put it:

> Murder, robbery and arson destroyed church and land from Denmark as far as Apulia, from France as far as Hungary. No one could withstand the disorders even if they wished to go united in loyalty,

for great campaigns were launched against family and household. The Empire thus turned its weapons upon its own innards. With victorious right hand it conquered itself, so that baptised corpses lay strewn about unburied for the baying, grey wolves to eat.[144]

The Saxon War and the War of Investitures certainly witnessed the movement of armies around Germany and Italy on a large scale. The sources show how, at first, the politics of warfare were regulated in the traditional manner of ducal leadership based upon the armed contingents raised in their provinces. In his anti-Salian *Book of the Saxon War*, Bruno of Magdeburg admitted that Henry IV, having fled from Saxony during the rising of 1073, was able to return to Saxony under arms because the Franconians, Swabians, Bavarians, Lotharingians, Czechs and even the Saxons of Westphalia and the march of Meissen were prepared to fight for him in the traditional manner.[145] Before the Battle of Homburg on the Unstrut where Henry IV then defeated the Saxons in June 1075, Lampert of Hersfeld claimed in words reminiscent of Widukind of Corvey's report about the Battle of the Lechfeld 120 years earlier that 'each duke made ready his own legion separately' and that they were then deployed under their individual ducal commands.[146] Duke Rudolf of Swabia's 'legion' led the charge, 'the peculiar privilege of the Swabians', but got into difficulties and had to be rescued by Duke Welf IV's Bavarians. But the day was carried for the king by Duke Godfrey IV and his Lotharingians supported by the Czechs under Duke Wratislav II of Bohemia.

As we have seen, Lampert of Hersfeld was hostile to the king, but he could not deny the effectiveness of Henry IV's tactic in sending in the ducal contingents in the traditional mode. The *Carmen de bello Saxonico*, enthusiastic for the king, preserves the same order: first the Swabians, then the Bavarians, and lastly the Lotharingians and the Czechs, with the Franconians mentioned as going in after the Bavarians.[147] In spite of the rhetoric and heavy reliance for colour upon the *Aenead*, the anonymous author of the *Carmen* bears out Lampert's well-informed report from the other side on the battle order and tactics of June 1075.

Yet in spite of these circumstantial reports, the 1070s and 1080s turned out to mark a shift from the real usefulness of the old duchies as the operational foundation for warfare. Why was this so? In the first place, the dukes who turned against Henry IV made a poor showing in the War of Investitures. By 1078 Berthold of Zähringen and Welf IV had been driven out of Carinthia and Bavaria respectively. The Swabians had to relinquish Rudolf of Rheinfelden as duke except in name when he was elected pro-papal anti-king in 1077, because his principal support was to be found in Saxony which he necessarily made his military and political base. The Saxon duke Magnus Billung (1072–1106) was not a notable military commander, and once Rudolf of Rheinfelden had been killed in battle in 1080 and Otto of Nordheim had died in 1083, there was no strong front in Saxony under ducal command. In other words, the Gregorian opposition to Henry IV in Germany found it much less easy than it expected to rally and to manipulate the traditional military capacity of the duchies when it was turned against the court.

The second reason was the gradual disintegration of political cohesiveness under the pressures of the war and its attendant propaganda. In all the duchies the episcopate was divided between Henrician and Gregorian supporters and their confusion, reflected in the rich letter-collections and other source materials, was mirrored in politics too. Much less is known about similar confusions among the secular aristocracy. Saxony itself was never wholeheartedly Gregorian and similar divisions were apparent in all the duchies. If Bavaria and Lotharingia were more inclined to Henry IV, there were strong Gregorian elements as well. Swabia was hopelessly divided.

But all these military, political and ideological influences were finite and might even be judged superficial compared with the long-nurtured inner identity of the German provinces laid down in the Frankish era. This is an extremely difficult problem to elucidate, because the coherence of provincial custom and dialect certainly went on. Yet the War of Investitures coincided with the rise of German dynasties and churches to a new level of local authority – fuelled by economic growth by no means incompatible with a long civil war – and it was their power which fragmented the old duchies into the territorial jurisdictions of the twelfth and thirteenth centuries without, however, destroying the identity of the peoples and their old provinces.

The politically disintegrative effects of the War of Investitures can clearly be discerned in the plight of Swabia. After his election as Gregorian anti-king in 1077, Rudolf of Rheinfelden who had been duke of Swabia since 1057 retired north to Saxony. In 1079 Henry IV attempted to align Swabia to his own side by appointing an extremely able proponent of the royal cause, Count Frederick of Staufen, as the new duke. Frederick was married to the king's daughter Agnes of Waiblingen, but he could at first set up realistic ducal authority only in northern Swabia and Alsace, where his own lands and jurisdictions were substantial. The Rheinfelden party did not give up, and King

Rudolf's son Berthold of Rheinfelden, the last of the line, managed to maintain himself as pro-papal duke from 1079 to 1090. Duke Frederick I's authority was further confounded by the ex-dukes of Bavaria and Carinthia, Welf IV and Berthold of Zähringen, who had retreated to their dynastic power bases in Swabia.

As a duchy, Swabia in effect fell apart in 1079. This state of affairs was never reversed, even when Henry IV intelligently achieved an uneasy peace between the parties by 1098. Berthold II of Zähringen, who had usurped the title of duke of Swabia as the successor to the Rheinfelden claim in 1092 or 1093, backed down and accepted another offer, the dynastic title of 'duke of Zähringen' within Swabia, encouraged by the grant of an extremely valuable imperial fief, the town of Zurich. Welf IV had already been reconciled by his restoration to the dukedom of Bavaria in 1096, but since he owned most of the south-eastern slice of Swabia into the bargain, his authority in practice matched that of Duke Frederick himself. By the end of the eleventh century there existed, in effect, three ducal authorities in Swabia: the Staufen in the north, the Zähringen in the west, and the Welfs in the south-east. The truce of 1098 tacitly confirmed the power of all of them, and was just a marker on the long road of Swabia's collapse from 1079 into the territorial and jurisdictional fragments typical of the thirteenth century there. As can be imagined, the lesser powers in Swabia, the churches and the counts, did what they could to make advantageous alliances with these parties, and the Swabian specialist Helmut Maurer has examined the compromises they had to make according to Gregorian principles or self-interest or vassalic relationship.[148] Not surprisingly, the sources of this time are full of the miseries of Swabia and its endless feuds.

In a slightly less dramatic way the complicated rivalries encouraged by the War of Investitures accelerated the disintegration of the other duchies. In Bavaria the archiepiscopal see of Salzburg was pedantically Gregorian, but the comital aristocracy broadly supported the Salian cause. Franconia provides another instructive example. The province was in principle imperialist – much to the annoyance of Lampert of Hersfeld, a pro-papal monk obliged to suffer in a pro-imperial community – so when Bishop Erlung of Würzburg went over to the Gregorian side in 1116, Ekkehard of Aura reports that Henry V was, naturally enough, enraged. He deprived the bishop of *ducatus* over eastern Franconia which, Abbot Ekkehard says, had belonged to the see of Würzburg by ancient commission of the crown, and conferred it upon his nephew Conrad of Staufen instead. Not much is known about this *ducatus* for part of Franconia, probably conceived as a peace-keeping device because the Conradine *ducatus* had been suppressed in 939. In the eleventh century Adam of Bremen did record that 'the bishop of Würzburg was the only one who was said to have no equal in his bishopric, since he himself holds all the comital powers of his diocese, and governs the land with ducal authority'. The nature of such ducal authority is uncertain before the imperial charter which recommissioned the duchy for Würzburg in 1168, but Adam of Bremen assumes it was confined to the one diocese.[149] What the incidents of 1116 show is that in Franconia as elsewhere the issues of the War of Investitures set the great men against each other, with politically disintegrative results at ground level.

Even in Saxony where the integrity of the duchy seemed more essential as a defence against royal armies, there were large-scale feuds between rival magnates. In 1088, for example, Bishop Burchard of Halberstadt, an ardent enemy of Henry IV ever since 1073, was assassinated at Goslar by Margrave Ekbert II of Meissen, who himself fell victim to a conspiracy in 1090. And there were several more such disturbances in Saxony.

When the Billung line failed in 1106, the Saxons were fortunate in being able to agree upon Count Lothar of Supplinburg as next duke, because he turned out to be a tenacious protector of Saxon rights both through political manoeuvre and upon the battlefield, so that the great sacrifices made for Saxon independence since the 1070s were not wasted.[150] But this did not endear Duke Lothar to those Saxon magnates disappointed in 1106: Count Otto of Ballenstedt who was husband of the elder Billung heiress and expected the reversion of the duchy, or Count Wiprecht of Groitzsch, the candidate preferred by the court. Descendants of Otto tried more than once to reverse the decision of 1106 – Albert the Bear was duke of Saxony from 1138 to 1142 – an aim at last achieved in 1180 when Bernhard of Anhalt and his descendants took the Saxon ducal title.

Such rivalries were not, of course, new to the era of the War of Investitures and its aftermath, but the bloodletting through which Germany had gone since 1073 certainly added to political tension in the duchies as well as the kingdom. The war had produced a new generation of successful dynasties such as the Staufen and Zähringen in Swabia, the Louvains in lower Lotharingia and the Supplinburgs in Saxony who, like many lesser families, did very well out of the conflict. But it is a moot point whether the war had in itself been necessary for creating the extended power of so many new families with dynastic names derived from their castles who now dominated the duchies and helped, in the interest of their own local jurisdictions, to break them up. As we have seen, the later eleventh century saw the initiation of programmes of internal colonisation which enriched the aristocracy and the Church. In the military sphere this meant that they were able to take new initiatives on the basis of the greatly expanded military retinues they could now afford to maintain, backed up by the castles they could likewise afford to build.

Agrarian expansion and military change thus played into the hands of the magnates and increased their power at the local level. But the dukes were able to switch into the new mode as well. Their authority came to rest upon their dynastic resources, their military retinues and their castles rather than upon ducal jurisdiction in the sense of peace keeping – although that duty was by no means given up – and the former military call-up from the whole province. The significance of the military changes was brought out by Bishop Otto of Freising when he wrote about his half-brother, Duke Frederick II of Swabia (1105–47), and his operations in Alsace and Rhenish Franconia in 1115 and 1116:

> Crossing the Rhine from Swabia into Gaul, he gradually subjected to his will the entire stretch of country from Basel to Mainz, where the principal strength of the realm is known to be. He thus made his way downstream along the bank of the Rhine, now building a fortress in some suitable place and subjecting all the neighborhood to his power, now proceeding again and abandoning the former stronghold to build another, so that it was said of him, 'Duke Frederick always hauls a fortress with him at the tail of his horse'.

The bishop goes on to explain that the duke was 'so generous of gifts that on this account a great multitude of warriors flocked to him and offered themselves voluntarily for his service'.[151]

From the text we can discern how the magnates were relying upon the expanding military technology of stone castles and large personal retinues of knights, a development widespread in Europe.[152] The castles and militias of the bishops and secular magnates come forward very strongly in the twelfth-century sources for Germany, and although their importance is becoming obvious in the eleventh century as well, the actual cases we have tend to refer to the ecclesiastical lords such as the bishop of Bamberg, who drew up a list of rules for his militia about 1060.[153]

Apart from specific rules for military retinues of *ministeriales*, several sources point to the enhanced significance of enfeoffed retinues. In 1136 Lothar III issued a diploma attempting to restrict the alienation of fiefs by military vassals because the practice vitiated the ability of their lords to supply forces necessary to the imperial *expeditio*. In 1154 Frederick Barbarossa referred explicitly to this injunction, and in 1158 again insisted that vassals in Germany and Italy were obliged to provide military service contingent upon their fiefs. Before this, the emperor had issued an ordinance to regulate and discipline imperial armies whilst encamped. Just at this time an edict was fabricated at Reichenau Abbey all about imperial armies, and it is widely accepted as providing a reasonably accurate picture of the twelfth-century military structure based upon retinues, with the fiefs and other resources which sustained them. In these sources it is the constitution of retinues and the function of enfeoffed knights which is emphasised, and there is hardly an echo of the paramount ducal role in military affairs one might have expected from the past. In other words, the enfeoffed chivalric retinue with its fiefs and castles had swept the outmoded and defeated ducal levy from the board, precisely matching what we know of the political decline of duchies at the same period of German history.[154]

Transformation of the Provinces after 1100

The multiplication of authorities within the traditional duchies and the relative decline of ducal military power from its tenth- and eleventh-century level did not dissolve the social integrity of the peoples in their provinces, described in 983 as 'dissimilar' in derivation, language and character. The distinctions between the peoples belonging to the German kingdom still had a future, particularly in the legal sphere, but the heyday of unifying ducal leadership was over. This was not perceived all at once. When Henry V could again open official negotiations with the Papacy after the death of his excommunicated father in 1106, he sent six bishops as ambassadors representing Lotharingia, Saxony, Franconia, Bavaria, Swabia and his kingdom of Burgundy. A similar arrangement was preserved when the magnates met King Lothar III and Pope Innocent II at Liège in 1131. The Franconians, Saxons, Bavarians and Lotharingians were formally presented to the court by their metropolitans, of Mainz, Magdeburg, Salzburg and Cologne respectively.[155]

The synchronism of the War of Investitures and its politically disturbed aftermath with economic expansion in Germany propelled the great churchmen and the secular aristocracy over a new threshold of regional power. This power had to work out compromises with the agents of the imperial fisc and with the newly apparent local authority of commercially successful cities. Everywhere in Germany the phenomenal increase in economic resources based upon the rational use of the demographic upsurge facilitated the emergence of a revised structure of ecclesiastical, dynastic and urban autarky within the old duchies. In consequence, the period from 1100 to 1300 revealed a transformation of the political map of the medieval German regions.[156] Yet the social sense of provincial identity felt by each of the German peoples and so tenaciously preserved in the duchies of the tenth and eleventh centuries was not eroded just because ducal authority was badly shaken during Henry IV's reign. Instead, the churches and dynasties which had given so much for the Henrician and Gregorian causes assembled local jurisdictional autonomy. As we shall see, the crown favoured this solution to the almost superhuman task of providing peace and order in the German provinces – a goal never properly achieved in the Middle Ages – under the aegis of local and imperial *Landfrieden* or peace-keeping associations. The real losers were the dukes. As the number of dukedoms increased by royal grant in the decades after 1098,[157] so dukes became much more like any other dynastic landowner possessed of castles, retinues and inherited jurisdictions. The power entrenched in the provinces by so many ecclesiastical and dynastic landowners in the twelfth and thirteenth centuries was not regarded as an institutional challenge to royal authority. In fact, royal officials were attempting to improve the fisc by similar methods, and the court in any case encouraged the jurisdictional efficacy of landowners in so large a kingdom where itinerant royal assizes were not a practical proposition. What did the post-1100 anatomy of regional dominion look like?

In spite of their addiction to partitioning their inheritances and to sustaining hereditary armed feuds, the magnates were methodical in defending their resources and in acquiring those of their neighbours by enfeoffment, inheritance or force. The Church was a loser by this since whatever the secular princes received in fief,[158] they generally kept for good. In spite of much spoliation, most of the German bishops survived as independent landowning authorities, a testimony to the huge grants of land, forest and other jurisdiction which they had been given ever since Carolingian times. Bishoprics also might well receive secular inheritances when aristocratic lines died out, and to some extent the enduring constitution of a cathedral church assisted in redressing the balance against dynasties subject to mortality. After long delay and difficulty, the archbishops of Bremen acquired the lands of the counts of Stade; the bishops of Regensburg were heirs of the margraves of Hohenburg; the archbishops of Salzburg were able to take over the best part of comital inheritances such as Plain and Lebenau; and the bishops of Eichstätt, after long and careful preparation, were heirs to the lands of the counts of Hirschberg.[159] There are records everywhere of such transactions.

Although the rhythm of local politics was dictated by feuds, the territorial contours of aristocratic power were also affected by the demise of dynasties. This is one way in which Duke Lothar of Saxony became so formidable. The Supplinburgs were not notably rich among the Saxon counts, but his wife Richenza was heiress of the Nordheim and Brunswick counts, who were very rich. Aristocratic inheritance explains a great deal about political change in the provinces. In 1192, for example, the dukes of Austria acquired the whole of the Styrian duchy under an agreement made in 1186. Several comital dynasties in Swabia were enriched by the demise of the ducal house of Zähringen in 1218. Feuds were motivated and fuelled by these dynastic accidents. When the landgraves of Thuringia failed in 1247, their enormous inheritance was claimed by Margrave Henry the Illustrious of Meissen, but after years of war, he could not prevent the other chief claimant, Henry of Brabant, from seizing Hesse and installing himself there as landgrave. Similar feuds disturbed Franconia and Bavaria when Duke Otto VIII of Andechs-Merania, the last of his line, died in 1248. The bishops of Bamberg claimed back his extremely extensive fiefs, but could not in the end prevent the burgraves of Nuremberg and their allies from occupying the best part of them. Lower Lotharingia was also torn by war after the ducal line of Limburg failed in 1283. The dukes of Brabant claimed Limburg as nearest heirs by blood, but had to fight off several challenges. The most serious of these came from the archbishop of Cologne; after his defeat and capture in 1288 the Brabantine claim was vindicated.

The Politics of Conflict in the Provinces

It it not difficult to discern from these examples how traditional aristocratic preoccupations with war and inheritance came to affect the political anatomy of the German provinces. As the duchies emerged from the War of Investitures, Saxony was probably in the strongest position of all of them after the long ducal reign of Lothar of Supplinburg (1106–37). In comparison with Swabia, where the dissolution of the old *ducatus* had tacitly to be accepted after 1098, it was not until 1180 that Saxony was formally divided up when Duke Henry the Lion was removed from power. Henry was recognised as duke in 1143, and his long career set most of the Saxon Church and aristocracy against him, because his ruthlessness in expanding the authority of the Welf dukedom so drastically threatened their own rights and authority.[160] Emperor Frederick Barbarossa did what he could to reconcile the Saxons with Henry the Lion, but by the end of the 1170s they were bent upon his removal, and he was indicted as a wrongful lord and as a peace-breaker. The emperor reluctantly concurred in his fall, and the duke was deposed in 1180. The Saxon ducal title was conferred upon the Ascanian magnate Bernhard of Anhalt, thus vindicating the Ballenstedt claim which went back to 1106,[161] as we have seen. A new dukedom, Westphalia, was set up for the archbishops of Cologne, and the Welf house was permitted to retain its allodial inheritances, namely Brunswick and Lüneburg, with a substantial territory in central Saxony, in effect a third Saxon dukedom but not officially recognised as such until the imperial grant of 1235.[162] In their results the feuds of Henry the Lion thus resembled the War of Investitures in its politically dissolvent aspect.

But a whole century notable for internal violence had done nothing to dampen the incurable energy of the Saxons, who began soon after 1100 to take over again the vast Slav lands, sparsely populated, east of the River Elbe, a programme of expansion which had stalled after the Slav rising of 983. There began a long history of confrontation and compromise between Slav and German down to the 1170s, vividly chronicled by Helmold of Bosau.[163] In political terms the move to the East confirmed three large territorial constructions in the hands of Saxon dynasties: the county of Holstein across the lower Elbe built up since 1110; the margraviate of Brandenburg set up by Albert the Bear between 1134 and 1170 on the basis of the Saxon Altmark and the Slav principality of Brandenburg which he took over in 1150; and, further south, the old march of Meissen reorganised by Conrad the Great (1123–56), the first of the new line of Wettin margraves. By 1200 the anatomy of Saxony as a province had thus changed almost out of recognition from the time of the Billung dukes, the colonial achievement of the twelfth century to some extent compensating for internal political collapse.

As in both Lotharingias, the churches of Saxony were political rivals of the secular dynasties; Bremen, Hildesheim and Halberstadt against the dukes of Brunswick, Magdeburg against the margraves of Brandenburg, Osnabrück against the counts of Tecklenburg, and so on. Such a pattern was just as significant in the Franconian centre of Germany as well: the abbots of Fulda against the landgraves of Thuringia; the bishops of Würzburg against the counts of Henneberg; and the burgraves of Nuremberg against the bishops of Bamberg. The Rhenish sees of Franconia, Speyer, Worms and Mainz also suffered depredations at the hands of the rising secular powers, notably the counts palatine of the Rhine and the counts of Nassau.[164]

In the province of Bavaria the twelfth century also witnessed the disintegration of the old *ducatus*, an experience shared with Swabia and Saxony. Welf IV was restored to the duchy in 1096, but the claim of his descendants was rendered insecure by Conrad III's appointment of the Austrian margraves as rival Bavarian dukes since 1139. This political impasse was resolved by Frederick Barbarossa in the 1150s by dividing rights according to the dynastic reality of that time: the Welf claimant Henry the Lion was confirmed as duke of Bavaria in 1156; the Austrian claimant Henry Jasomirgott was created independent duke of Austria;[165] and the comital houses of Dachau and Andechs, in effect promoted over the heads of the other Bavarian counts, were entitled dukes of Merania from 1152 and 1178 respectively. Merania was a colonial district on the Adriatic claimed by the Empire, but the power bases of its dukes were their comital inheritances, which lay in the heart of Bavaria. In other words, *ducatus* in Bavaria had been divided into three in the 1150s, driving further the subdivision of Bavaria initiated in 976. Then the fall of Henry the Lion in 1180 occasioned the promotion of the march of Styria into another duchy in this quarter of the Empire.[166]

Henry the Lion was replaced as Bavarian duke by another cousin of the emperor, Count Palatine Otto V of Wittelsbach, quite a substantial landowner in his own right. But like Bernhard of Anhalt's position in Saxony after 1180, the realistic authority of the new ducal house was at first matched by many other magnates, notably the dukes of Andechs-Merania, the archbishops of Salzburg, the margraves of Vohburg, the landgraves of Leuchtenberg, and the counts of Bogen, Falkenstein, Hirschberg, Ortenburg and Wasserburg.[167] Although he was an able man, Otto of Wittelsbach was not, according to the sources, very highly regarded by the Bavarian magnates, because they were long used to him as one of themselves. But the next generation went in for astute marriages, and upon this basis the Wittelsbachs were able to acquire the Vohburg (1204), Bogen (1242), Wasserburg (1247) and Ortenburg (1248) inheritances.

The new ducal house also employed the feud, continually usurping jurisdictions from the see of Salzburg and seizing much Andechs land after 1208 and nearly all the Falkenstein estates after 1248. They also acquired crown lands, particularly after the execution in 1268 of Conradin, to whom they were closely related. They took over the advocacy of a large number of Bavarian monasteries, and various other valuable jurisdictions such as the Hirschberg *Landgericht* in 1305. In other words the Wittelsbach dukes became formidable by dynastic or territorial methods, not on the basis of the old *ducatus* over Bavaria. Nevertheless, they modernised the peace-keeping role of the duchy by issuing a comprehensive *Landfriede* in 1244, virtually a refashioned Bavarian code of custom in nearly a hundred chapters.[168] Before 1273 Abbot Hermann of Niederaltaich listed about thirty dynasties great and small of which the Wittelsbachs had become heirs, and before this Abbot Conrad of Scheyern had noted of Duke Louis I (1183–1231) that he 'became richer than the rich, more powerful than the powerful, and resolution sustained him as sole prince of the princes in his land, and they respected his ascendancy'.[169]

People, Province and Jurisdictional Subdivision after 1100

The duchies which were put into place in East Francia at the end of the ninth and the beginning of the tenth centuries to answer critical political needs facing the ancient *gentes* certainly had an important future in the military and peace-keeping spheres. But then the duchies showed very rapid signs of disintegration between the late 1070s when the south German dukes were expelled from their dukedoms and 1180 when Saxony, following the experience of Swabia, Lotharingia and Bavaria, was subdivided. This decline was much hastened by the rivalries produced by the War of Investitures and showed up markedly in the tripartite division of Swabia between 1079 and 1098.

But the crown did not therefore adopt any specifically anti-ducal policy,[170] and the functions of the *ducatus*, however diluted, continued to seem useful to the court. This is partly the explanation for the number of dukedoms doubling between 1098 and 1181 by imperial grant. Yet the dynamic behind it was actually the enrichment of the princely dynasties and the evolution of their inheritances and jurisdictions into a more 'territorial' dimension during the great age of internal colonisation.[171] This dynamic was fully shared by the bishops and richest abbots and was challenged, not by the court which did not regard the jurisdictional inference of autonomy with distaste, but by the formidable evolution of the larger towns which reached out for jurisdictional autonomy of their own, to safeguard their new economic and political needs. This the traditional lords, especially the bishops, found it irksome to concede, but in the process, so often marked by violent confrontations stretching over decades, some of the cities achieved *de facto* independence under the distant overlordship of the crown.

One significant conclusion is that these processes by no means dissolved the identity of the peoples in their provinces. Dukedoms might multiply or be subdivided; bishops might extend their local jurisdictions; and towns might take over portions of the surrounding country. But according to references in the charters, the legal custom of the Bavarians and Saxons, Franconians and Swabians went on even if our knowledge of continuity in German regional law is dismayingly thin before the thirteenth century, a point stressed by the legal scholar Gerhard Theuerkauf.[172]

So the political process saw the survival of the *gentes*, then the establishment and decline of the *ducatus* in their midst, and then the evolution inside the crumbling duchies of dynastic, territorial, episcopal and urban jurisdiction. The duchy was deflated into a much smaller principality comparable with the counties, bishoprics and margraviates sometimes called *terrae* or lands in the sources of the late twelfth century and thereafter.[173] This is why the vocabulary of jurisdiction tended towards the ubiquitous *Landgerichte*, regional magistracies, which emerged by the thirteenth century to deal with the most serious offences, namely murder, rape, robbery, incendiarism and grievous bodily harm. To their place in the German kingdom we will return in Part III. Unfortunately for us, the fragmentary nature of the sources makes the political interpretation of the rise of *terrae* rather like looking at a storm-obscured landscape through the wrong end of a telescope. Be that as it may, by the third and fourth decades of the thirteenth century, the royal chancery began to use the expression *dominus terrae*, 'lord of the land' to describe the magnate who actually exercised the jurisdiction.[174] Such men were the real heirs of the eleventh-century *ducatus*.

Part II: Germany and its Neo-Roman Empire

When Emperor Otto the Great resided in Italy between 966 and 972, Widukind of Corvey recorded that Archbishop William of Mainz 'ruled the *imperium* of the Franks' as regent north of the Alps. To some extent the phrase reflects Widukind's prejudice against Rome. He did not approve of the Roman definition given to Otto the Great's imperial title assumed in 962. For him, Otto was emperor or *imperator* in the Roman military style by virtue of his victory over the Magyars at the Lech in 955, not as a consequence of coronation at the hands of the pope.[1] What Widukind's expression also conveys is that Otto the Great's *imperium* was visualised by him as the continuation of the Carolingian Empire of the Franks. This was made possible by his theory that Charlemagne's conquest of Saxony turned Franks and Saxons into one *gens*. But whatever nuance Widukind preferred to give to the imperial restoration of the 960s, the new emperor's chancery proclaimed him *imperator augustus Romanorum ac Francorum*, 'Emperor Augustus of the Romans and Franks' in so obvious a reference to the Carolingian emperors that their conception of Empire was what the Ottonian regime hoped to restore.[2] The medieval Germans rightly sensed that just as it was the Frankish conquest which initiated the possibility of their cooperating as 'one people' in Widukind's sense, so it was the foundation of Charlemagne's Roman Empire in and after 800 which was the model and basis for the restoration of 962. This is why we need to consider the military and ideological transformation of the Frankish realm into the neo-Roman Empire of 800,[3] and more especially how this affected the peoples of East Francia.

Eighth-Century Foundations for the Neo-Roman Empire

The *Lorsch Annals* for 801, among other sources, pointed out that since Italy, Gaul, Germany and Rome itself had submitted to Charlemagne's authority, it was enough to justify his elevation into a Roman emperor.[4] So the new Empire was perceived as an empire by conquest whether it was Roman or Frankish in name, and this was what was to appeal to Widukind of Corvey as well. Imperial history in the ninth century was to show by contrast that the expansive military tendency could not be kept up, so the Carolingian Empire declined in consequence.[5] The transition from Frankish realm to neo-Roman Empire had relied heavily upon military success, and this to some extent upon the institutional reform of the army. Nevertheless, the degree to which Carolingian military force may be related to grants of land in benefice to vassals has recently been questioned,[6] and the problem of military reform will have to be re-examined. But there were changes which indicate an ever greater reach to Carolingian military force. According to several sources, Pepin the Short changed the date for opening the annual campaign from March to May, certainly to solve supply problems for the expanding cavalry arm of Frankish armies.[7] So the eighth century witnessed much more formidable campaigns and the consequent dilation of the kingdom under competent commanders. This inspired Einhard to claim, with some exaggeration, that the large and powerful realm of Pepin was almost doubled in its extent by Charlemagne's efforts.[8]

Without military success of this nature it is hard to conceive of a new western Empire being initiated in 800, but even so religious and ideological motives probably outstripped the material. After the collapse of Byzantine support for the Papacy against the Lombards in 730, the Roman Church experimented with aligning itself with the aspirations of the Carolingian dynasty; for example, in setting up the new ecclesiastical apparatus east of the Rhine which we considered in Part I. The Papacy was invited to contribute to transforming the Carolingian mayors of the palace into kings. Pope Zacharias gave his consent, and on his visit to Francia in 754, Pope Stephen II anointed Pepin the Short and his sons at the Abbey of St Denis.[9] The reference was to the prestige of Old Testament kingship and to the prophet Samuel's anointing of Saul and David as Heaven's chosen kings. At the Carolingian court explicit references were later made to the Davidic, victorious, celestially approved kingship of Charlemagne.

In return for papal support, the Carolingians offered to underwrite Roman claims to temporal authority in Italy, a step seen as necessary to stem the Lombard threat to papal possessions. In 754 the court issued the 'Donation of Pepin' to guarantee Roman rights, and twenty years later it was confirmed by Charlemagne after he had overthrown the Lombard kingdom.[10] By 774 their alliance with the Papacy and their hostility to the Lombards had thus established the authority of the Franks in Italy, but there was nothing specific in this to suggest that a western Roman Empire ought to be restored. Since 754 the Frankish rulers were in any case entitled 'patricians of the Romans', encompassing a protective role for the Papacy which Pepin and Charlemagne had taken seriously in confronting the Lombards at papal request.

Since the defection of Byzantium into iconoclasm in 730, the Papacy may have needed a new protector, but according to the interesting but palpably forged 'Donation of Constantine' probably confected in Rome some time in the eighth century,[11] this could hardly be a new emperor. The source asserts that Roman imperial authority had migrated to the east under Constantine the Great, leaving the dominion of the west to the Papacy:

> . . . in order that the prestige of the Papacy should not deteriorate in any way, but on the contrary should shine even more brightly than the honour of the Empire and its power and glory, we hereby concede and confer to the blessed Sylvester, our father, the universal Pope, not only our palace of the Lateran, already mentioned, but also the city of Rome, and likewise all the provinces, districts and cities of Italy and the Western regions, so that they may be held by him and his successors in their power and under their guardianship.[12]

Obviously such an extravagant claim was hardly intended to be taken literally, but read in its eighth-century context it reveals a train of thought that surfaces in the 'Donation of Pepin' too: that the Roman pontifical dignity included secular as well as religious authority. If the pope could be considered as something like an emperor at least in theory, then there was no immediate reason why Rome's temporal authority established as St Peter's republic should abandon its autonomy to some reconstituted western Empire.[13] This argument was fortified when the eastern Roman Empire returned to catholic orthodoxy in abandoning iconoclasm at the second council of Nicaea in 787, and Pope Hadrian I (772–95) was quick to extend recognition to Constantinople again.

This changed in the 790s and culminated in the Frankish king being turned into a Roman emperor. But why? Everyone knew that an emperor was something more than a king, the prestige of the Byzantine rulers proving the point. As the French historian Robert Folz pointed out, when a barbarian king towered over his contemporaries, then the chroniclers liked to suggest a quasi-imperial status for him.[14] This can be detected in Gregory of Tours for Clovis as king of the Franks; in Cassiodorus and Jordanes on Theoderic as king of Italy; and in Adamnan of Iona for the victorious Oswald of Northumbria. This attitude was divorced from Byzantine pretensions to universal rule and from notions of Roman power cherished by the Papacy, but it was crucial to promoting Charlemagne as an emperor in 800 and Otto the Great in 962. By the 790s the Frankish king had acquired the requisite status by conquering the pagans, Saxons due for conversion and Avars ripe for slaughter, but perhaps the shrewdest testimony to his charisma is provided by a later biographer, Notker Balbulus of St Gallen, writing in the 880s, because it is conjoined with the current theory of a final, divinely commissioned Empire needed to take mankind through the last stages of world history towards the Apocalypse:

> He who ordains the fate of kingdoms and the march of the centuries, the all-powerful Disposer of events, having destroyed one extraordinary image, that of the Romans, which had, it was true, feet of iron, or even feet of clay, then raised up, among the Franks, the golden head of a second image, equally remarkable, in the person of the illustrious Charlemagne.[15]

Such imagery derived from the Book of Daniel was a constant preoccupation in medieval historiography, and Charlemagne's decisive role in inaugurating the 'Last Empire' contributed to his legend as the model ruler for the entire Middle Ages.[16]

The Coronation of 800 as the Formative Event

In 799 Charlemagne's adviser Alcuin of York minuted his opinion of recent events and sent it to the king. Pope Leo III had fallen victim to a conspiracy in Rome, a hazard frequently endured by the Papacy in medieval politics, and had fled to the protection of Charlemagne at

Paderborn in Saxony. Secondly, the Byzantine emperor Constantine VI had been deposed and blinded by his mother in 797. As Alcuin remarked, 'the news has spread everywhere of the impious manner in which the head of this Empire has been deposed . . .'. Alcuin then put forward his version of the mantle of heaven falling upon Charlemagne in these circumstances:

> Thirdly, there is the sovereign status which Our Lord Jesus Christ has reserved to you in order that you may govern all Christian peoples. This status is higher than the two others, eclipses them in wisdom and surpasses them in power. It is now on thee alone that the Churches of Christ depend, from thee alone they await their salvation, from thee, avenger of crimes . . . .

Since Charlemagne's Christ-given authority outstripped, according to Alcuin, the powers of the Papacy and the court of Constantinople, the way was clear for the resumption of a western imperial title. The year before, Alcuin had in any case referred to a superior *imperium christianum* committed by God to Charlemagne and his sons to govern, in an obvious signal to policy-makers that the Frankish realm and the Danielic 'Last Empire' in its western Roman guise were one and the same thing.[17]

In modern historiography it is widely assumed that Pope Leo III acquiesced in creating Charlemagne a Roman emperor in order to restore papal authority in Rome. There is much to be said for this argument, but it is hard to see why Charlemagne's title of *patricius* of the Romans, held as we have seen by the Carolingian dynasty since 754, would not have served just as well. The sources for 800 are in fact somewhat fragmentary and contradictory. In 817 Einhard claimed that the king was taken aback and was subsequently annoyed to have been proclaimed emperor by a pope, possibly because it seemed to place his authority in some kind of position subordinate to the papal name, against what Alcuin had just told him in 799. The semi-official *Annales regni Francorum* did not record an unfavourable reaction from Charlemagne, and ascribed the management of the occasion to the pope, just as Einhard does. This agrees closely with the official Roman account given in the *Liber Pontificalis*. The Byzantine chronicler Theophanes rightly perceived that the coronation was, in part, a 'deal' with Pope Leo III in exchange for his restoration to the Holy See: 'In order to repay Charles, Leo crowned him Emperor of the Romans in the church of the holy apostle Peter, anointing him with olive oil from head to foot and clothing him in the imperial regalia and crown.' Theophanes could not resist poking fun at the western rite of unction.[18]

The fact is that so extraordinary a series of events in 799 and 800 excited different opinions, memories and interpretations. If Charlemagne appeared to abdicate some of his power by accepting a coronation at papal hands, then Leo III was obliged to concede a portion of the Papacy's secular claims by elevating a new Roman emperor. The 'Donation of Constantine' was certainly back in the drawer.[19] As Theophanes put it, 'Rome has been under the power of the Franks ever since.' Perhaps the most judicious opinion was recorded in the *Lorsch Annals* (Vienna manuscript), because it combines the advanced 'Frankish' views of Alcuin and Einhard with the 'Roman' interest reflected in the Royal Frankish Annals and the *Liber Pontificalis*:

> Since there was no longer an emperor in the country of the Greeks, and the imperial power was in the hands of a woman [Irene, mother of Constantine VI], it seemed to Pope Leo and to all the holy fathers who were at that time assembled in council, and also to all other Christian people, that it would be fitting to give the title of emperor to King Charles, who held in his power the town of Rome, where the Caesars were always accustomed to reside, and the other towns of Italy, of Gaul and not just those of Germany. Since God Almighty had thus permitted all these places to be placed under his authority, it seemed right to them that, in accordance with the will of God and the request of all Christian people, he should in addition bear the title of emperor. Charlemagne did not wish to oppose this request and, submitting humbly to God, as well as to the wish expressed by the priests and all Christian people, he received his consecration from Pope Leo and along with it the title of emperor.[20]

As a definition for the neo-Roman Empire as a God-given gift, things could hardly go further.

Some understanding of the coronation of 800 as a formative event is crucial because it already contains ideological implications for the relative status of papal power and imperial authority, and for the future cooperation or conflict between them. If Pope Leo III had been rescued from his difficulties and had acquired an effective protector modelled upon Constantine and Theodosius, then the price was, as Theophanes perceived, accommodation to the political domination of Italy by the Franks. In 796 Charlemagne had already written to Leo III to spell out his conception of royal power sustaining the Catholic faith:[21]

> It is for us, in accordance with the help of divine goodness, out-wardly to defend by force of arms the Holy Church of Christ in all places from the incursions of pagans and the ravages of infidels, and inwardly to fortify her with our confession of the Catholic faith. It is for you, most holy father, raising your hands to God with Moses, to aid our armies, to the end that with you as intercessors and with God as guide and giver our Christian people may in all places have the victory over the enemies of its holy name, and that the name of Our Lord Jesus Christ may be renowned throughout all the world.

The ruler did the work while the pope turned the prayer wheel.

In 813, near the end of his reign, Charlemagne arranged for his heir Louis the Pious to be crowned emperor in the palace chapel at Aachen. A coherent explanation is that Charlemagne had initially regarded the imperial title as a personal accolade which could not conveniently be passed on to his three sons. But by the end of 811 Charles and Pepin were dead, so the decision was taken after laborious consultation with the Frankish Church and aristocracy to make Louis into an emperor after all. As Thegan's *Vita Hludowici* pointed out, Charlemagne was too infirm to delay the event, so the coronation at Aachen rather than at Rome may not after all refer to any dissatisfaction with the Roman coronation of 800 upon which Einhard insisted in his biography of Charlemagne composed in 817. If the coronation of 813 did bear out some preference for a Frankish rather than a Roman interpretation of the imperial name, then it did not last long in that form. In 816 Pope Stephen IV recrowned Louis the Pious as emperor at Rheims, and in 823 his eldest son Lothar – coopted as emperor in 817 – was reconsecrated in Rome by Pope Paschal I. The new emperors then went further than Charlemagne's conclusions in his letter to Pope Leo III in 796. Since it was the pope's duty to cultivate prayer, the faith and morals while Frankish power governed the Empire, Rome itself was placed under a Frankish commission by the *Constitutio Romana* of 824.[22]

The Western Imperial Ideal in the Ninth Century

The convergence of Frankish and Christian authority in the form of a neo-Roman western Empire was taken with the utmost seriousness by Louis the Pious,[23] but the ideals rehearsed in 800 and 813 soon ran into difficulties. The invincible hand which authors of the ninth century liked to ascribe to emperors fell foul of Carolingian dynastic politics and resulted in 843 with the effective tripartite division of the Empire at the Treaty of Verdun which we considered in the Introduction. The imperial name certainly retained its outward form and prestige, and the ideal of protecting the faith in general and the Papacy in particular could not be eroded. In fact the obvious decline of Carolingian political power in the ninth century had the effect of concentrating the imperial focus upon that alignment of celestial, secular and religious authority adumbrated by Alcuin of York in 799.

As an illustration of this, Emperor Louis II (850–75) towards the end of his reign addressed a letter to his Byzantine rival Basil I (867–86). It was almost certainly confected by Louis II's adviser Anastasius Bibliothecarius, who had served briefly as pope in 855 and was subsequently the secretary and librarian of the Holy See. Few other figures from the papal and imperial households can have come so close to understanding the new ideology of the ninth-century West. The letter asserts the following:[24]

> It is fitting that thou shouldst know that if we were not emperors of the Romans we should not be emperors of the Franks either. We have received this name and this title from the Romans, among whom the pinnacle of such great sublimity and such a distinguished appellation first shone with a brilliant light; it was the decision of God which caused us to assume the government of the people and of the city, as well as the defence and exaltation of the mother of all the Churches, who conferred authority, first as kings and then as Emperors, on the first princes of our dynasty. Indeed, it was only those of the Frankish princes whom the Roman pontiff consecrated for the purpose by means of the holy oil who bore the royal and then the imperial title.

But in spite of their unique status as the Lord's Anointed, 'the government of the people and of the city' in reference to Carolingian authority over Rome was no longer realistic.

In the second half of the ninth century the nobility of Rome and central Italy entrenched its power to the detriment of the Papacy and the Carolingians alike. Several imperial successors to Louis II still visited Rome, but the last vestige of Frankish influence there eventually came to an end with the death of Emperor Arnulf in 899. The actual title of emperor survived among Italian potentates until 924. By that time the papal see was controlled by the Roman aristocracy, and it seemed unlikely that imperial power from the sub-Frankish north or from the traditional Byzantine east could ever reappear in Italy to sort out the problems of the Roman Church as Charlemagne had done in 800 and 801.

Imperial Restoration in the Tenth Century

The last of Charlemagne's direct descendants to wear the imperial crown was Berengar of Friuli, who reigned as king in Italy from 888 to 924 and was made emperor by Pope John X in 915. But with the rise to power in Rome of the comital dynasty of Theophylact,[25] there was no immediate future for the ninth-century tradition of imperial protection over the Holy See, although the idea by no means died out of the possible political repertoire. The west Frankish kings, distracted by dynastic rivalries and internal political fragmentation, and the new Saxon dynasty in East Francia, its regal authority remote from Rome and its power threatened by the Magyars and Slavs, were surely not likely to be able to interfere in Italian politics in the style of Charlemagne, Louis the Pious and Lothar I. But this proved to be wrong. Otto the Great inaugurated the German imperial age in 962 on the basis of Carolingian tradition, and it was to last in various guises until the abolition of the Holy Roman Empire of the German Nation in 1806.

As the German scholar Percy Ernst Schramm pointed out long ago,[26] the powerful myth proclaiming the City of Rome as head of the world did not wither just because the neo-Roman emperors of the period 800 to 924 had, in the end, failed to establish a lasting political link between Rome and Francia. But the question remains: when did Otto I of East Francia crystallise his ambition to turn himself into an emperor, and what were his motives? It is not possible to provide a completely convincing answer, because the principal sources are at odds about the king's political propulsion towards imperial status. In his *Liber de Ottone rege* Bishop Liudprand of Cremona presented the imperial coronation of 962 as the culmination of a rescue-package for the Italian kingdom in general and for the Papacy in particular.[27] In this respect the account clearly resembles the tradition for the events of Charlemagne's reign, telescoping the conquest of 774 and the coronation of 800 into a much shorter span, Otto's conquest of Lombardy in 961 and his Roman coronation in 962. But Widukind of Corvey, as we have seen, presented a completely different explanation for Otto the Great's rights as an emperor, a revival of the classical idea that 'the army creates the emperor'.[28] Widukind's earnest devotion to this explanation is borne out by his account of Henry I's victory over the Magyars in 933, where he claims that the army then proclaimed the king as *pater patriae, rerum dominus imperatorque*, 'father of his country, lord of all things and emperor.'[29]

After his victory at the River Lech in 955 Widukind also ascribed the *pater patriae* and emperor epithets to Otto I as victor,[30] and thereafter calls Otto emperor even though the Roman coronation was not to take place for another six and a half years. That event Widukind refused to mention, claiming that Otto's glorious campaigns in Italy in the 960s including his triumphant entries into Rome were beyond his powers to describe! In his text Widukind would not permit the Saxon rulers to receive any kind of honour at the hands of popes or Romans. For him, Saxon glory justified itself and its new imperial heroes. But in his epitaph for Otto the Great, he did label him *imperator Romanorum*, emperor of the Romans, which was a title not often used by Otto himself, whose chancery preferred the more neutral title *imperator augustus* while negotiations with the Byzantine court were being undertaken. Widukind rounded out his phrasing with another epithet, *rex gentium* or 'king of the peoples', in itself another justification for crediting imperial stature to Otto the Great.[31]

Whatever preferences Widukind may have aired, the politics which actually brought Otto I to Rome for his coronation in February 962 did look remarkably like one of the motives for Charlemagne's coronation in 800: a manoeuvre by the Papacy for restoring its own authority under a new protector. Pope John XII (955–64) was himself a member of the aristocratic house of Theophylact which had dominated Rome since the early tenth century, but his secular authority was threatened by Berengar II of Ivrea, who had reigned as king of Italy since 950. One option was to play another claimant, Otto the Great, who had in 951 married Adelheid of Burgundy, widow of the previous Italian ruler Lothar (948–50), against Berengar II. It was the solution adopted, and papal envoys visited Germany in 960.

It is possible that the pope did not appreciate how effective the German seizure of Italy in 961 might then turn out to be. With a relatively settled state of affairs in Germany and the Magyar threat behind him since 955, Otto the Great was ready to extend his reach as far as the imperial title. After consecrating the new emperor, Pope John XII announced that one motive was to reward Otto as conqueror of the heathen nations and as defender of the Christian Church with a triumphal crown bestowed by the apostolic prestige of St Peter.[32] This comes extremely close to Carolingian conceptions of what the neo-Roman imperial office was for. In a sense Otto the Great did accept that papal participation was necessary and desirable for the restoration of the western Empire. A military acclamation in the style proposed by Widukind of Corvey and the *de facto* domination of several peoples were not quite enough. It is not difficult to see where Otto the Great found the models: in the coronation and *imperium* of Charlemagne.[33]

The sources which directly report Otto's proclamation as emperor, Adalbert of St Maximin's continuation of Regino of Prüm's chronicle and Liudprand of Cremona's *Liber de Ottone rege*, take a radically different approach from Widukind of Corvey in that the event is celebrated as a positive achievement for pope and emperor.[34] But both chroniclers are weak on the Carolingian precedent. Its significance is testified by one of the most important productions of Otto I's chancery confected with papal assistance, the diploma known as the *Ottonianum*, which confirms the rights and resources of the Roman See in Italy.[35] The source is based upon the pact between Pepin the Short and Pope Stephen II (754) repeated by Charlemagne for Pope Hadrian I in 774 about papal rights in Italy. The 962 version inaccurately refers to the Carolingian kings as though they were already emperors, but this error simply reinforces the ideological importance of the past to the restoration of the neo-Roman Empire in 962.

In spite of unresolved difficulties in interpreting the *Ottonianum*, it represents the closest we can confidently approach to the East Frankish court's understanding of the restoration of the Empire. It was a renovation not only of Roman but of Frankish *imperium*, memories of the latter probably being easier to comprehend in tenth-century Germany than materials about the classical Roman past. The Saxon nun Hroswitha of Gandersheim, in her own account of Otto the Great's reign, followed Notker Balbulus of St Gallen in employing the theory of imperial *translatio* or devolution in order to make a similar point about the proximity of the Carolingian Empire to the East

Frankish regime of her day, turning in due course into the renewed Ottonian *imperium*:[36] 'the King of kings, who alone rules forever, by His own power changing the fortunes of all kings decreed that the distinguished realm of the Franks be transferred to the famous race of the Saxons' . . . and so on.

Whatever the protagonists of the time hoped to gain from restoring the neo-Roman Empire in the west in 962, the Papacy got more than it bargained for in the way of imperial protection. This is because the emperors gained the right of scrutiny and virtually of confirmation in papal elections, and several times used these powers to secure pontiffs to their liking. This kind of influence was repudiated in the eleventh-century phase of ecclesiastical reform when papal elections were confined by decree to the college of cardinals in 1059.

Pope John XII regretted his arrangements with Otto the Great, renounced them in 963 and had to be driven out of Rome. If the sources are anything to go by, then it was Emperor Otto who enjoyed the moral edge in politics over the papal court. Pope John XIII (965– 72) admitted that of all emperors Otto was the most august after Constantine the Great and Theodosius the Great, and Bishop Liud-prand of Cremona ascribed a panegyric duly delivered by the Romans and encapsulating the supposed imperial virtues: 'The emperor, as we have learned by experience, knows, works and loves the things of God: he guards the affairs of church and state with his sword, adorns them by his virtues, and purifies them by his laws',[37] possibly referring to the *Ottonianum*.

These are tainted sources in the sense that John XIII and Liud-prand of Cremona were close associates of the imperial court. But they do testify to the fact that after a turbulent and successful reign north of the Alps, Otto the Great was able to build upon the Italian claims opened up for him by his marriage to Adelheid of Italy and to go so far as to restore the Empire. The recriminations amongst Otto's suppor-ters and adversaries bring to mind the controversy in evaluating the coronation of 800: the murky mixture of ecclesiastical, Frankish and Roman traditions and ambitions. For a century the German court would, on balance, enjoy a reasonably secure hold over papal politics, and would use it, as we shall see, in an ecclesiastically reformist sense which was high-minded if not always popular in Italy.

Nevertheless, the German emperors found plenty of admirers in Italy, such as Liudprand of Cremona, who asserted that the disorders of the period before 961 were destroying the future health of Italy. But his opinions were by no means universal. Some Italians bewailed the

advent of the Germans as a disaster, and viewed the achievement of
Otto the Great as a foreign conquest. Percy Ernst Schramm drew
attention to the way in which the chronicler Benedict of Monte Soratte
relied upon the classical image of Rome's greatness in the opposite
sense, to bewail its submission to Otto I and Otto II as barbarian
despoilers:[38]

> Woe to Rome oppressed and trampled upon by so many peoples,
> taken prisoner by the Saxon king, your townsfolk ruled by the
> sword, and your strength all gone. They carry off your gold and
> silver by the sackful . . . At the height of your power you triumphed
> over the peoples, threw the world into the dust, and throttled the
> kings of the earth. You held the sceptre and the highest authority,
> now you are thoroughly pillaged and plundered by the Saxon kings.

And so on, with more rhetoric in the same colourfully effective vein.

Ideal and Reality under Otto II and Otto III

Obviously Otto the Great was satisfied with what the imperial title
had done for Saxon prestige in Germany and Italy, because he
arranged for Pope John XIII to co-opt his young son Otto II as
emperor in 967. The immediately perceived problem, however, was to
gain recognition from the resurgent Byzantine Empire. For the
purpose, Bishop Liudprand was sent to Constantinople in 968 to
secure a political settlement and a Greek princess as Otto II's bride.
The mission was a failure. The Byzantine emperor Nicephorus I
Phocas (963–9) is reported to have spoken of 'the impiety of your
master [Otto I], who in the guise of an hostile invader has laid claim to
Rome'; and again,

> Do you want a greater scandal than that he should call himself
> emperor and claim for himself provinces [Italy] belonging to our
> empire? Both these things are intolerable; and if both are insuppor-
> table, that especially is not to be borne, nay, not to be heard of, that
> he calls himself emperor.[39]

It is not difficult to see why the Byzantine court, which considered
itself the true heir to the Roman name ever since 330, disapproved of

Otto the Great's new title. Liudprand of Cremona was obliged to return empty-handed to the western emperor, but the fall of Nice-phorus Phocas motivated a change of attitude in Constantinople. Since the reconquest of Italy seemed at that time to be beyond the capacity of the Byzantine Empire, John I Tzimisces (969–76) resolved to recognise the new imperial regime in the west, and despatched to Italy a bride for Otto II after all. Theophanu's identity has never been established beyond doubt, but probably she was a niece of Tzimisces.[40] Whether Bishop Liudprand lived to see the outcome he had tried to negotiate in 968 we do not know, but the account of his legation to Constantinople does reveal the complexity of the political issues once the East Frankish king attempted to rule south of the Alps as well. Since the arrival of the Arabs in Sicily and of the Germans in Lombardy, one has to add two more powers to the Roman, south Italian Lombard and Byzantine interests in Italy.

Otto II (973–83) sought to resolve such problems by incorporating the rest of Italy south of Rome into the western Empire, at the same time reducing or eliminating the threat which the Muslim emirate of Sicily posed to the Italian mainland. Otto II cast himself as a military emperor in the mould of his father. Writing early in the eleventh century, Bishop Thietmar of Merseburg sought to explain Otto II's motivation:

> The Caesar so ruled the Roman Empire that whatever his father had previously possessed he held as well, stoutly resisting the Saracens' attack and driving them far from his boundaries. Ascer-taining that Calabria was suffering heavily from frequent incursions by the Greeks and pillage by the Saracens, Caesar summoned the Bavarians and battle-trained Swabians to reinforce his army.[41]

Otto's efforts to occupy southern Italy were overthrown in July 982 in battle against a Sicilian expeditionary force. At an unknown place by the sea in Calabria, the imperial army was overwhelmed by the Muslims. The traditional site is Cape Colonna.[42] The emperor man-aged to escape by plunging his horse through the waves to a Byzantine ship. So the early 980s marked a low point for western imperial power which relied heavily on the military potential provided by the East Frankish duchies. Failure of the Calabrian campaign was followed by the loss of a large proportion of Sclavinia in the revolt of 983. Otto II died unexpectedly at the end of 983, and this required a regency for the infant Otto III at an already perilous time.

Otto III attained his majority in 994 and was crowned emperor in Rome in 996. His short personal reign has always attracted attention, because he appears to have been interested in shifting the political focus of the Empire from the military emphasis given by the sources to his father and grandfather over towards the ideological. In his examination of the rich sources about Otto's *renovatio* in chapter IV of *Kaiser, Rom und Renovatio*, Percy Ernst Schramm showed how Otto and his circle were concerned to promote the literal Roman name and the missionary duty of Christian Roman emperors more eagerly than had been possible for his predecessors. For long periods the emperor resided in Rome and directed his court according to practices thought at the time to match classical antecedents. But the motive was more earnest than superficial political borrowing. Otto III evidently thought that the Roman Empire had been bestowed upon him by celestial providence for religious reasons: to reform and to expand the Christian faith and, possibly, to save the world from imminent destruction by renewing the Roman Empire which was destined to coexist with the Christian Church until the end of time.

So it is not hard to see why Constantine the Great and Charlemagne served, in spite of their political and military ruthlessness, as models for Otto III's exercise of *imperium*. But probably because the limits to an expanding military empire brutally felt in 982 and 983 on the Italian and Saxon fronts were well understood at the court in which Otto III was brought up, it was their legendary services to the faith and to the Church which appealed to Otto III and his circle. The cult of Charlemagne was taken seriously by the emperor, who adopted the Carolingian slogan *renovatio imperii Romanorum*, 'renewal of the empire of the Romans', for his own seals.[43] Otto's personal streak of ascetic religiosity is well attested, and what interested him above all was the religious renewal of the Roman Empire. In 996 Otto III appointed his cousin Bruno of Carinthia as first German pope. He adopted the reign-name of Gregory V in deference to one of the reforming fathers of the Church, Pope Gregory the Great (590–604). In 998 Bishop Leo of Vercelli, who had been one of the chaplains of the court, addressed a rhapsody to the pope and the emperor as the luminaries of the age, including many extravagant expressions about their devotion to *renovatio*, culminating with 'the times are reformed by the pope under the aegis of Caesar'.[44]

But it is likely that the churchman who best understood the programme of *renovatio* and its implications was Otto III's tutor from France, Gerbert of Aurillac, archbishop of Ravenna. Succeeding

Gregory V as pope in 999, he took the reign-name of Sylvester II, evoking the supposed collaborative relationship of Constantine the Great and Pope Sylvester I (314–35) when Christianity had first been proclaimed the official religion of the Roman Empire. What was actually a myth from the fourth century was intended to become reality in the tenth. Leo of Vercelli's verses had looked to the Byzantine Empire and to the traditional patriarchates of the East as the field for the renewal of Roman power. But this was a pure fantasy. Otto and Sylvester developed much more specific and practical plans for promoting the *renovatio imperii Romanorum* as a Christian enterprise in northern and western Europe instead, the outcome shown in the establishment of archiepiscopal sees and suffragans in newly-converted countries, Poland and Hungary, under the direct auspices of pope and emperor.[45] It is thought that the programme was intended to be extended to Scandinavia and Russia.

Otto III's adoption of new titles, 'servant of Jesus Christ' and 'servant of the Apostles', testifies to his enthusiasm for the religious style of reform indicated by Leo of Vercelli. The high point of the *renovatio* as we know it came about in 1000 when Otto set out for Poland. Travelling to the tomb of the martyred missionary bishop Adalbert of Prague (983–97) at Gniezno, he was received by the Polish duke Boleslav I Chrobry (992–1025), and together they inaugurated Gniezno as Poland's metropolitan see. The duke was presented with a copy of the Holy Lance, the most potent of the relics in the imperial treasury, and then he accompanied Otto III back to Germany to visit Aachen, where the emperor is reported to have exhumed the remains of Charlemagne in order to rehouse them in a new tomb in the palace chapel. The transmission of the pallium from Rome to Gniezno, the exchange of relics – Otto received a portion of the body of St Adalbert – and reverence for Charlemagne's memory illustrate something of that blend of the sacred with the political to which Sylvester II and Otto III appealed in their programme of renewal.

The symbolic importance of Aachen's connection with the prestigious Carolingian *imperium* was a well-understood dimension of Otto III's *renovatio*. For example, the *Annals of Quedlinburg*, in reporting the emperor's visit in 1000, described Aachen as the place which stood above all others with the exception of Rome itself.[46] On his deathbed in Italy in 1002, Otto insisted upon his corpse being transported all the way back to Aachen for burial in the same chapel as Charlemagne, the first protagonist of *renovatio imperii Romanorum*. The success of the mission to Poland was followed by the official conversion of Hungary, the coronation of Stephen as its first king with a crown sent by Otto III and Sylvester II, and the elevation of Esztergom as the first Hungarian archbishopric in 1001. The sources about these events are sparse, but in any case the emperor could not himself visit Hungary because he had become entangled in plans to suppress a revolt by the Roman nobility against the imperial court.

It would not be reasonable to dismiss Otto III's and Sylvester II's aims as chimerical, even though so much of the programme remains opaque. *Renovatio* remained a constant inspiration in the politics of Germany's neo-Roman Empire, so the experiment about the year 1000 counts as more than a wasteful interlude between the more military understanding of imperial politics as exercised by an Otto II or a Conrad II before Henry III reverted to a specific programme of Roman reform in 1046. Otto III's intentions of making Rome into the imperial as well as the papal capital foundered upon the hostility of the Romans themselves, in a city where the political strength of the nobility had increased since the end of the ninth century. If Leo of Vercelli was not averse to some sort of renewal of the city's political significance, then it was to be subordinate, in his view, to German control: 'Christ, hear our prayers, look down on thy city of Rome; in thy goodness, revive the Romans, reawaken the strength of Rome; let Rome rise again under the rule of the Emperor Otto III.'[47]

The sources are not clear about Otto III's long-term intentions. At one point he even threatened to resign and to retire to Jerusalem in what may have been intended as an apocalyptic scenario for Christian history. In East Francia there was some disapproval of the emperor's long absences south of the Alps. Early in 1001 Otto III was expelled from Rome. The biographer of Bishop Bernward of Hildesheim who was visiting Rome at the time ascribed the following words to Otto III in his address to the Romans before he left, and they may well give some insight into how the emperor thought that adopting Rome as the principal imperial residence was necessary to the programme of renewal:[48]

Are you not my Romans? For you indeed I left my fatherland and also forsook my kin. For love of you I rejected my Saxons and all the Germans, my blood. I led you into remote parts of my empire in which your fathers, when they ruled the world, never set foot, that I might spread your name and glory to the ends of the earth. I adopted you as my sons. I preferred you to all. For your sake, because I put you before all, I brought on myself the envy and hatred of all.

Otto III was never able to retake Rome. A year later he was dead, and in 1003 Sylvester II followed him to the grave.

Imperial Rule and Ecclesiastical Reform, 1002–56

As Timothy Reuter wrote in 1991 of Ottonian hegemony,[49]

> Until comparatively recently it could be debated whether the Italian and imperial involvement of the Ottonians was a Good Thing or whether it hindered German development, but this question, whose answers were heavily influenced by the contemporary debate about the nature and purpose of a unified Germany, no longer seems very interesting.

It used to be thought that the Saxon kings, misled like their Salian and Staufen successors by the Carolingian example, somehow expended German assets in Italy which might better have been put to use in centralising their realm north of the Alps. But this seriously misundstands what could have been achieved with the resources at hand, which did not in any case include the mental picture of centralisation that appealed to theorists in the sixteenth and seventeenth centuries.

Once Otto the Great had settled Saxony, the duchies and the Magyar question to his satisfaction, then there was nothing to lose by acquiring the Lombard kingdom, the alliance of the Papacy, and the imperial title of Charlemagne and his successors. In other words Otto I, his son and grandson may have invested some expenditure of German resources, but it returned a great gain to their prestige and no diminution of their authority. In any case, the neo-Roman Empire sponsored from East Francia did not face the same levels of internal diversity and external pressure which accelerated the disintegration of the Carolingian Empire.

Conceptions of Otto III's immediate successors as exponents of the German imperial theme are necessarily coloured by our understanding of the sources, notably Bishop Thietmar of Merseburg's not entirely uncritical account of Henry II's time (1002–24) and Wipo's adulatory biography of the first Salian emperor Conrad II (1024–39), written in part as a 'mirror of princes' for Conrad's son Henry III (1039–56). In their quite different characters the three emperors of this time were all noted for their committed piety and for their military and diplomatic skills. The demise of Otto III and Sylvester II by no means devalued the ideal of religious and imperial *renovatio* under German auspices. Nevertheless, some of the ground had to be won afresh. In 1004 Henry II descended upon Lombardy and secured recognition as king against his rival, Margrave Arduin of Ivrea, who claimed the Italian crown from 1002 to 1015.

The expulsion of Otto III from Rome and the career of Arduin of Ivrea reveal that German authority in Italy was not sustained by a sound institutional foundation. Instead, successive emperors had relied upon cliques among the Lombard and Roman aristocrats and churchmen to rally to the support of their claims. In Rome itself, Henry II was able to take advantage of the rivalry between the dynasties of the Crescentii and of the counts of Tusculum, descendants of the house of Theophylact so prominent in the tenth century. When the latter regained power in 1012 and installed one of their own as Pope Benedict VIII (1012–24), the German king was able to enter Rome in 1014 for his imperial coronation. Hitherto Henry II had very modestly echoed Otto III's programme of imperial renewal by using Charlemagne's seal as a prototype with the downbeat inscription *renovatio regni Francorum*. But once his imperial coronation explicitly confirmed him as advocate of the Holy See, *patronus* and *defensor* of the Roman Church in the chosen words of Thietmar of Merseburg,[50] then pope and emperor exhibited vigorous cooperation in holding reforming synods which foreshadowed the reform of the Church undertaken from 1046. Synods were held at Rome and Ravenna in 1014 and at Bamberg in 1020 during the pope's festive visit to Germany. Henry II committed himself to the imperial tradition of Otto the Great and Charlemagne by confirming the *Ottonianum*,[51] a concession from which even Otto III had drawn back. On Henry II's next visit to Italy, pope and emperor held another reforming council at Pavia in 1022.

The activities of Henry II and Benedict VIII have not achieved the status in historiography enjoyed by the reforms of Otto III and Sylvester II, followed by those of Henry III's German popes after 1046. But they are significant in revealing that the ideals of *renovatio* were by no means moribund. Church and Empire were committed by God to emperor and pope for the improvement of Christian order and its faith, however rapidly they might be approaching the dreaded millenial consummation. Imperial protection of the Roman See was by no means regarded with political cynicism, as a mechanism for the control of Italy, but as a celestially invented relationship expounded through Pope Gelasius I's theory of the Two Swords governing

Christian society, one symbolising papal power, the other Roman imperial authority. At this time ecclesiastical art and literature in Germany and Italy inclined to the view that the emperor was as much a Vicar of Christ on earth as was the pope,[52] and so long as they could co-operate in programmes of ecclesiastical reform and imperial renewal, then this view of the Christian order sustained the dominion of both parties until Gregory VII saw good reason to reject it in 1076. Henry II's own reputation as a reformer, both of the German episcopal and monastic establishments and of the Italian church, was quite impeccable. He was canonised in 1146 and his cult is still valid in the see of Bamberg, which he founded in 1007.

Upon his election to the German throne in 1024, Conrad II took vigorous steps in promoting propaganda about the Salian family as the new *stirps regia* or royal dynasty chosen by God for its imperial and ecclesiastical duties.[53] In 1026 his young son Henry was already elected as next king, whereupon Conrad left for Italy to take over the Lombard kingdom and to proceed to his imperial coronation in Rome. This event, in March 1027, was attended by King Rudolf of Burgundy and King Cnut of Denmark and England. Controversy has always gone on in modern scholarship about the exact date of the magnificent octagonal imperial crown, one of the very finest examples of medieval gold, enamel and jewel work to survive, now in the Vienna *Schatzkammer*. The German art historian Mechtild Schulze-Dörrlamm, after an exhaustive study of the crown's typology, has concluded that it was actually made for the coronation of 1027, and this would certainly fit with the high view Conrad II took of the office for which he was convinced Heaven had chosen him.[54] Debate will go on, but the arc of the crown in any case bears his name and title picked out in pearls: Conrad by the grace of God August Emperor of the Romans. Conrad was also responsible for the resplendent imperial processional cross encrusted with pearls and precious stones which served at the same time as the reliquary for the Holy Lance, with its crucifixion nail acquired for the royal treasury by Henry I in the 920s.

Conrad's imperial authority was advertised not just in the realm of celestial ideals made manifest in costly materials. When the royal house of Burgundy died out in 1032, he was able to vindicate Germany's claim to the kingdom against Count Odo of Champagne, who thought he would be the next king, and by 1034 Conrad II had extended the frontiers of the Empire in the territorial sense to the Rhône and to the coast of Provence. As one of his diplomas expressed it, 'our imperial authority is more and more asserted and strengthened in the realm by the grace of God.'[55] The emperor was also interested in the promotion of the Roman ideal as the foundation of Empire in the style of his predecessors. From an Italian source he adopted for his seal the long-lasting inscription also continued by his Staufen descendants: *Roma caput mundi tenet orbis frena rotundi*,[56] 'Rome as head of the world holds the reins of the Earth.'

Conrad II's biographer may have characterised him as a new Charlemagne, the best credential for a new man, but the fact is that the ruler's experiences in Italy resembled those of his immediate predecessors: riots in Rome and other cities, and military resistance to German rule throughout the country. It is telling that so large a proportion of Wipo's biography is devoted to the unsettled condition of Italy, almost the norm of medieval political endeavour there.[57] Nevertheless, Conrad II was a capable exponent of the inherited imperial ideal, to such an extent that Wipo claims he was the inspiration for a new proverb: 'The saddle of Conrad has the stirrup of Charles.'[58] The chaplain was a known hand at inventing saws.

The actions and plans of emperors such as Charlemagne, Otto the Great and Otto III demonstrated that imperial political power ought to defend, to sustain and, if necessary, to reform papal authority. The idea that the Roman Empire existed in part to defend the Roman Church outlasted the Middle Ages, and it was in this spirit that Henry III patronised a new reform of the Papacy from 1046. But thirty years later a real divergence opened up between papal power seeking ecclesiastical autonomy based upon the vicariate of St Peter and the imperial powers of protection over the Church as traditionally understood by the German court and its attendant bishops. The quarrel between Gregory VII and Henry IV over making the correct appointments to the archbishopric of Milan and other Italian sees, and the much wider argument about the scope and limits of pontifical and imperial powers which that issue raised, motivated a reappraisal of the meaning of the Empire itself in the years after 1076. The reformed papacy could rely upon and develop the tradition of Rome as the apostolic city of St Peter. But the German court certainly did not relinquish the notion of Rome in the physical sense as the keystone to the neo-Roman imperial structure in the West. Ironically the city itself continued to suffer from internal political faction to the detriment of papal authority and imperial claims.[59]

When the recurrent rivalries of Roman ecclesiastical and urban politics resulted in three rival popes by the mid-1040s, Henry III descended upon Italy and held synods in Sutri and Rome which annulled their claims and deposed them in 1046. Partly under the influence of Abbot Odilo of Cluny, Peter Damian of Fonte Avellana and other high-minded churchmen, the king used the opportunity to sponsor yet another reform of the Papacy which in the event inaugurated the great age of Roman reform in the medieval Church. One of the German bishops in the king's entourage, Suidger of Bamberg, was installed as pope, taking the reign-name Clement II in reference to the earliest days of the Papacy's pristine purity. The next day he crowned Henry III and Agnes of Poitou as emperor and empress. The new emperor also received the ancient title of *patricius* of Rome in order to give him the right to approve future popes. Clement II's three successors were also German bishops trusted by the emperor as reformers, but the motive behind his powers as *patricius* had more to do with diluting the undue Roman secular influences which had resulted in the papal schism just ended than in deliberately attempting to create a 'German' Papacy.

Shortly after the events of December 1046, somewhat reminiscent of the measures taken by Otto III and Gregory V in 996, pope and emperor held a reforming synod in Rome early in 1047. Like Henry II and Benedict VIII, Henry III viewed synodal reform as an essential duty of emperors and encouraged the most successful of his popes, his cousin Bishop Bruno of Toul, who reigned as Leo IX from 1049 to 1054, into holding such meetings. Lotharingian and Italian reformers advised the pope on tackling the problem of simony, the sale of clerical offices, which was perceived as the principal cause of corruption in the Church. Leo IX toured Italy, France and Germany to hold synods, including a grand meeting at Mainz with the emperor, nearly forty bishops and the secular magnates of Germany, as Hermann of Reichenau reported.[60] Henry III's understanding of the imperial office thus brought to fruition another tradition stretching back to Charlemagne: as protector of the Papacy, the emperor underwrites its ecclesiastical endeavours. But this serene era of cooperation was about to end.

The Rupture Between Empire and Papacy

The content of the papal reform movement was not at first politically controversial. The German court was itself in the lead in appointing reform-minded bishops and abbots, and this had provided an impetus for Roman reform. But Henry III's unexpected death in 1056 did alter the character of the Roman programme, because its decisions were no longer monitored by the German court during Empress Agnes's troublesome regency for the under-age Henry IV. Canonically the Church had always maintained the theoretical superiority of papal power over any secular authority including the imperial and had, for example, backed it up by forging the Donation of Constantine. After 1056 the more radical reformers such as Archdeacon Hildebrand, Cardinal Humbert of Silva Candida and Bishop Anselm of Lucca might well have perceived that a strong-minded emperor like Henry III was not after all essential to the practical and effective functioning of the papal court for the fulfilment of its reformist ambitions.

Given the long history of cooperation between Papacy and Empire since 800, it is at first sight difficult to comprehend the savagery of their confrontation in and after 1076. At the time the conflict soon became encrusted with large bodies of propaganda from open letters in rapid circulation to learned tracts defending the liberty of the Church or the rights of the German ruler, both sides appealing to precedent, the Bible and to their own interpretation of the Divine Will. The initial disagreement (1071–75) over the best candidate for the vacant see of Milan obviously pinpointed ecclesiastical investiture by the German court as a potential problem. In order to secure a loyal episcopate it was an ancient tradition for kings, and not only in Germany and Italy, to choose the bishops, to direct them to be elected by their cathedral chapters and other local interests, and to invest them with some sign of their episcopal authority. It was not at first perceived that such a system when operated by high-minded emperors such as Henry III, who personally invested his bishops with their episcopal rings and staffs, might thereby be trampling upon the canonically established liberties of the Church.

But when Henry IV and his advisers insisted upon their own candidate for the see of Milan, a man considered below par as a reformer, then Popes Alexander II (1061–73) and Gregory VII did come to view the court appointment of bishops as a hindrance to the ecclesiastical programme of reform. It is highly likely that sooner or later the growing authority of a Papacy invigorated by reform would have collided with the traditional powers over the Church exercised or claimed by every royal court, and would therefore have condemned them as uncanonical and a source of corruption. But the German case was the first, and it was the issue of the Milan appointment, as Zachary Brooke pointed out long ago in a classic article,[61] which suddenly opened up the real gap between the scope and limits of sacerdotal as opposed to secular power, not only in the Church as an institution but in Christian society as well. It is also possible to ascribe some conflict of personality between Gregory VII and Henry IV, although their personal meeting, at Canossa Castle in January 1077, passed off with diplomatic correctness.

In December 1075 Gregory VII despatched a firm letter to Henry IV reproaching him with his incorrect proceedings in the case of the appointment to Milan and to other Italian sees. The pope required of him 'more respectful attention to the master of the Church, that is, to Peter, prince of the Apostles' whose representative Gregory VII claimed to be: '. . . we, unworthy sinner that we are, stand in his place of power'.[62] St Peter's vicar had chosen his moment badly. Fresh from his victory over the rebellious Saxons, Henry IV reacted to the pope's letter by asserting the traditional imperial claim to authority over the Roman See and the Italian Church. Troublesome popes had been deposed before: John XII in 963 and Benedict V in 964 by Otto the Great; John XVI in 998 by Otto III; and Benedict IX, Sylvester III and Gregory VI in 1046 by Henry III. In what he must intemperately have thought was the same spirit, Henry IV summoned a synod of German bishops joined by a couple from Burgundy and Italy to Worms in January 1076. They renounced obedience to Gregory VII as a pernicious disturber of the Church and as a usurper of the papal dignity, as well as accusing him of other crimes.[63] Evidently the king expected the Romans to rise and expel the pope, to be followed up by his own expedition to Italy to sort out the politics of the Italian churches, including Rome, in the style of Otto the Great, Otto III and Henry III, installing a more subservient pope who would also crown him emperor.

But Gregory VII, relying upon his commission as Vicar of St Peter, reacted at his own synod held in Rome in February 1076 by excommunicating Henry IV, suspending him from his office as king, and necessarily releasing his subjects from their oaths of allegiance to him. In terms of papal and imperial politics and of expectations inherited from the past, this was a truly revolutionary act. But it was defended, like subsequent measures, by the pro-papal parties as the legitimate and justified use of ancient canonical rights, powers and privileges of the papal office. Gregory VII took great interest in the canonical rights of the Papacy and had, for example, ordered a list of canonical headings pointing up papal authority to be inserted into his register of correspondence in 1075.[64] Although Henry IV was not yet an emperor, the war of propaganda which now broke out highlighted the access of power enjoyed by the papal court as an attack upon the imperial prerogative. In one of the earliest of Henry IV's propaganda circulars, usually attributed for its composition to his able scribe Gottschalk of Aachen, the traditional status of the Empire directly under divine providence is stressed as wrongfully under threat from a misuse of papal authority.[65] Henry IV is called king 'not by usurpation [of which Gregory VII was accused], but by the pious ordination of God'. The pope is reproached with being 'emboldened to rise up even against the royal power itself, granted to us by God. You dared to threaten to take the kingship away from us – as though we had received the kingship from you, as though kingship and empire were in your hand and not in the hand of God.' This circular also quoted the First Letter of St Peter 2, 17 which was a verse much loved by the imperial supporters because it was believed to have emanated from the first pope himself: 'The true pope Saint Peter also exclaims, "Fear God, honor the king." You [Gregory VII], however, since you do not fear God, dishonor me, ordained of Him.' The study of the polemic between papal and imperial power is a fascinating task based upon a wealth of source literature stretching well away into the twelfth century and later.[66]

Henry IV's excommunication and suspension from kingship proved much more effective than Gregory VII can have dared to hope in that it revived the recent political opposition to the king's rule in Germany in a much more virulent form. As we saw in Part I, four of the dukes formed a new alliance against him. By October 1076 Henry IV was obliged to submit to the magnates of Germany seconded by papal legates, and to the pope himself at Canossa in January 1077. But the fact is that between 1077 and 1084, the king tenaciously got the better of his enemies in spite of Rudolf of Rheinfelden's election as German anti-king in March 1077 and a final decree of deposition aimed at Henry IV by the pope in March 1080.[67] The king reacted by convening a synod at Brixen in June 1080 which again deposed the pope, and in October 1080 Rudolf of Rheinfelden was killed in battle. With the rebellious dukes outfaced in Germany, Henry IV was ready to turn his attention to Italy, and after several sieges of Rome, he was able to drive Gregory VII out in 1084. The pope was rescued at the last moment by his Norman allies, and died at Salerno in 1085 reportedly with the words 'I have loved justice and hated iniquity, therefore I die in exile.' He was canonised in 1605. If the *Libelli de lite* are anything to go by, then the Gregorians got the better of the moral argument, but there were plenty of dissenting voices. One commentator remarked that every time Gregory VII opened his mouth, he divided the Church. Another said that much of the reform programme was pursued not out of religious zeal but out of hatred for Henry IV. As an annalist remarked, 'Everything's mixed up.'[68]

Iniquity in the form of the excommunicated Henry IV celebrated his imperial coronation in St Peter's Basilica in 1084 at the hands of his anti-pope Clement III (1080–1100). As Archbishop Guibert of Ravenna, the new pope was himself a respected reformer, but like so many of the Italian clergy, he regarded the powers claimed by Gregory VII as a threat to the ancient rights of bishops, a fear also expressed for the Germans by Archbishop Liemar of Bremen, who complained that Gregory VII pushed bishops around as though they were his bailiffs. Clement III's reign-name was intended to reflect the harmonious relationship of Henry III with the inception of the new reform under Clement II in 1046, and this was no cynical appropriation. The anonymous *Vita Heinrici Quarti* composed by a churchman early in the twelfth century celebrates Henry IV as personally pious like his father, and Clement III held serious reforming synods. The point is that the imperial cause was much in favour of the varied programme of ecclesiastical reform. The contentious issue was about the relative extent and limits of imperial and papal powers within the Church, and one of the concomitant problems concerned the correct investiture of bishops.

The Ideology of Conflict and the Progress of Compromise

It took a long time before a *modus vivendi* could be negotiated between the papal and imperial courts, because the newly-found liberty of the Church from all unwanted secular influences had to be reconciled with the realistic authority of all rulers over their own bishops. The French bishop Ivo of Chartres (1090–1116) perceived that there was a technical distinction between the spiritual authority inherent in the episcopal office – and this, as a good reformer, he thought could only be conferred by canonical election – and the temporal trappings of bishoprics which could, without any sin, be held by homage from the kings whose predecessors were thought to have donated them in the first place. Once this crucial distinction was accepted as canonically correct, then the Papacy could reconcile itself to the peace arranged with Emperor Henry V at Worms in 1122, on the very spot where the quarrel had broken out in January 1076. In Germany and Italy bishops were to be elected canonically, but their temporal resources were still to be conferred upon them by the emperor in return for the military, fiscal and political services seen as essential to the welfare of the Empire. This was not a compromise which could possibly have recommended itself to purists such as Humbert of Silva Candida or Gregory VII, but we are on the threshold of the age when St Bernard denounced the Papacy for fishing for gold rather than the souls of mankind. From 1122 bishops were to be invested with a sceptre, not the actual episcopal ring and staff, at the hands of the emperor.[69]

The *pax* of Worms was a success, but there remained the poisoned question of the relative meaning of papal and imperial rights of command within the Christian structure. This is the real sense in which the pontificate of Gregory VII was a turning point. All the specific points in church law and the custom of the Empire could in some way be accomodated, as the *pax* of Worms revealed, but what could not be settled until the fall of the Staufen dynasty in the thirteenth century was which of God's puppets, pope or emperor, had the last word of command over baptised Christians. The pope won.

In fact the recriminations went on into the fourteenth century, but there is no better way of understanding what was at issue than returning to the polemics of Gregory and Henry at the start of the struggle. It is not surprising that well-trained imperial bishops were bewildered by the sudden conflict of loyalty placed upon them. For example, Bishop Hermann of Metz had subscribed to the decree deposing Gregory VII at the synod of Worms in 1076, and then regretted it. The pope saw his chance and wrote more than once to explain his point of view. In 1081 he put forward an Augustinian argument about the essential evil of all secular government, in itself a radical devaluation of the theocratic *imperium* for which Henry III, a ruler of whom Gregory VII actually approved, had stood:[70]

> Who does not know that kings and princes derive their origin from men ignorant of God who raised themselves above their fellows by pride, plunder, treachery, murder – in short, by every kind of crime – at the instigation of the Devil, the prince of this world, men blind with greed and intolerable in their audacity?

Repudiating the tradition of imperial protection which goes back to the revival of the Empire in 800, the pope went on with more invective against the 'kings and emperors who, swollen with the pride of this world, rule not for God but for themselves'.

This is far too strong to make sense, but the Gregorian movement certainly did its best to devalue theocratic kingship in such polemics. It is not therefore surprising that, as early as 1076, Henry IV's court turned to the traditional Gelasian doctrine of the Two Swords of authority bestowed by God upon Christendom, the sacerdotal and the regal, which were intended to support each other under the command of Christ. Again it appears to be Gottschalk of Aachen who was making good use of this image in an encyclical addressed to all the German bishops in 1076, and the majority of them did, after all, rally to Henry IV's cause.[71] The argument is a little strange to modern ears because we do not live with the passage from Luke's Gospel in which Christ discovered that his disciples had brought two swords with them to the Last Supper. The encyclical explained that Gregory VII

> held in contempt the pious ordinance of God, which especially commanded these two – namely, the kingship and the priesthood – should remain, not as one entity, but as two. In his Passion, the Savior Himself meant the figurative sufficiency of the two swords . . . He was teaching that every man is constrained by the priestly sword to obey the king as the representative of God but by the kingly sword both to repel enemies of Christ outside and to obey the priesthood within. So in charity the province of one extends into the other, as long as neither the kingship is deprived of honor by the priesthood nor the priesthood is deprived of honor by the kingship.

Live and let live.

Even in referring briefly to just a few of the arguments rehearsed at the time – the Petrine commission to popes; the divine ordination of kings and emperors; the symbolic significance of the two swords taken to the Garden of Gethsemane; the potential wickedness of secular rule; the spiritual pride of the higher clergy; the canonical distinction between the temporal and sacerdotal authority of bishops – one can at once perceive how rich an ideological debate about Empire and Papacy was opened up by the confrontations of the 1070s. But there certainly survived on both sides the contention that in a properly regulated Christian order of society, Papacy and Empire were designed from on high to complement each other's powers. It was upon this understanding – reintroduced with the *pax* of Worms in 1122 – that future German rulers, Lothar III from 1125, Conrad III from 1138 and Frederick I Barbarossa from 1152, were able to base their pro-papal policies down to the Council of Pavia in 1160, which attempted to depose Pope Alexander III after the double election to the Papacy in 1159. The fact is that just as the Papacy had welcomed strong intervention by a regal power from north of the Alps in 774 or 800 or 962 or 1014, so the twelfth-century Papacy badly needed support against the expansionist aims of the Norman counts and kings of Sicily. This the Germans were prepared to provide.

The Western Imperial Ideal in the Twelfth Century

However skilful the Salian chancery had proved in defending imperial rights and powers on parchment, it could not be concealed that the rise of the papal reform movement had changed for good the formidable protective powers over the Roman See enjoyed by the German emperors from Otto the Great to Henry III. To some extent the German court compensated for this by referring more systematically in the royal diplomas to imperial authority as the basis for rulings. This was at a time when, almost providentially for the Empire, the renewed study of Roman law gave an autocratic flavour to legal powers which emperors might claim.[72] It was certainly the case that Frederick Barbarossa was advised by Bolognese lawyers learned in Roman law when he sought to restore imperial rights, jurisdictions and incomes in Italy during the court meetings at Roncaglia in November 1158. They are reported to have assured him of an almost unlimited prerogative, yet the emperor was not deluded into imagining that boundless legal authority could be wielded in practice. A letter to the bishops claims that 'There are two things by which our Empire should be governed, the sacred laws of the emperors and the good practices of our predecessors and ancestors. We neither desire nor are able to exceed those limits; we do not accept whatever is not compatible with them.'[73]

Fine language was nevertheless employed to glorify the status of the Empire, the words imbued with legal, historical or biblical symbolism. An imperial diploma stated that the emperor followed 'our sacred predecessors, namely the emperors Constantine the Great, Justinian and Valentinian as well as Charlemagne and Louis the Pious . . . venerating their holy laws as though they were divine oracles.' This was the time when the imperial chancery was introducing the phrase *sacrum imperium*, 'Holy Empire', into its formal usage in order to achieve parity with the Holy See and with the eastern Empire to a sacred pedigree. So it is not surprising that another chancery product proclaimed that 'the imperial majesty reigns on earth as Vicar of the King of Kings and Lord of Lords', adapting Deuteronomy 10:17.[74]

The chancery also emphasised the Two Swords theory which had served Henry IV's cause well enough. In summoning the German and other bishops to the Council of Pavia (1160) to judge between the rival popes elected in 1159, Frederick Barbarossa's letters proclaimed

> That at the time of His passion Christ was content to have two swords, was, we believe, a marvelous revelation regarding the Roman Church and the Roman empire, since by these two institutions the whole world is directed in both divine and human matters. And although one God, one pope, one emperor, is sufficient, and there should be also but one Church of God, we now have – we cannot speak of it without sorrow – two popes in the Roman Church.

The emperor's solution was yet another synod – shades of 1046, 1076 and 1080 – and he had already threatened one of the parties (Alexander III) with the words

> if you are unwilling to accept God's justice and that of the Church in so solemn a council, may God see it and judge. But as for us, by the grace of Him who giveth salvation unto kings [Psalm 144:10], we shall honor God's justice, as beseems none more than the emperor of Rome,

implicitly referring to his powers as advocate of the Holy See to enforce whatever the council might decide.[75]

If the German court can be credited with promoting a consistent imperial policy in the twelfth century, then it was to build upon the earlier concept of *renovatio* and to achieve proper recognition of the 'honour of the Empire', a term widely used by the chancery,[76] to renew rights and prestige in need of repair after the bad days of the War of Investitures. In modern historiography it is usually conceded that this ideal was to a great extent achieved by Frederick Barbarossa in spite of his setbacks in Italy,[77] and by his son Henry VI in spite of his short reign, 1190 to 1197. Then, after the feuds to win the German throne and the imperial title between 1198 and 1214, imperial ideology achieved its apogee under one of the most versatile of all medieval emperors, Frederick II (1212–50).[78] Frederick Barbarossa has the advantage of a convincing eulogy by Otto of Freising and

Rahewin, but their work concerns only the first nine years of his reign. In fact Henry V, Lothar III and Conrad III – who was prevented by circumstance rather than intention from actually being crowned emperor – were also competent exponents of imperial renewal with shared perceptions about restoring the Empire's prestige after Henry IV's death in 1106.[79]

But this was not quite a question of taking up the reins in the style of Otto III or Henry III, because the Papacy had formidably promoted the apostolic and ecclesiastical reputation of the Roman name by means of the reform movement since 1046.[80] Frightened by Henry IV's measures against Gregory VII, and more so by the concessions which Henry V had tried to extort from Paschal II in 1111, [81] the papal curia had reason to be suspicious of the German presence in Italy. Still, no one could deny that the German ruler was also the rightful king of Italy; the elected German king – normally called *rex Romanorum* or 'king of the Romans' from the mid-eleventh century – was the proper candidate for the imperial title; and Lothar III and Conrad III were deferential to the Roman See, offering protection against such threats as King Roger II of Sicily (1130–54) and the Roman Commune of 1143 to 1155. In 1153 this form of protection was explicitly stated by Frederick Barbarossa and was accepted by the papal legates in the Treaty of Constance as advocatial, that is, implying rights of administration over what was to be protected. According to the Gelasian theory of the Two Swords, the Papacy had no good reason to object to a German ruler committed to defend 'the honour of the Papacy and the secular properties of St Peter as the devoted and particular advocate of the Holy Roman Church'.[82]

The revival of interest in things Roman during the renewal of learning in the twelfth century[83] was bound to make an impact upon the uses of the imperial name just because it had been under adverse pressure during the War of Investitures. The papal court busied itself with the apostolic importance of Rome, and the Roman Commune revived classical paraphernalia including the SPQR signature, inviting Conrad III and Frederick Barbarossa in turn to receive the imperial title on its own terms.[84] But the German court was well aware of its Salian antecedents and its view of the imperial office remained tied to its obligations to the Papacy, not to the city of Rome with its dubious, perhaps dangerous, republican tendency after 1143.

This did not prevent misunderstandings with the Papacy either. For example, German and papal leadership disagreed more than once upon the best method for dealing with the Norman threat. And when papal legates visited the imperial court at Besançon in 1157, it caused an uproar when the letters they brought with them were translated to say that the Empire was little more than a fief from the Papacy. The word in the text was *beneficium* and it was open to misinterpretation, since it could mean a favour in general or a fief in particular. Through new legates sent in 1158, the court was informed that the former had been intended, referring to the imperial coronation in Rome in 1155. But Frederick Barbarossa had already circulated his bishops about the truly independent status of the Empire under God alone, shrewdly quoting the same passage from the First Letter of St Peter employed by Gottschalk of Aachen for Henry IV;[85]

> And since, through election by the princes, the kingdom and the empire are ours from God alone, Who at the time of the passion of His Son Christ subjected the world to dominion by the two swords, and since the apostle Peter taught the world this doctrine: 'Fear God, honor the king,' whosoever says that we received the imperial crown as a benefice (*pro beneficio*) from the lord pope contradicts the divine ordinance and the doctrine of Peter and is guilty of a lie.

One consequence of the more scientific study of Roman law was to revive for the Empire another claim to domination, not just over the German, Italian and Burgundian kingdoms, but over the entire Christian order. The Staufen dynasty displayed a certain sobriety about attempting to make more of *dominium mundi*, lordship over the world, than a useful diplomatic handle. According to the Italian lawyer Otto Morena of Lodi, one of the Roman law professors from Bologna did assure Frederick Barbarossa in 1158 that he was in effect lord of the earth, with virtually unlimited powers.[86] No more than an idea, it had a certain appeal. For example, a literary figure known as Archipoeta who belonged to the entourage of the imperial chancellor, Archbishop Rainald of Cologne, claimed of Frederick Barbarossa 'No rational being disputes that thou art, by the will of God, constituted king over the other kings and that thou hast deservedly acquired the sword of vengeance and the buckler of guardianship over all Christian people.'[87] Such ideas were perhaps taken a bit more seriously by Henry VI. More than one source ascribes to the crusade planned for 1198 the aim of conquering the Byzantine Empire as the prelude to the downfall of Egypt and the subsequent recovery of Jerusalem lost to Saladin in 1187. But all that Henry VI lived to achieve in the line of world dominion was to receive homage from foreign kings, of England, Cyprus and Cilician Armenia.

The revival of German imperial power in the twelfth century was not necessarily perceived as a threat to the new papal monarchy so long as the advocatial rights of the emperor in no way threatened the religious leadership of the Roman Church in Christian society. But after the papal schism of 1159, it did appear to the majority in the Church that the secular sword of Gelasian theory was improperly used by Frederick Barbarossa to sustain Victor IV and his successors after the Council of Pavia, convened by the emperor, rejected Alexander III as true pope in 1160.[88] The dangerous apparition of Henry IV's anti-popes rose up again to bedevil German and Italian politics, and it is to the credit of emperor and pope that after a long schism, their differences could be settled by the Peace of Venice negotiated in 1177.[89] It would be hard to prove that memories of the Council of Pavia and its aftermath motivated Pope Innocent III (1198–1216) into engineering the virtual end of Gelasian 'Two Swords' theory by proclaiming papal plenitude of power over all aspects of Christian existence, sacred and secular. Like most reformist ideas emanating from the papal court, it actually had a very long prehistory. But many of Innocent III's measures were, as we shall see, explicitly designed to curtail imperial power on the grounds that 'Just as the moon derives its light from the sun . . . so, too, the royal power derives the splendour of its dignity from the pontifical authority.'[90]

In spite of the fact that Conrad III and Frederick Barbarossa served the Church as crusaders, and that Henry VI was preparing to do so, the imperial tradition of protection and advocacy over the Papacy as practised in the twelfth century did not ultimately suit papal preten-sions to liberty and authority proclaimed as far back as the 1070s. Just before the Council of Pavia which decided against his claim to the Papacy, Alexander III was informed by the emperor that

> since we are obliged to protect all churches established in our Empire, we ought so much the more readily provide for the most sacred Roman Church, because the care and defence of it are believed to have been more particularly committed to us by divine providence.[91]

But when the decision at the council went against the pope, it is not surprising that the Roman curia perceived such obligations as a menace.

Emperor Henry VI, Pope Innocent III and the Future of the Empire

As we have seen, the opinion on Frederick Barbarossa as a more successful exponent of the imperial ideal than his immediate predecessors is undoubtedly distorted by the panegyric upon the early years of his reign proposed in Otto of Freising's and Rahewin's *Gesta Frederici*. Yet it does appear that the prestige of the western Empire increased in the later twelfth century, perhaps raising fresh fears about too powerful an imperial court in the thought of the Papacy, the Lombard communes, and cliques amongst the German secular and ecclesiastical princes. Because Henry VI's unexpected death in 1197 was followed by a disruptive civil war in Germany between rival candidates for the throne, it is often inferred that Henry VI had somehow overplayed his hand and that the Staufen dynasty ought to be removed as representing too great a threat to the interests of the German magnates. But the fact is that in 1198 the great majority of the princes backed the Staufen candidate, Henry VI's brother Philip of Swabia, and he had virtually mastered Germany by the time he was assassinated in 1208.

Henry VI did nevertheless endeavour to improve the potential of imperial authority in two directions. In 1186 his marriage to Constance of Sicily gave them a direct claim to the Norman kingdom of Sicily which was activated upon William II's death in 1189. The Norman barons' preference for the illegitimate Tancred of Lecce followed by his son William III as their kings would therefore have to be reversed by force if the Staufen claim was to be validated. In 1191 Henry VI's invasion was a failure, but in 1194 he was able to seize the Norman kingdom. It is not clear whether the new king was intending to integrate the Sicilian kingdom into the western Empire as the fourth realm after Germany, Italy and Burgundy. In 1191 he inconsistently advertised his claim to Sicily both by ancient imperial right – the goal which had eluded Otto II in 982 – and as his wife's inheritance. But the acquisition of Sicily certainly turned Henry VI into such a formidable power in Italy that in the thirteenth century it became a fixed point in papal diplomacy to keep the crowns of Germany and Italy constitutionally separate from that of Sicily, although they were in fact all held together by the Staufen dynasty between 1212 and 1254.

The acquisition of Norman Sicily marked the material zenith of Henry VI's imperial rule, but in 1196 he sought to introduce a major reform into the legal structure of the Empire as well. At court meetings held in Mainz and Würzburg he proposed to the princes that the traditional electoral procedures should be abolished and that the imperial title should become hereditary in the Staufen dynasty.[92] This proposal appears not to have been motivated by fears of the German princes' right to elect their kings – after all, the Staufen rulers had come to power by election, and its theoretical grounding had been used to good effect in outfacing the papal legates at Besançon in 1157 – but to sustain a novel theory that since the Staufen constituted the providential imperial line destined to last until the end of human history, then a hereditary Empire was both logical and appropriate as well as pleasing to the Divine Will. The plan was not conceived as an attack upon princely rights as such and, as a result of lengthy negotiations, the sources indicate that the majority of the magnates were cautiously in favour of the scheme. The emperor offered concessions. The secular princes' fiefs from the Empire would become hereditary in both lines, or pass to collateral heirs should the main line of a princely family fail. Such methods were already familiar from the constitution of the new duchy of Austria set up in 1156. To the episcopate the emperor was prepared to surrender the right of *spolia*, the escheat to the crown of a bishop's personal property upon his decease. In the end Henry VI's scheme had to be shelved at the insistence of a powerful clique, and the emperor had to settle for his infant son Frederick II's election as king in the traditional manner.

As conqueror of Sicily, protagonist of a hereditary Empire, and potential crusader, Henry VI can certainly be assessed as a vigorous interpreter of the prestige of the western Empire. It is difficult to measure how far the attempt by Archbishop Adolf I of Cologne and his party to shake off the Staufen dynasty in and after 1198 was motivated by a perception that imperial authority should be trimmed back. Another explanation is simpler: that the rivalry during the twelfth century between the sees of Mainz and Cologne for effective primacy in the German Church culminated in the archbishop of Cologne's attempt in 1198 to seize from Mainz the privilege of *prima vox*, the first voice, in German royal elections.[93] Whatever the interpretation, the struggles between 1198 and 1214 over the right to the German crown obviously represented a setback for imperial might. But the future of the Empire and its status were in any case on the verge of change as Pope Innocent III, elected in 1198 like Otto IV and Philip of Swabia, undertook a revision of the relationship between Papacy and Empire.

Since both parties in Germany after the double election to the throne appealed to the pope for recognition and support, Innocent III had good reason to take up the matter of the Empire and to turn it to Rome's advantage. But it would be a mistake to discern in this pope an enemy of imperial or any other properly constituted secular authority as such. He did, however, take a lofty view of his own position as Vicar of Christ,[94] and proclaimed that adjudication in the German quarrel came well within the canonical authority of the pope to decide what was for the best in Christian society. After long deliberations preserved by the pope in the dossier entitled *Registrum super negotio Romani imperii*, visits backwards and forwards by ambassadors and legates, and the exchange of many letters, Innocent III felt able to vindicate his view that a pope had the right to decide which was the best candidate, a claim which dismayed the Germans so used to the notion that God alone chose the ruler through the mechanics of an election by the princes, which both German parties claimed had correctly taken place in 1198. In 1201 Innocent III chose Otto IV and in 1202 issued the bull *Venerabilem*, which explained and summarised the powers he had used. This document was important in that it was enshrined in canon law, asserting practical papal plenitude of power over imperial affairs. For the average German it was too much. As the poet Walther von der Vogelweide put it, the shepherd of Christ's people had turned into a wolf.

Innocent III did concede, in the spirit of the Besançon circular of 1157 and its tacit confirmation by the legates in 1158, that the German princes did legally elect the king who would later be promoted to emperor by ancient custom. But in the spirit of the Donation of Constantine, he seized upon the theory of *translatio imperii* for himself: that the Germans' right to imperial rule had been conferred by the Apostolic See when Pope Leo III transferred the Roman Empire from the Greeks to the Germans in the person of Charlemagne. This, of course, was the extreme pro-papal interpretation of the events of 800 which was feared at the time and later. Innocent III therefore inferred that the *ius et auctoritas examinandi*, the right and authority to weigh up the suitability of candidates, even when elections were unanimous, rested with the Papacy: how much more so when the German electors were in discord! Various reasons were then given to the effect that Philip of Swabia was unworthy and that Otto IV had been confirmed, the pope being careful to reject the idea that his legate had in some way acted as an undercover elector. The pope also played upon the fears raised by Henry VI's proposal of 1196 for a hereditary Empire, claiming slightly unscrupulously that the Staufen succession from Conrad III to Philip of Swabia 'makes it seem that the Empire is owed not to election but to heredity'.[95]

This theoretical subordination of kingdoms and empires to the sacerdotal authority of the Papacy was one result of the dramatic increase in canonical, biblical and historical speculation about and application of papal power ever since Gregory VII's *Dictatus Papae*, twenty-seven chapters about Petrine rights drawn up in 1075.[96] But the gap between theory and reality remained a serious problem for the pope. By 1206 Philip of Swabia's hold upon Germany was so efficacious that Innocent III undertook negotiations to try to persuade Otto IV to withdraw from the contest in spite of *Venerabilem*, and to recognise Philip as the papal candidate after all. Philip of Swabia would be required to make great concessions to papal regional authority in Italy, including a marriage alliance with the pope's family subvented by a principality. This stage of the game was wrecked by Philip's murder in 1208 and Otto IV's acceptance as king in Germany for the sake of peace, followed by his imperial coronation upon terms favourable to the pope in 1209.

But once again Innocent III found himself upon shaky ground. As Bernd Ulrich Hucker, the recent biographer of Otto IV, has pointed out, the new emperor slavishly took up all the imperialistic ambitions of Henry VI,[97] including an attack upon the kingdom of Sicily in 1210 in order to wrest it from the pope's ward and Henry VI's rightful heir, Frederick II. This did not suit the pope at all, since one idea behind the promotion of Otto IV's claims in the first place had been the separation of Germany and Sicily: the Welf dynasty would rule in Germany, the Staufen in Sicily. In his disappointment Innocent III excommunicated his new emperor and wrote to the German bishops that 'the sword we ourselves forged has dealt us grievous wounds'. Reluctantly the pope saw little alternative but to put forward his Staufen ward as the next German king, and upon papal instructions he was duly elected by a party of princes in 1211.[98]

The Rise of Frederick II

As practical diplomacy the post-1198 policy of the Papacy towards the Empire was not a success. In the background stood the theory of the papal plenitude of power, knowledge of the Donation of Constantine, and the better attested privileges donated by the Carolingians, to which Innocent III specifically referred. The decretal *Venerabilem* of 1202 and oaths extracted in turn from Otto IV and Frederick II were intended to guarantee the parity of the Roman See with the Empire. In fact this policy declined into a wrangle with Frederick II about ensuring the separation of the German and Sicilian crowns. When Frederick II adventurously took advantage of his election in 1211 and travelled to Germany to seize the throne in 1212, his infant son Henry was left behind as king of Sicily with the child's mother Constance of Aragon as regent. After the Fourth Lateran Council of 1215 had killed off Otto IV's claim to the Empire for good, Frederick II opened negotiations with Innocent III about his own imperial coronation. The pope insisted upon the separation of the crowns, but in the year of Innocent's death, Frederick II summoned his son Henry to Germany and eventually had him elected king of the Romans as Henry VII in 1220.[99]

The fact that both father and son now bore both the Sicilian and German regal titles certainly aroused the suspicions of Pope Honorius III (1216–27). But Frederick II claimed that his son's German election was a spontaneous decision by the German princes, and that the advantage for all parties was that it released him to return to Sicily to prepare for the crusade upon which the pope had set such store. So Honorius III accepted the arrangement, and on his way south, Frederick II was duly consecrated emperor by the pope in St Peter's in November 1220. It was to be the last imperial coronation for nearly a century. Constitutionally the new emperor did stick to the technical separation of his crowns – to which he added that of Jerusalem in 1229 – and the Sicilian kingdom never was subordinated to the Empire. But since he certainly envisaged the descent of Sicily and the Empire first to Henry VII and then to Conrad IV as his sons and heirs, it is hard to see what difference was made in practice.

The bull *Venerabilem* was certainly designed to demote the status of the Empire in relation to papal authority, perhaps even to the extent, as suggested by the American scholar James Muldoon, of turning an emperor in theory into an official of the Church. *Venerabilem* still took the traditional view of what an emperor was for: he was 'advocate and defender of the apostolic see'.[100] The argument, of course, turned upon what this implied. Pope Innocent III was convinced that the Roman curia should run its own jurisdictions in central Italy, and Pope Honorius III knew very well what they were from his time as papal chamberlain since 1188. As usual in papal history the claims went back for centuries, but Innocent III and his successors are generally credited in the historiography with placing the papal state in central Italy upon a new material footing.[101] But Frederick II regarded this as a threat. He reverted to the policy of his father and grandfather in assuming that the papal possessions beyond Latium, the original 'patrimony of St Peter' based upon the Byzantine duchy of Rome, that is, the exarchate of Ravenna, the Pentapolis and the march of Ancona, and the duchy of Spoleto, were to be administered by imperial officials. This contentious issue, which went back in some form at least as far as Lothar I's *Constitutio Romana* of 824 which had placed papal property under imperial supervision, contributed to Frederick II's disastrous confrontations as emperor with Popes Gregory IX and Innocent IV.

A further result of the disruptions in imperial politics between 1198 and 1214 was Frederick II's strong motivation in restoring the glory of the Empire for which the dynasty had worked so hard under his father and grandfather. Frederick II has been regarded by some commentators as the greatest of all the medieval German emperors, perhaps because of the many-sided nature of his activities, from writing a fine book on falconry and his patronage of the arts to his formidable legislative record and his success in regaining Jerusalem for Christendom in 1229, albeit temporarily. Everyone had to be impressed with his capacity for the grand gesture in politics and upon parchment.[102] In a careful study of Frederick II's 'imperial idea', the Austrian historian Hans Martin Schaller drew attention to the almost inexhaustible interplay between the real and the theoretical in this emperor's thirty-year incumbency, 1220 to 1250,[103] and we will be returning to the details.

For most of this time Frederick II actually lived south of the Alps, building fine new residences such as Castel del Monte in Apulia, and like Otto III he regarded Italy with the city of Rome as the Empire's terrestrial centre of gravity. But much more important was the assertion to be found again and again in his charters that his true authority was celestially bestowed: '. . . the Lord of lords, glorious in his majesty, who created the kingdoms and established the Empire, . . . who placed us above kings and kingdoms and raised us to the imperial throne' . . . and so on.[104] It is probable that the emperor was in any case familiar with such concepts from his Sicilian upbringing, because his maternal forefathers had deliberately employed Byzantine imperial imagery and materials to underpin the prestige of their own parvenu kingship.[105]

Hans Martin Schaller has pointed out how the actual events of Frederick II's reign then shaped his conception of imperial rule. For example, on the eve of his departure for the crusade of 1228 and 1229, he commissioned decorations for the cathedral at Foggia, the principal imperial residence in southern Italy, which included a relief of Constantine the Great's victory over paganism, just as Frederick had vowed to free the Holy Land from Muslim domination.[106] In Jerusalem itself he staged a crown-wearing ceremony in the Church of the Holy Sepulchre, and issued a long manifesto which proclaimed his imperial mission as bestowed directly by God in the manner of King David's kingship, a theme inherited from the Carolingian tradition of imperial rule. In adapted biblical style we hear that 'all those who honour the true faith shall from henceforth know and shall publish it far and wide to the ends of the earth that he who is blessed for all time has visited us, has brought deliverance to his people, and has raised up an horn of salvation for us in the house of his servant David'.[107]

Upon the emperor's return to Italy, he heard a triumphal sermon in Bitonto Cathedral delivered by Nicholas of Bari, which again explicitly compared the imperial dynasty with that of King David; Frederick Barbarossa with Jesse, the founder of David's line; and Frederick II himself with Jacob's son Judah, ancestor of Christ and one of his prefigurations in medieval biblical exegesis. Expanding upon Jacob's blessing to Judah in Genesis 49 and using the messianic 110th Psalm, the preacher concluded that

> *The sceptre shall not pass from* the hand of the Lord Frederick *nor the mace from between his feet*, which means 'nor the *imperium* from his heirs' *until he comes to whom it belongs*, that is, Christ in judgement; so Frederick's lineage will rule until the end of the world, because *Royal dignity was yours from the day you were born*, like Christ's in all his representatives, kings and emperors.[108]

This view of the divinely commissioned *imperium* had already been aired by Godfrey of Viterbo, an Italian educated at Bamberg and subsequently working as chaplain and chancery official for Frederick Barbarossa and Henry VI. In his works, Godfrey proclaimed that the Staufen dynasty, the *imperialis prosapia*, was the last and greatest of all imperial lines in world history, direct heir of the Caesars, and destined to rule until the end of the ages.[109] He is likely to have been the source for Henry VI's ideas in this line when the plan for a hereditary Empire was presented in 1196. Later on in Frederick II's reign the Davidic theme was developed a bit further when the emperor expressly described Jesi, his birthplace in the March of Ancona, as 'our

Bethlehem' and went on to adapt the prophet Micah's teaching as quoted in the second chapter of St Matthew:

> And you, Bethlehem in the land of Judah,
> you are by no means least among the leaders of Judah,
> for out of you will come a leader
> who will shepherd my people Israel.

By direct analogy the emperor states that Jesi is by no means the least of cities because it produced the *princeps* of the Roman Empire.[110]

In another direction, the projected conquest of Prussia by the Teutonic Order was also fitted ideologically into the cosmic purpose of the Empire as a proper religious and political protector of mankind until the end of the ages. At Rimini in 1226 Frederick II authorised the conquest of Prussia *sub monarchia imperii*, 'under the sole rule of the Empire', with the support of the Papacy and the duke of Masovia. This enterprise was placed squarely within the universal and ever-lasting imperial mission of Rome which had been established by Augustus Caesar just at the same time as Christ was born into the world, both authorities providing legally for the ultimate goal of all history, the salvation of mankind:

> God has sublimely constituted our Empire over the kings of the earth and has extended the limits of our sovereignty throughout the diverse latitudes of the world in order to glorify His name through-out the ages and to propagate the faith amongst the peoples. Just as he provided the sacred Roman Empire for the purpose of spreading the Gospel, so our administration is anxious to bring about not only the conquest but also the conversion of the heathen nations. . . .[111]

Whatever the meaning of all these messianic sources, in his letters Frederick II did not neglect the useful tradition that emperors protected the Roman Church, and there was more to this than opportunism. For example, the emperor was as genuine in his desire to defend the Church from heresy as any pope, preacher or inquisitor, partly because he regarded heresy as sacrilege against Christ's word which upheld the authority of kings and emperors.[112] Frederick II was also educated in the notions sustained by Roman law that an emperor was virtually *lex animata*, 'the living law',[113] but like his grandfather he did not intend to overturn the customs of his kingdoms in favour of a kind of legal autocracy, which was not desirable or practicable.

Instead, the legislative material for Sicily as well as Germany stresses the greatness of the imperial office in its guardianship of law. At Mainz in 1235, when Frederick II issued his *Landfriede* or peace-ordinance for the whole Empire in twenty-nine chapters, the motivation expressed in the prologue reflects the supreme duty of all medieval rulers to purvey justice and peace to their peoples:[114]

> Having obtained the throne of imperial eminence by the command of divine providence, we have taken care to strengthen our plans for the government of our subjects with the double bond of peace and justice so that the renown of our name has something with which to promote both its own glory and the welfare of our subjects. For the authority of the ruler will especially be fortified when, in the observation of peace and in the execution of justice, it is as fearful to the wicked as it is welcome to the obedient.

Peace and justice – the style in which they are invoked is far from rhetorical in intention, and conveys an exact statement of the political duty of German emperors apart from the protection of the Church, which features later on in the same source.

From the Downfall of the Staufen to the Peace of Lausanne in 1275

Pope Gregory IX's excommunication of Frederick II in 1239 for his supposed mistreatment of the Church in his Sicilian kingdom was sustained by other fears. In 1237 the emperor had beaten the Lombard cities, traditional allies of the Papacy, at the Battle of Cortenuova. He had designated his illegitimate son Enzio as king of Sardinia, although the island was in theory a papal fief. Imperial occupation of the lands in central Italy claimed by the papal curia provided an ongoing wrangle. One consequence of the excommunication was a sharpening of polemic. The pope even went so far as to state that Frederick approved of being compared to Antichrist's precursor.[115] By contrast, the emperor and his circle emphasised the messianic nature of imperial authority, and continued to raid scripture and the liturgy for all the references to the celestially bestowed nature of secular power.[116]

  As the convoluted language of propaganda travelled to the extremities – the German scholar Peter Herde has suggested that the more ridiculous letters were never actually sent out – Gregory IX's successor Innocent IV declared at the First Council of Lyons in 1245 that the emperor was irrevocably deposed. Frederick held back from the countermeasures undertaken by his predecessors Henry IV, Henry V and Frederick Barbarossa in promoting or supporting anti-popes, undoubtedly hoping for better days because there was widespread opinion that the pope had gone much too far. Matthew Paris of St Albans claimed that the French aristocracy hatched an abortive plot against Innocent IV, and in any case that the loyalty and affection which Christians ought to entertain towards their spiritual father had 'turned into execrable hatred and secret maledictions'.[117] But the reign of the last emperor before the fourteenth century ended in 1250 and his family had by 1268 suffered virtual extinction, including Conradin's execution at Naples, at the hands of the papacy's allies, armies and agents.

The sobriety of Frederick II's death in 1250 clad in Cistercian habit was reflected in his will.[118] From the point of view of the Empire, its most significant provision was to underline the internal tradition of devolution; that Conrad IV, elected king of the Romans in 1237, would be consecrated as the next emperor according to the pattern established by the end of the tenth century. Of course this was a political impossibility after the First Council of Lyons, but it was from the imperial angle legally irreproachable. Another entry concerned the current quarrel between the papal and imperial courts, and simply reflected many similar declarations of good intent stretching back to the treaty made at Worms in 1122: that the Holy Roman Church should have all its rights restored, but without compromise to the rights and honour of the Empire, Frederick's heirs and his followers, and only on condition that the Roman Church restore the Empire's rights. It sounds well, but since it was designed to cover everything about which the two sides were at loggerheads, it was bound to remain a dead letter.

In spite of the political differences and polemical recriminations experienced ever since the excommunication of Frederick II in 1239, the Papacy's attitude towards the Empire became more optimistic in the 1270s, partly because the Roman Church discovered that its new protector, Charles of Anjou, who had taken over the kingdom of Sicily in 1266, was almost as onerous in handling ecclesiastical rights in Italy as his Staufen predecessors. Pope Gregory X (1271–6) approved the election of Count Rudolf of Habsburg as king of the Romans in 1273 and began to negotiate about his coronation as emperor. Gregory X took a broad, traditional view of papal needs; a protective alliance with a well-disposed German emperor and the union of the Greek and

Latin Churches under his own auspices as a prelude to the definitive crusade for rescuing Jerusalem. The union was supposedly achieved at the Second Council of Lyons in 1274, and the obvious sequel was to reconcile the Roman See and the Empire, particularly for the purpose of facilitating the crusade. But before meeting King Rudolf at Lausanne in 1275 to set a date for the imperial coronation, the pope had secured assurances about the real bone of contention in the thirteenth century, the status of the papal possessions in central Italy. Although he would have liked to have reneged on the agreement later, King Rudolf was far-sighted enough to perceive that imperial rights over the duchy of Spoleto, the march of Ancona and the province of Romagna would have to be renounced. In territorial terms the imperial frontier was shifted to the north, although the Empire still encompassed Tuscany and most of the Lombard plain. Germany also renounced any further interest in the kingdom of Sicily. So weak had the Empire become since 1239 that Gregory X was able to secure for Rome what Henry VI, Otto IV and Frederick II had for some sixty or eighty years denied to his predecessors.

As so often in diplomatic history, a change of cast was almost enough to change minds as well. At Lausanne Gregory X assured Rudolf of Habsburg that just as the *sacerdotium* offered a salvatory direction to the Empire, so the latter was still the *defensor* and protector of the Holy See.[119] There was nothing new in this as theory. It restated the expectations surrounding the role of Empire enjoyed by the educated elites of Italy and Germany. For example, in the political memorandum he drew up in 1281, Alexander of Roes proclaimed that Rudolf of Habsburg's election in 1273 demonstrated the grace of God returning to His people after the long tribulation since 1239. He thought that it proved that just as the Roman Church was the Church of God, so the Roman Empire was the Kingdom of God and ought to be understood in this advanced mystical and messianic sense, obviously building upon the idea of Godfrey of Viterbo, Nicholas of Bari and those Joachite thinkers favourably disposed to the imperial cause. Returning to the same theme a few years later, Alexander thought that after the gross abuses of power by the Papacy and the consequent abasement of the Empire, the elections of Gregory X and Rudolf of Habsburg symbolised a return to the just equilibrium between their God-given rights.[120] We can see from speculations of this kind that the neo-Roman western Empire had lost little of its appeal as an ideological force in Christian society, whatever the future reality for imperial political power within the European structure may have been.[121]

Economic Rationale for the German Imperial Experience

Although Rudolf of Habsburg never made it to Rome for an imperial coronation, the German version of the western Empire had a protean future for many a century until its dissolution in 1806. For the neo-Roman imperial structure since the ninth century we have seen the ways in which the political, ecclesiastical, military, ideological and territorial dimensions of the Empire could all change quite rapidly. The western Empire had very little to do with any notion of German statehood or nationhood. Such concepts are too modern for a reasonable match in the sources, but in the history of empires we do generally expect to find some economic rationale as an explanation as well, at least early on in their history. Did this exist in our case? There are several pioneering studies on the Empire's economy, and they indicate that the economic fabric was potentially stable.

The end of large-scale tribute and plunder proved dangerous for the integrity of the Carolingian Empire. The Saxon dynasty of East Francia was not capable of robbery on such a large scale, but the subjection of Sclavinia from the 920s was significant. Bishop Thietmar of Merseburg preserved a report on how Henry I extended Saxon power over the Slavs on the upper Elbe by establishing the fortress of Meissen in 929, and then used it to force tribute or *census* out of the Slavs further east.[122] Several sources through to the twelfth century reflect a guilty conscience about tithes and tribute outstripping the concern for missionising in the Slav lands. Although tribute from the Slavs inevitably fell off after 983, there was still enough to make a difference. From Wipo we hear that in 1025 Conrad II, in 'exacting tribute payments from the barbarians who border on Saxony, . . . received all the income owed him'.[123] Italy as a Christian country could not be looted in the same manner, in spite of Benedict of Monte Soratte's remarks about sackfuls of silver being hauled off to Germany, which may in any case have been metaphorical. As Karl Leyser pointed out, the extraordinarily rich royal silver mines in the Harz mountains, especially the Rammelsberg near Goslar, were seriously exploitable from the 960s. Supply dried up in the twelfth century when the shafts could no longer be pumped out properly before the advent of technologically more advanced equipment in the fifteenth and sixteenth centuries. This flood of silver 'was like a second wind. The Carolingians had not been so fortunate'.[124] And if archaeological finds are anything to go by, then much of the money minted was sent abroad to pay for all the materials which Scandinavia, the Baltic coasts and the Slav East could provide. For example, the enormous hoard buried after

1079 at Vichmjaz on Lake Ladoga in Russia consisted of 12,472 German coins out of a total of 13,398, with English (147), Danish (107), Islamic (53), Hungarian (27) and other mintings trailing a very long way behind.[125]

As successors to the Lombard and Frankish kings of Italy, the German emperors claimed substantial services and revenues there, some of them under the ancient Lombard heading of *fodrum*. The ability to collect renders was obviously linked to the variable military and administrative capacity of the emperors as Italian kings, although the marked increase in the use of the word *fodrum* in the sources from the end of the tenth century indicates an upsurge in the German ruler's tax-gathering efficacy in Italy. Frederick Barbarossa's endeavours to restore full royal rights to Italian revenues after the hiatus caused by the War of Investitures induced dismay amongst the Lombard cities. But after years of warfare in which the Lombard League eventually got the better of the emperor, the treaty agreed between them at Constance in 1183 still preserved imperial rights to the customary *fodrum* wherever it was due. A substantial list of manors owing revenues to the king of the Romans known as the *Tafelgüterverzeichnis* was drawn up in the twelfth century and included a group of them in Lombardy.[126] To the significance of this source we will return in Part III.

Although the German emperors were supported by significant annual subventions from the Church, the crown did not raise a general tax in Germany. There were, however, many towns upon the royal fisc and if the tax list which survives from 1241 is anything to go by, then over eighty towns could be charged by the imperial treasury.[127] It is thought that from the end of the tenth century Germany became a relatively rich country, so that the maintenance, expansion and exploitation of the fisc was a matter of moment to the successive dynasties.[128] But the windfalls due to imperial might were also worth having. One source reports that the ransom which Henry VI charged Richard I of England in 1194 was so huge that it took fifty packhorses to deliver the barrels containing the cash. That very year the emperor also seized the treasure of the Sicilian kings, its richness causing astonishment when it was displayed in Germany.

Eschatology and Empire

Carolingian tradition, military success and economic opportunity go some of the way towards explaining why the Saxon dynasty took up the pretensions of the neo-Roman *imperium*. But for collecting tribute, for securing frontiers, for keeping control over the *gentes* in the duchies, for managing groups of secular and ecclesiastical magnates in the crown's interest, it is not at first sight at all obvious why the name of emperor was a great improvement upon that of king. Political explanation rightly focuses upon Otto the Great's entanglement in Lombard politics after his marriage to Adelheid of Italy in 951, and then in Roman and *a fortiori* Byzantine politics from 960. Another dimension was eschatological, to set right the relationship of the Christian faith, political authority and the chronology of the human race in light of the approaching end of the world at the Last Judgement.

The consummation of human history at the onset of the Christian Apocalypse was a constant preoccupation of the medieval mind. Speculation was both encouraged and restricted by the obscurity of the numerous biblical proof-texts and by the ambivalent theology of the Church about the eventual Apocalypse.[129] Presiding over the marriage of Church and Empire, Constantine the Great had rendered the notion of the providential installation of the Augustan *pax Romana* and the Christian revelation at the same point in human history into a new political reality some three hundred years later.[130] It was held that the Christian Church and the Roman Empire were designed by God to endure until the end, the latter protecting the former and both fulfilling parallel functions; for example, in subduing and converting by sword and mission the nations of the earth. Such duties were high on the political agenda of the medieval Roman empires, Byzantine[131] and western. As we have seen, one justification for Charlemagne's restoration of a western neo-Roman Empire in 800 had been his successes in conquering the heathen, and Otto the Great had already achieved something similar against the Slavs and Magyars by 955. Otto III inclined by preference to emphasise the theme of conversion, and the explicit motive for Henry II's foundation of the new bishopric at Bamberg in 1007 was 'so that the paganism of the Slavs would be destroyed, and the memory of the name of Christ would always be remembered there'. It proved an uphill task. As late as 1059 a local synod complained that since the inhabitants of the bishopric were Slav for the most part, they clung to pagan rites and abhorred the Christian faith.[132]

The close association of the Christian Church with the Roman Empire under divine providence also gave rise to an understanding of the imperial office functioning as a kind of guarantee against the dissolution of the cosmos and the Last Judgement as outlined in several

New Testament passages. Relying upon some verses in 2 Thessalonians, several medieval commentators thought that the end of the world could not come about until some great revolt had taken place against the Empire. In 1018, for example, Bishop Thietmar of Merseburg warned his readers that the recent threat of invasion of Saxony by the Slavs was precisely not this dreaded event, but still pointed out that 'No one should question the coming of the Last Day or wish for its swift arrival either, because it is to be feared by the just and much more so by those worthy of punishment.'[133]

In other words, the ideological dynamism of the neo-Roman Empire in the West was largely eschatological, that is, concerned with the end of history and the Last Judgement, and the proper regulation of Christian society in relation to these expected but terrifying events. The effect of neo-Roman rule was seen as preservative. The American historian Richard Landes has shown how fear of the Last Judgement or according to some theologians, the millenium which would precede it, which was scheduled for the six thousandth year from the supposed creation of the world, naturally aroused anxiety about establishing the correct computation. In the eighth century

> the *Annus Domini* took its place as the third major dating system in the Church's struggle against apocalyptic enthusiasm. . . By dating the Coronation AD 801, then, they [the Carolingians] publicly affirmed *urbi et orbi* this new system which, like its predecessors, promised a reprieve of several centuries.[134]

The sense of living in the last days and the duty of rulers to reckon with this was already recorded by Charlemagne in the *Admonitio Generalis* of 789 with a warning against the consequent evils.[135] The restoration of the western Empire in 800 was designed in part to steady the chronological decline of humanity towards the Last Judgement.

Recently the German scholar Johannes Fried, among others, has perceptively reviewed the recrudescence of apocalyptic fears at the end of the tenth century,[136] and there is a sense in which the *renovatio imperii Romanorum* patronised by Otto III and Sylvester II was intended to pilot Christendom under the aegis of Church and Empire safely over the thousandth year. The theoretical eschatological function of the Empire was sustained by an amazing variety of prophecy and speculation, some of which was based upon a legend, the supposed visit by Charlemagne to Jerusalem as a pilgrim or crusader. It is known that at one point Otto III did actually plan to go to Jerusalem, but in all the literature there was a certain incoherence about the implications of such undertakings. Would an imperial visit to Jerusalem herald the messianic consummation of human history or guarantee, on the contrary, the continuation of Empire, Church and Christian order against the threatening appearance of Antichrist? Bishop Benzo of Alba, for example, who had probably been trained as chaplain by Henry III and was a committed supporter of Henry IV against the Gregorians, hailed the latter emperor as the last and greatest of the Caesars and encouraged him to undertake the apocalyptic progress to Jerusalem. But the general tone of his writings is politically restorative rather than dissolvent.[137]

Naturally the crusades revived the focus upon Jerusalem as a centrepiece of the Christian experience in politics, and encouraged further examination of the imperial role in salvatory history. One text providing details was the *Ludus de Antichristo*, probably written at Tegernsee Abbey in Bavaria about 1160,[138] spelling out the scenario to the limit. The western Roman emperor travels to Jerusalem and achieves the subjection of all other terrestrial authorities, pagan and Christian, by consent or force. Still in Jerusalem, the emperor resigns his crown and Antichrist, the harbinger of the End according to several New Testament passages, begins his reign instead. After many devious successes he is destroyed by Christ's Word, and the true Church emerges triumphant over the whole world. The *Ludus* is distinctly solvent in that imperial rule gives way to Antichrist before the new reign of the Church which is now beyond the need for any temporal assistance. But the *Ludus* was a play, not a political programme. It is thought that it may have been acted before the imperial court at Augsburg.

The manipulation of eschatological thought for political purposes returned in strength in the thirteenth century, revived by both parties in the ideological conflict between the papal and imperial courts in Frederick II's time.[139] Another cause was the prophetic output of Abbot Joachim of Fiore, which became popular in the thirteenth century. He forecast an imminent 'third age' in human history, the reign of the Holy Spirit scheduled to begin in 1260, but to be preceded by Antichrist's persecutions. So it can be imagined that Frederick II, the official enemy of the Church since his excommunication in 1239, fitted the bill according to some of his opponents.[140] If the papal curia was not Joachite, then it still played upon apocalyptic fears in order to blacken Frederick's reputation. More than one of Gregory IX's encyclicals between 1239 and 1241 apostrophise the emperor as the Great Beast of the Book of Revelation or as the Antichrist:

> What other Antichrist should we await, when as is evident in his works, he is already come in the person of Frederick? He is the author of every crime, stained by every cruelty, and he has invaded the patrimony of Christ seeking to destroy it with Saracen aid,

probably a reference to the emperor's garrison of deported Sicilian Muslims at Lucera. Frederick II's chancery returned the compliment:

> from the time of his election he [Gregory IX] has been not a Father of mercy, but of discord, an eager promoter of desolation rather than consolation. He has scandalized the whole world. Construing his words in the true sense, he is that great dragon who leads the world astray, Antichrist, whose forerunner he says we are. . . He is the angel coming from the abyss bearing vials full of bitterness to harm the sea and the earth.[141]

Bedevilled by controversy, the eschatological theme as an explanatory device still remained extremely popular well into modern times. But the poisoned atmosphere after 1239 eroded the restorative meaning of eschatological *imperium* developed ever since Charlemagne's time for the neo-Roman West.

The Western Imperial Ideal by the End of the Thirteenth Century

When Bishop William of Champeaux and Abbot Pontius of Cluny assured Emperor Henry V in 1119 that he would lose nothing by surrendering his rights to invest bishops with ring and staff,[142] then the relation of Papacy and Empire could in theory return to the harmony enjoyed by Otto III and Sylvester II, Henry II and Benedict VIII, and Henry III and Leo IX. But this did not happen. Since Gregory VII's time the Papacy had done much to devalue the theocratic prestige of the imperial office and to make its own temporal claims explicit. Used to a more traditional subordination of patriarchs to emperors, the ambassadors from Constantinople who arrived in Italy to visit Lothar III in 1137 were shocked to discover that the Roman pontiff acted more like an emperor than a bishop,[143] and one of them even thought the Roman clergy as worthy of excommunication in consequence. Accusations of this kind would not have frightened a pope such as Innocent III, who recorded in the Lateran's file on the German election dispute that the Empire belonged in any case *principaliter et finaliter*, from start to finish, to the papacy's sphere of authority. These ideas and their application did little to endear the Papacy to the Germans. According to Walther von der Vogelweide, the angels themselves bewail the Donation of Constantine for turning honey to gall, and as for the pope, he was no less a traitor than Judas Iscariot himself.[144]

We have already observed how such recriminations decorated the renewed confrontations of Empire and Papacy from 1239, but in the main the papal curia achieved its object with the elimination of the Staufen dynasty after 1250.[145] Early in the fourteenth century an animal fable was adapted to illustrate the newly restricted focus of the Empire's power. It was said of Rudolf of Habsburg that, as a wily fox, he shrewdly avoided going into the lion's den, representing the lure of Italy.[146] He was, notwithstanding, interested in the prospect of the traditional coronation in Rome. But the fable was right in the sense that imperial domination of Italy rehearsed by the Carolingians and practised by Otto the Great and his successors was orchestrated for the last time by Frederick II.

Yet the grandeur of the western neo-Roman ideal still appealed to the great minds of the age. It is well known how Dante Alighieri (1265–1321) argued in his *De Monarchia* for the restoration of a Roman and Christian Empire similar to that envisaged by Frederick II and his propagandists. But Dante took the argument a stage further in divorcing Roman imperial power from the pretensions of the Papacy as well as the Germans. For him, the Roman people had already won the right to world governance through their own efforts and sacrifices by the time of Christ's incarnation. And Christ, according to Dante, confirmed Rome's rights by accepting the validity of Roman law when he voluntarily submitted to judgement by Pontius Pilate.[147] But how such a theory could actually be translated, in fourteenth century politics, into the universal *monarchia* required by Dante now entered the realm of fantasy.

Part III: Kingship and Governance in Medieval Germany

Ever since the expulsion of the house of Tarquin, the Romans claimed to despise the very name of king. But in their relations with their Hellenistic, Persian and barbarian neighbours, they continued to be perfectly well acquainted with the institutions of kingship in all their variety. As Germanic pressures upon the Roman frontier became more apparent in the third century CE and resulted in the armed migration of German tribal configurations into the Roman Empire in the fourth and fifth centuries as supplicants, confederates or conquerors, so the Roman governing and literary elites learned perhaps more than they would have liked about Germanic military kingship.[1] In restoring the functions of kings to the mainstream of political history in western and southern Europe, the Germans changed the nature of governance, but without replacing the classical Roman state with any true version of statehood of their own. The political ideal continued to be Roman and imperial, which explains the deference paid by barbarian kingship to Constantinople as well as the appeal of the western neo-Roman revival of the ninth and tenth centuries. The barbarian kings in sub-Roman Europe endeavoured to govern through such institutions inherited from the Roman and Christian past which could be salvaged or adapted for the purpose,[2] and through their own conceptions of loyalty to their dynasties from powerful military or landowning figures. Our understanding of such political systems, often frustrated by the fragmentary nature of the written sources but helped out by archaeological and art-historical discovery,[3] inevitably fluctuates with the modern scholarly ideas about medieval lordship, political continuity and legal identity.[4]

126

Legacies of Germanic Kingship

The last thing which migratory Germanic kingship contemplated was institutional stasis. The opportunities to develop military, judicial and fiscal functions as well as an emphasis on sacral and dynastic kingship, so often disappointed, were taken up.[5] The king's household, whether peripatetic or fixed at a convenient residence, was the centrepiece of governance. It was a legal institution in that it acted as the ultimate court of judgement and appeal. In spite of some division of military and judicial function in origin, the Germanic king became the supreme magistrate of his people in sub-Roman Europe, even if the subjects might live under a variety of civil or tribal codes which were not his own. The royal household was also a military organisation in that the political method of last resort was warfare. After the settlements, the Germanic kings developed their role as leaders of military aristocracies, and took it for granted that normally there would be an annual campaign, and more if necessary, against external or internal enemies.

The sacral dimension of kingship may well have emerged, in some cases, from a belief in descent from a pagan deity. Naturally this was unacceptable to Christian belief, yet the idea persisted that royal lines stood above ordinary mortals, their virtue discerned by the celestial powers and rewarded by success in battle and in consolidating the dynasty. An obvious inference was that the Christian Church ought to support kings and pray for them, and later on, to provide them with more specific political and material support.[6] Another ingredient essential to the stability of early medieval kingship was the possession of extensive landed estates to provide the economic underpinning for the royal court and all its activities because the Roman tax system had, in spite of some exceptions, reached the virtual end of useful productivity in the fourth and fifth centuries, apart from the provinces governed from Constantinople.

There were, of course, immense variations in the scope of the Germanic kingdoms and in the ways in which the rulers, the landowning aristocracy, and the Christian prelates shared out power, influence and resources. It is striking to reflect upon the methods with which a new royal dynasty, the Carolingian, did manipulate the essential ingredients of barbarian kingship after 751 to establish their authority: guardianship of the laws in their various forms, some of which were written down and revised; a programme of justice and order for all subjects; an extremely vigorous version of military leadership; acquisition of a new sacral status through unction and other ecclesiastical ceremonies of installation; patronage of the religious and diocesan activities of the Church which underlined the theocratic nature of their rule; and ownership of a vast fisc, which was further expanded in new provinces taken over by conquest.

It has been pointed out that one reason why the Carolingians found it relatively easy to remove the Merovingian dynasty was that as mayors of the palace of Austrasia, they had already outstripped in resources all the other landowners in the Frankish realm, and that the Merovingian dynasty had itself been rendered virtually landless. It was also reported that the last Merovingian, Childeric III, was deprived of hereditary charisma by having his long hair shorn, extravagant chevelure apparently signifying a sacral status going back to the origins of the dynasty. But Einhard also betrays the fact that the Merovingians tried to hang on to their juridical and political duties to the very last:

> Whenever he [Childeric III] needed to travel, he went in a cart which was drawn in country style by yoked oxen, with a cowherd to drive them. In this fashion he would go to the palace and to the general assembly of his people, which was held each year to settle the affairs of the kingdom, and in this fashion he would return home again.[7]

Carolingian Kingship in Germany

In Part I we have already seen some of the ways in which Frankish kingship was extended into Germany, by conquest in the eighth century and through the formation of Louis the German's successor-kingdom in the ninth. Royal residences such as Frankfurt, Ingelheim and Regensburg were supported by substantial fiscal resources. There was a rich establishment of subordinate bishoprics and abbeys, the majority of them founded from scratch or re-endowed since the advent of Carolingian power east of the Rhine after 700. There was a substantial landowning aristocracy, some of the members bearing titles of count or margrave, but it is a difficult and controversial question to determine whether this was essentially a newly introduced Frankish imperial following or an admixture of Austrasian and Burgundian grantees with the older noble groups to be found in Saxony, Alemannia and Bavaria.[8] Differing historiographical perspectives about the function and descent of the aristocracies within the Frankish Empire and its successor kingdoms are influenced by opinions about whether noble status was based primarily upon high birth or upon royal service.

The ninth century was a period of rapid political change for kingship because the conquest era of Frankish history came to an end, and this implied a relative impoverishment of royal resources just when external threats were on the increase.[9] One response was an elaboration of the political responsibilities of the Church, which also increased its jurisdictional authority by enfeoffing military retinues and by building fortifications to cope with internal feuds in East Francia, with the Viking and Slav menace, and eventually with the invasions of the Magyars.[10] We hear, for example, of Corvey Abbey's *militia coenobii* in 897, military protection for the monastery consisting of the abbot's vassals, and in 908 the bishop of Eichstätt was granted leave to fortify his cathedral town against attack by the Hungarians.[11] The *Annals of Fulda* are full of the new ecclesiastical militarism. In 883, for example,

> the Northmen came up the Rhine and burned many places lately rebuilt, taking not a little plunder. Archbishop Liutbert of Mainz came against them with a few men; but he killed not a few of them and took back the plunder. Cologne was rebuilt apart from its churches and monasteries and its walls were provided with gates, bars and locks.[12]

In the ninth century the titles carried by the most prominent aristocrats – duke, margrave and count – seem to have implied a mixture of military, fiscal and juridical duties under the aegis of the crown. But there is some difficulty in disentangling the influence which landowners exercised in their regions, as opposed to the benefits of royal offices such as counties which they might hold.[13] Evidence is hard to come by, but the East Frankish secular aristocracy with the dukes in the lead had, by 900 or 910, based themselves quite securely upon local and autonomous foundations consisting of lands, military retinues, fortifications and the use of a variety of jurisdictions other than counties, of which advocacy or right of protection over ecclesiastical resources was probably the most effective and lucrative. In other words, the decline of royal governing authority was matched by a necessary attitude of *sauve qui peut*, so that by the beginning of the tenth century the bishops and secular landowners of East Francia were realistic political heirs of fragmenting Carolingian authority.

Bishops and abbots were further sustained by grants of juridical immunity against interference by local counts and margraves.[14] They also possessed forests and towns with appropriate jurisdictions, although one difficulty for them was that, according to ecclesiastical custom and canonical regulation, the actual exercise of the jurisdiction had to be delegated to aristocratic advocates who all too often abused their powers. But bishoprics and abbeys enjoyed one advantage in that, as undying corporations, their resources might pass almost intact from generation to generation, whereas the secular aristocracy was addicted to the division of family inheritances. On the other hand, all the resources including offices granted by the crown to the lay aristocracy were normally to be regarded as hereditary by the beginning of the tenth century.

The gradual transformation of precarial tenure into hereditary right proved advantageous to local aristocratic power at a dangerous time. The best-documented moment in the process is Charles the Bald's court held at Quierzy in 877, when a conditional grant of heredity to regally bestowed offices paved the way for his expedition to Italy in pursuit of the imperial crown. For both Frankish realms, western and eastern, hereditary right to counties as well as other fiefs and offices was outlined.[15] This recognition at Quierzy set the tone for the hereditary dukedoms, margraviates and counties of the tenth-century Frankish successor kingdoms.

The Carolingians of East Francia and Itinerant Kingship

We are not well informed about the politics of royal governance in the ninth-century East Frankish kingdom. But we can see how itinerant kingship facilitated formal meetings with bishops and secular magnates as well as carrying on the military business of the crown, which was very demanding considering the advance of the Northmen and the Slavs, the rivalries with the other Carolingian kingdoms, and the internal predilection for major feuds to work out regional political rivalries. Yet the *Annals of Fulda* do testify to the vigour of the royal *iter* or perambulation as an essential method of governance in a realm where administrative techniques were so primitive. The years 873 and 874, for example, demonstrate the king's journeys out of the two principal residences, Frankfurt and Regensburg, and how kingship was exercised on the move.[16] After wintering in Frankfurt, Louis the German went after Easter in 873 to

the *villa* of Bürstadt near Worms, where he had his sons, Louis that is and Charles, judge individual cases; and what they could not resolve themselves they left to their father's judgement. Whence it came about that all of those who came from various parts returned with joy with their grievances lawfully settled.

This idyllic report of the dynasty successfully fulfilling its professional duties as the highest magistracy constituted, of course, a vital legacy to its successors.

Then the king went to Mainz and took a boat down the Rhine to visit Aachen before heading south again for Metz. From there he went to Strasbourg and by the late autumn of 873 was back in Regensburg. In January 874 he set out for Augsburg, going on to Frankfurt in February and visiting Fulda Abbey before returning to a general assembly at the royal manor of Tribur on the Rhine. Then he travelled to Italy to meet his nephew Emperor Louis II and the pope near Verona before heading back over the Alps to Forchheim in Franconia to meet his sons. After an excursion back to Bavaria, he went to Frankfurt yet again and on to Aachen via the manor of Biberich before going on to Liège (or possibly Herstal) to see his half-brother, King Charles of West Francia. Back in Mainz by December, he once again spent Christmas in Frankfurt nearby. The source reveals a great deal of diplomatic business with friends, family and enemies (notably envoys from the Northmen and the Czechs) undertaken on these journeys, and shows up why incessant perambulation was a significant source of royal power: constant meetings and discussions kept the network of *amicitia* or royal friendship, almost the equivalent of a political party, in good repair and also allowed for defusing potentially dangerous conflicts across the frontiers by receiving ambassadors and through interviews with other Carolingian rulers. As we have been able to observe, itinerant kingship was another of the most efficacious legacies of the Carolingians to the later rulers of medieval Germany.

The Last Carolingians of East Francia

The deposition of Emperor Charles III in 887 and his replacement as king in East Francia by his nephew Arnulf of Carinthia serves as a reminder of two related political realities about late Carolingian kingship. The first is the disintegration of the myth of imperial unity as new kings salvaged realms of their own out of the debris of Carolingian collapse: notably Berengar of Friuli (888–924) and Wido II of Spoleto (888–94) as rivals in Italy; the Welf count Rudolf in upper Burgundy (888–912); Louis, son of Boso of Vienne, as king of Provence (890–928) and the Robertian count Odo of Paris in West Francia (888–98). In spite of his imperial coronation in 896, King Arnulf as senior representative of the Carolingian house was in no position to reverse such usurpations, and they help to explain why the election of Conrad of Franconia as king of East Francia in 911 was not an anomaly. Rather than attempt another union under the Carolingians, the only realistic candidate being Charles the Simple, king of West Francia (893–923), the eastern Franks chose their own man. The other point, made again by the *Annals of Fulda* for 888, simply reminds us of the internal diversity of the East Frankish realm:[17] 'King Arnulf received at Regensburg the leading men of the Bavarians, the eastern Franks, the Saxons, the Thuringians, the Alemans and a great part of the Slavs, and celebrated Christmas and Easter there with honour.'

Endangered as it was by the Magyar menace and by the severity of internal feuds, the governance of Arnulf of Carinthia, Louis the Child and Conrad I stuck to the norms of Carolingian rule in East Francia, shaken again by the demise of imperial unity in 887. Arnulf relied heavily upon the bishops and abbots – twenty-six bishops met the king at the royal residence of Tribur in 895 and issued extensive ecclesiastical legislation[18] – but it is no longer thought that Arnulf intended to use episcopal influence as a counterweight to the aristocracy. Churchmen and secular magnates co-operated in establishing Louis the Child as his successor in 900, although the royal court was inevitably a household of bishops during the king's minority (he was born in 893).[19] In spite of the confusion caused by the Magyar raids, this court was not inert. Its most interesting surviving instrument is the toll ordinance of Raffelstetten drawn up after a visitation to the eastern marches.[20] The agents of the court, two bishops and a count, interviewed at least forty noblemen to establish the rightful tolls for ships proceeding down the Danube, and what ought to be paid as duty upon goods leaving Bavaria or coming in from Bohemia, the Moravian principality and Russia. The principal export was salt, the most valuable imports being slaves, horses and wax.

The politics of royal governance in East Francia in the ninth century were seminal in that certain traditions and expectations were developed which were taken up almost automatically by the successors, the Liudolfings and the Salians. These were: an elective kingship which was also sacral in character; itinerant kingship which facilitated the military and judicial business of the crown; reliance upon the support offered by the Church, and upon the principle of political friendship with the secular aristocracy; the use of an extensive fisc and the palaces upon it, and the limited use of counts to administer it; possession of an efficient chancery staffed by churchmen; and above everything the royal *bannus* or protective jurisdiction over all the regions and inhabitants of the realm, including rights to use or tax certain material resources.[21]

Military and Theocratic Kingship: Henry I and Otto I

Since Conrad I left no direct heir, his reign is often regarded as an interlude between the Carolingian era and the onset of Ottonian kingship and *imperium*. Yet Conrad I appears to have been an able exponent of Frankish royal governance in spite of the perils posed by the power of the dukes. Ever generous with its resources, the episcopate rallied to the king's side. The synod in Carolingian style assembled at Hohenaltheim in 916 and attended by a papal legate not only issued decrees of interest to the Church but also declared the king to be the Lord's Anointed, *Christus Domini*, against whom it would be sacrilege to raise the spectre of rebellion.[22] Later narrative sources were quite favourable to Conrad, but his short reign and his childlessness still confer upon him a certain political transitoriness.[23]

A purpose behind Widukind of Corvey's compelling and inexhaustibly interesting account of the tenth-century Saxons[24] was to promote the prestige of Henry I as the founder of a triumphant *stirps regia*. One of the methods was to dramatise by contrasts Henry's military record *vis-à-vis* the Magyars. For 924 Widukind reported that the Hungarians 'inflicted such carnage and burned down so many monasteries at that time that we have judged it better to keep quiet about our calamities than to reveal them in words.' According to the source, King Henry then adopted tactics reminiscent of the Frankish and Anglo-Saxon reactions to the Vikings; payment of tribute, construction of fortifications, and the training up of more effective armed forces. The fruits of these endeavours became apparent in 933 with victory over a Magyar army invading Saxony and Thuringia, and Widukind made the most of its political potential for advertising the successful military kingship of the Saxon ruler:

> The victorious king returned and gave thanks as was due to God for a victory granted by heaven over his enemies. He could devote to religion the tribute he used to pay to the enemy, and could

command the resources to be devoted to the poor. He was hailed father of his country, the lord of all, and *imperator* by the army, and the fame of his power and his strength was spread far and wide to all peoples and kings.

No reader or hearer of Widukind's work could then fail to pick up the connection with his comment upon Otto I's victory in 955 at the Lechfeld:

Glorified by his distinguished triumph, the king was acclaimed father of his country and *imperator* by the army; then he ordered honours and fitting praises to the highest God in all churches ... He returned as victor to the Saxons who danced for joy, and he was welcomed with the utmost goodwill. No victory of this kind had so gladdened a king for two hundred years.[25]

Naturally Widukind had a great deal more to say about how his heroes, Henry I and Otto I, rose to greatness as kings, yet the neatness of his accounts of military affairs, essential to the medieval perception of effective kingship, has raised some doubts amongst modern commentators.[26] For example, Widukind's account of the programme of fortification, corroborated from other written sources,[27] has always aroused great interest. After arranging a truce with the Magyars underlined by paying them an annual tribute, Henry I established

one out of nine agrarian warriors (*ex agrariis militibus*) to live within a fortification, to build dwellings for the other eight of his companions and to look after a third of the produce duly put aside. The other eight cultivated the soil, reaped and collected the grain and stored it in the fortification. Court meetings and all markets and festivities he ordered to be held inside fortifications. They worked day and night to construct the forts and learned in peace what to do against the enemy in time of war. Apart from these fortifications there were trifling defences or none at all.[28]

The inference is that the Saxons were safe from the Magyars behind walls until they could return fire with a new cavalry army of their own in the 930s. But the archaeological record, after diligent excavation of Saxon sites, cannot relate the undertakings to Henry I's time in any purposeful way which might bear out Widukind's account.[29]

A consequence is that an approach being developed in modern historiography is to look beyond Saxon military and triumphalist interest to Henry I's exercise of traditional Carolingian methods of establishing networks of friendship within and beyond the boundaries of the realm, as incentives towards peace and order.[30] Several sources, including Widukind's own account, indicate that Henry I was more sensitive in this respect than Otto I, who appears to have changed the agenda in favour of confrontation, a strategy which paid off in the end. Abbot Adalbert of St Maximin preserved an interesting report from 931, which recorded that Henry I 'was invited by Eberhard and the other Frankish counts and bishops to Franconia, each and every one honouring him as befits a king in their houses or episcopal seats with banquets and gifts',[31] rather like a modern state visit.

Widukind also asserted the warmest understanding of *amicitia* for Otto I, among whose many virtues were 'refusing nothing to his friends and loyalty to them beyond the human norm'. At least this is accurate for his Saxons such as Hermann Billung and Margrave Gero; faced by a new rising in 953, the king retreated from the Rhineland to Saxony where he was consoled by his friends and the presence of his own people.[32]

In order to understand the duties of East Frankish kingship in the tenth century, it is necessary to return to Aachen and the installation of Otto I in 936 for which Widukind confected commentaries upon the royal insignia with which the new king was endowed. This harks back to his report of Conrad I's deathbed scene in 918, when insignia are symbolically given equal weight with the other material and psychological signs of successful kingship. The king speaks to Eberhard:[33]

We dispose, brother, of large military retinues to call up and to lead; we have fortifications and weapons as well as the royal insignia and everything else due to royal status except for the fortune and fitness for it.

Fitness he discerned in Duke Henry of Saxony and, as we saw in Part I, recommended him as successor to the throne.

Good fortune, military paraphernalia, royal insignia – there are classical as well as Germanic prototypes behind Widukind's thinking here, but it is realistic for appreciating the style of tenth-century kingship and its prestige. Henry I thought it a great thing to acquire from King Rudolf II of Burgundy a wonder-working relic, the supposed Holy Lance with a nail from the crucifixion, to incorporate with the East Frankish royal insignia. Bishop Liudprand of Cremona attributed Otto I's victory at the Battle of Birten in 939 in part to prayers offered up before this relic. Widukind says that the king also carried it into battle against the Magyars at the Lechfeld. It outstripped all other relics in the royal collection, and the great processional cross of the Empire, a marvel of gold and precious stones commissioned by Conrad II, was designed at the same time as the reliquary in which the lance was to be stored. His grandson Henry IV embellished it with a silver casing and an inscription.[34]

Henry I has been credited with some novel approaches to the Carolingian inheritance of kingship. He seems to have realised that the *fortuna atque mors* generously ascribed to him by Conrad I would not stretch in the Frankish mode to kingship divided between four sons, on the narrow basis of a kingdom where the other dukes were so formidable. This is thought to have been the motive for designating Otto as sole royal heir, and the chief cause for the opposition which he then was obliged to overcome between 937 and 941.[35] It is difficult to deny that in former times Otto I's brothers could have expected a better deal, apart from Bruno who was in any case dedicated to the religious life. Thangmar, the eldest brother, was killed and Henry was, as we have seen in Part I, compensated with the rich duchy of Bavaria in 947.

Henry I also broke with tradition in declining consecration in any kind of religious ceremony, a decision which has never been satisfactorily explained. According to Widukind of Corvey, the new king politely explained to the archishop of Mainz that God's will and the archbishop's piety – this prelate was the principal elector – had designated him a king; for unction and coronation he was not worthy.[36] This strange reaction has often been taken to mean that Henry I shrewdly distrusted bishops, since their notorious political wranglings had distracted East Francia since the end of the ninth century. This explanation has something to recommend it, but may simply be a rationalisation.

Yet from the very start of his reign, Henry I was entitled king in theocratic terms, 'by the favour of divine clemency'. He confirmed the great churches of the realm in their rights and privileges and, like his predecessors, gave handsome properties to the Church. And he continued the tradition of royal participation in ecclesiastical synods, as practised by the Carolingians and carried on by Conrad I as at Hohenaltheim in 916. At Coblenz in 922 the synod was also attended by King Charles of West Francia, and at Erfurt in 932, Henry I met more than a dozen abbots and bishops from all over Germany.[37]

In comparison, Widukind of Corvey's account of Otto the Great's inauguration at Aachen in 936 is obviously an ideological statement about the religious dimensions of royal office, rather than an exact report. It looks back to the Carolingians and to Old Testament kingship as well as forecasting the new king's imperial future. The conduct of the ceremony was undertaken by Archbishop Hildibert of Mainz (927–37), a man to whom Widukind attributed prophetic powers because of his sanctity and intellect, in all likelihood an allusion to Samuel's role in the inauguration of Saul and David as kings. It is the insignia which are used in the monk's report, to point out the sacral nature of royal tasks:

> Accept this sword, with which you may chase out all the adversaries of Christ, barbarians, and bad Christians, by the divine authority handed down to you and by power of all the empire of the Franks for the most lasting peace of all Christians.

The royal cloak with its *armillae* was taken to symbolise the king's duty as faithful guardian of the peace. The protective and judicial function of kingship, the *bannus*, was given formidably religious colouring when investing Otto I with sceptre and staff:

> With these symbols you may be reminded that you should reproach your subjects with paternal castigation, but first of all you should extend the hand of mercy to ministers of God, widows, and orphans. And never let the oil of compassion be absent from your head in order that you may be crowned with eternal reward in the present and in the future.

Unction, coronation and enthronement ceremonies then followed.[38]

The Symbiosis of the German Church and Medieval Kingship

Archbishop Hildibert's words are no doubt freely found fancies, but they would have sounded credible to Widukind's audience because of the growing mutual commitments of Church and secular governance, at least since the time of Pepin the Short and Charlemagne.[39] But the use of churchmen in the service of the German *Christus Domini* was the subject of some debate. To the pope, Archbishop William of Mainz observed in 955 with a hint of disapproval that the dukes and counts were doing the work of bishops, and bishops were exercising authority like counts and dukes. The delegation of counties to the bishops is a well-attested phenomenon.[40]

Later commentators thought that the method had worked well enough. During the bad times of conflict after 1076, Sigebert of Gembloux asserted that

> I rightly call the times of Otto (the Great) fortunate when the *res publica* was reformed by renowned prelates and wise men restored peace to the churches and integrity to religion. One could then see and, indeed, experience the truth of the philosopher's saying: 'Happy the state whose rulers are philosophers and whose philosophers rule!'[41]

The American historian C. Stephen Jaeger has illustrated how such Ottonian churchmen with Archbishop Bruno of Cologne in the lead were the creators of a revived religious, political and courtly culture which was to have widespread influence for the next two centuries.[42]

Right from the start of Otto I's reign, just when he was in deep trouble with his own family and its allies amongst the dukes and other magnates, there survive over forty royal diplomas[43] indicating the material relationship between sacral kingship and support from the Church. They concern the foundation of important royal abbeys in Saxony, Quedlinburg and Magdeburg, and their endowment with property. They confirm the legal privileges, notably jurisdictional immunity, and rights of tithe and other material resources assigned to bishoprics and abbeys, not only in Saxony such as the monastery of Corvey and the sees of Halberstadt and Osnabrück, but throughout Germany: Kempten Abbey in Swabia; the monasteries of Fulda, Hersfeld and Lorsch in Franconia; and bishoprics such as Utrecht and Würzburg. The diplomas also conferred royal property outright upon the churches favoured by the court and whose support was required the length and breadth of the kingdom, from the archbishopric of Bremen in the north to that of Salzburg in the south, as well as the sees of Worms and Speyer in the Rhineland and the richer abbeys and collegiate churches: the palace chapel at Aachen, St Alban at Mainz, St Emmeram at Regensburg and St Gallen in Swabia. There was nothing very novel in the type or content of these charters, of which more have no doubt been lost. But they constitute a witness to the spiritual and pragmatic relationship of throne and altar inherited from the Carolingians and developed further in the Ottonian and Salian practices of kingship.[44]

In Germany the pope was revered as the father of the Church and the living embodiment of St Peter, but the king was Christ's vicar for the actual terrestrial organisation of the Church. In an elaborate preamble to a diploma issued in 1020, Henry II asserted that having taken up the burden of kingdom and Empire, *regni et imperii fasces*, by divine command, he was obliged to heed the words of the Gospel, 'For unto whomsoever much is given, of him shall much be required: and to whom men have committed much, of him they will ask the more.' This is diagnosed to mean that it was his duty to enrich, to promote and to direct the Church of Christ, through whose person and for whom he reigned.[45] This theocratic programme justified the huge investment of land and other resources confided by the crown to the German Church because the bishops were committed to the *Christus Domini* as their temporal sovereign worthy of their devoted service. As another charter of Henry II's expressed it, a king could therefore lighten his 'burdens in the course of this life by imposing them on the bishops'.[46] In other words, the duty of the secular *rex* and the sacred bishop had convergent aims in the salvation history of Christian people, Church and Empire as they hurried towards the end of time.

Specific Cases: Magdeburg and Bamberg

Henry II's great-uncle Otto I had already demonstrated that such a relationship contained political and material purposes beyond the general protective role of kings over the visible Church, and the spiritual functions of the bishops in their dioceses alluded to by Sigebert of Gembloux. Having been founded by Otto the Great in 937, the monastery of St Maurice at Magdeburg became one of his favourite residences, and as emperor he carried out the plan of promoting it into an archbishopric. The rationale was provided by the Slav conquests since the 920s. A new archdiocese with suffragan sees would complement the structure of military marches under the Saxon margraves, and provide the cultural means for incorporating Sclavinia into the East Frankish *regnum* and the Roman *imperium*. Magdeburg's geographical position at an important crossing of the River Elbe fitted it in any case as a political, military and economic gateway to the East, although its full potential was not to be realised until the twelfth century.[47]

The establishment of the new archbishopric took time, largely because it was at first opposed by the sees of Mainz and Halberstadt, which rightly foresaw a diminution of their own diocesan authority. But the necessary papal authorisations were secured in 962 and 967, and in 968 Otto the Great was able to send the necessary letter of command from Italy to Germany. The preamble states the motive for creating the archbishopric in terms of the interconnected invisible authority of God and the visible authority of the earthly ruler: 'Since we believe that the augmentation of the divine religion affects the safety and welfare of our kingdom and empire, we intend and desire to amplify it in all possible ways.'[48] The Austrian historian Heinrich Fichtenau has drawn attention to the importance of preambles or *arengae* in royal documents as statements of policy and intent.[49] They were quite the opposite of pious or inconsequential formulas, and encapsulated the politico-religious mentality of kingship at that time.

The new archbishop, Adalbert of St Maximin, abbot of Weissenburg and a notable chronicler, was undoubtedly chosen as a fluent Slavic linguist who had already been sent to Kiev on an unsuccessful mission to investigate the possibility of converting the Russian court to Latin Christianity. Three new suffragan sees were set up in order to assimilate the Slav lands to Germany itself; this is one reason why Brun of Querfurt later referred to Magdeburg as *Theutonum nova metropolis*, 'new metropolis of the Germans'.[50] The bishoprics were equivalent to three of the marches; Merseburg, Zeitz and Meissen. Two other colonial bishoprics founded in the 940s, Havelberg and Brandenburg, were added to the archdiocese at the expense of Mainz as previous metropolitan. Since the authority of the conquering Saxon nobles preceded that of the Church by many years, the margraves were admonished by name to co-operate with the ecclesiastical establishment and to offer material support. In spite of the setback represented by the Slav rising of 983, the politics of governance in the German north-east were changed forever by the royal foundation of Magdeburg.

Although the sources are full of abrasions and confrontations between secular magnates and bishops about material resources, the former had to accept that cooperation between the court and the Church provided essential infrastructure to royal governance. To some extent this is demonstrated by the foundation of Bamberg as a bishopric by Henry II in 1007. There is no reason to doubt that one motive, the conversion of quite a substantial Slav population in the region, was genuine. But the king also marked out Bamberg in the political sense, by setting it on the path of exemption from any archiepiscopal authority, and by endowing it with a huge amount of the royal inheritance all over the south-eastern quarter of the German kingdom.[51] Another political motive was to replace the power of the aristocratic house of Schweinfurt in upper Franconia with the agency of the Church. In 1003 Margrave Henry of Schweinfurt had revolted against Henry II because he thought he had been denied the reversion of the duchy of Bavaria, which was in the king's hands. His counties were transferred to the new bishopric.[52]

Another aspect of sacral kingship which the foundations of Magdeburg and Bamberg assist in illuminating is the predilection of German kings for certain localities with distinguished monastic, collegiate or cathedral churches which were used to display the glory of kingship by patronage or royal residence or court festivities. For such purposes the palace chapel at Aachen was always of prime significance, but Otto the Great also favoured Quedlinburg and Magdeburg after their establishment in 936 and 937 respectively. Such purposes also lay behind the foundation of Bamberg and the refoundation of Merseburg as a bishopric in 1004 by Henry II. The latter was the residence most favoured by him as king. Conrad II cultivated Speyer, with ambitious plans for the cathedral, as we have seen. Henry III developed Goslar in Saxony, where the new collegiate church of Saints Simon and Jude was consecrated in 1051.[53]

The modes of governance meant that medieval Germany did not possess an administrative capital, but these semi-sacred places with their important churches were somehow regarded as special centres of God-guarded kingship. One method by which this was made explicit was through the ceremony of crown-wearing.[54] So the sources sometimes attest that when German kings spent principal feasts of the Church, notably Easter, Whitsun and Christmas, at such places, then they wore their royal crown as a part of the religious ceremonies for the day. Quedlinburg, for example, featured quite often in the Easter celebrations of the Ottonian dynasty. But the best-known example of the crown-wearing is Philip of Swabia's at Magdeburg at Christmas 1199, because it was put into verse by Walther von der Vogelweide, with an extravagant comparison of the royal person with the Holy Trinity itself.[55] As Hans-Walter Klewitz demonstrated, such ceremonies were more or less divorced from coronations, which took place, with unction, at the outset of the reign after election. Yet another way in which sacral kingship was tied to specific places with prestigious churches was through the custom whereby German kings were recognised as canons of cathedral and collegiate chapters.[56] The origins and significance of such arrangements are still the subject of considerable debate, but the drift is clear enough. An anointed king was not a priest, but his sacral status conferred a proximity to the altar which was understandably symbolised by his holding canonries.

Bishops as Servants of the Crown

It used to be thought that Otto the Great deliberately promoted the political importance of bishops and abbots as a check upon the unruly ambitions of dukes, but this theory no longer enjoys much credence. Instead, the presence of churchmen at court – also as the staff of the chapel and chancery, as we shall see – the royal *iter* which included episcopal and abbatial residences, and the pursuit of *amicitia* to include the cathedral churches rewarded on a large scale by grants of land and juridical immunity simply served to integrate the Church into German politics. It also helps to explain why the crown took so close an interest in the election of bishops, usually nominating the candidate and expressing approval by investiture with the insignia of episcopal office. It also explains why church reform was of professional interest to kings and was encouraged by them – another Carolingian tradition not permitted to fall into disuse – making the readjustments demanded by the Gregorian papacy after 1076 all the more painful to realise.[57]

Long before the age of Hildebrandine reform, commentators had observed that it was necessary though difficult to reconcile the roles of good politician and good bishop in Germany. It was something of a literary exercise to discuss the issue. The tenth-century biographies of Bishop Ulrich of Augsburg by Gerhard and of Archbishop Bruno of Cologne by Ruotger are designed as *vitae* of saints, but manage to integrate the virtues and effectiveness of these bishops in all the affairs of the high political world with their excellence as churchmen.[58] Bishop Thietmar of Merseburg was not so sure that this game could always be played out successfully, so his generally favourable picture of the German episcopate of the tenth and early eleventh centuries is sometimes punctuated by acid remarks. In his portrait of Archbishop Adalbert of Bremen (1043–72), Adam of Bremen did not try to square the circle, portraying the archbishop first and foremost as a powerful and ambitious politician. As a regent of the Empire during the minority of Henry IV, and as architect of plans to turn Bremen into the ecclesiastical patriarchate of Scandinavia, Adalbert certainly

possessed political vision. He was also greedy for the secular improvement of his see in Germany, but Henry III's early death in 1056
deprived him of essential support. His schemes recruited him too many
enemies, resulting in his expulsion from court in 1066 and the downfall
of his authority in Saxony itself.[59] But like the other prelates, Adalbert
of Bremen certainly understood the attractions and prestige of ecclesiastical reform as well, and it is significant that he was the first to be
offered the Papacy by Henry III when Roman reform was inaugurated in 1046.[60]

The prosaic account of Bishop Benno II of Osnabrück (1068–88) by
Abbot Norbert of Iburg gives us a good idea of how the well-trained
courtier bishops of Germany reacted to the distracting political
challenges of the 1070s and the 1080s. Bishop Benno was certainly
one of the most talented churchmen of his time.[61] He was a learned
scholar who made his mark in the cathedral schools of Strasbourg and
Hildesheim. He was a competent administrator entrusted with high
offices by the crown and by the archbishop of Cologne. He was well-
known as an expert architect of churches and castles, working on the
great imperial project at Speyer Cathedral and designing Henry IV's
unpopular castles in Saxony. When he became a bishop, he energe-
tically defended and extended the rights of his see, cultivated monastic
reform, and played the respected politician at court. By professional
instinct most of the German bishops inclined to support Henry IV
against Gregory VII, but the pope had strong arguments of which he
did not fail to remind the German episcopate in his circular letters.
Benno II certainly saw the point, and was unusual in advocating
compromise. In 1080, when Henry IV convoked the episcopal synod of
Brixen in order to depose Gregory VII for the second time, the bishop
prudently hid himself inside a hollow altar in the church where the
proceedings were taking place, and so he avoided signing the decree.
The biographer noted that hatred had got the better of reason and
sound judgement on both sides with the exception of Benno II, who
always managed to reconcile fidelity to the king with a proper
episcopal obedience to the pope. Henry IV soon forgave the bishop
for his amusing deception; a model of the altar was gratefully installed
in the bishop's foundation, Iburg Abbey; and as Abbot Norbert noted,
Benno II's political skill fulfilled the apostolic instruction of St Paul in
Romans 12:18 – 'If it be possible, as much as lieth in you, live
peaceably with all men.'

Since they were magnates in possession of lands and jurisdictions,
there was in any case a structural inheritance from the past which

rendered the combination of prelate and politician inseparable in the German Middle Ages. Pope Paschal II recognised this with disapproval in 1111, listing the temporalities with which the German Church had been gradually endowed ever since the time of Charlemagne:[62] urban, advocatial and hundredal jurisdictions; ducal powers, marches and counties; towns with mints, tolls and markets; manors, estates and villages; military retinues and castles. And there were other valuable assets such as forests and mines. Again the biographies of the twelfth-century bishops make the connection plain: those of Bishop Otto I of Bamberg (1102–39), the apostle of Pomerania, and of Archbishop Norbert of Magdeburg (1126–32), the founder of the Premonstratensian Order, are good examples. Already regarded as saints in their lifetimes, they were able to combine reforming zeal and administrative efficiency with the political and military duties in which members of the German episcopate were bound to be involved as vassals of the Empire.

All this is taken for granted in Balderich of Florennes's biography of Archbishop Albero of Trier (1131–52).[63] A noted reformer and a friend of Popes Innocent II and Eugenius III, the archbishop also put down secular opposition to his regime in the town of Trier. He accompanied Emperor Lothar III on the Italian expedition of 1136–7 with sixty-seven knights of his retinue. We hear of the feuds he conducted against the secular magnates, during which castles of his own were defended and those of his enemies besieged and destroyed. The archbishop also had time to visit reforming synods in France and to attend the German royal court, where he was welcomed as a learned raconteur. He knew how to advertise his political prestige through the splendour of his retinue and the magnificence of his expenditure. For 1149 Balderich describes how the clerical and secular notables of the diocese travelled by river to visit Conrad III at Frankfurt in forty houseboats, with innumerable guard-boats, barges with provisions, and boats for use as kitchens. Apart from the usual crowd of clerics and knights, the archbishop was accompanied by two dukes and eight counts as his guests. On the way home, they had a laugh when the flotilla gave the rival archiepiscopal city of Mainz quite a fright by sailing past in full war array, banners unfurled, all the knights on deck in armour, and trumpets blaring. They saw the men running about and the women screaming, as though the town were about to be assaulted. But not all the great German sees could keep up the same sort of profile as Trier. Just at this time the Bavarian archbishopric of Salzburg was virtually bankrupt after a series of feuds stretching back to the 1070s, and could hardly take advantage of the economic upsurge until the re-organisation and extension of its material resources by Archbishop Ebcrhard II (1200–46).

The image of the bishop in close association with the crown is essential for understanding the impact of sacral kingship in medieval Germany and the ordinary business of royal governance. This is why investiture with the sceptre, accepted at the Peace of Worms in 1122, was so significant a compromise after the Hildebrandine onslaught upon royal authority. Otto of Freising, a reforming bishop as well as grandson of a king, understood the ideological relationship to perfection. In his account of Frederick Barbarossa's consecration as king in 1152, he explained that a second Frederick, the bishop-elect of Münster, was ordained by the same bishops who had just sanctified the king, so that 'in one church the same day saw the induction of the only two persons who are sacramentally anointed according to the procedures of the New and Old Testaments and are solemnly called the Lord's Anointed.'[64]

The Royal Chapel and Chancery

The nature of the material services provided by the German Church to the royal court, the *servitium regis*, we will consider along with itinerant kingship and with the general scope of royal resources later on. Yet perhaps the most obvious and ordered constitutional link between the Church and the court was represented by another inheritance from the Frankish past, the single institution of royal chapel and chancery. Several classic studies by Austrian and German historians have shown up not only the continuity of the Carolingian writing-offices with the German royal chancery, but also the scheme in which the personnel acted as court chaplains as well as chancery clerks, and on the other business of the crown such as diplomacy.[65] Meticulous investigation by the editors of the volumes of royal diplomas in the *Monumenta Germaniae Historica* series stretching back for many decades, and by various other scholars, has revealed a profile of chancellors, their clerks, and their work reign by reign, even if we do not always know their personal names.[66] The constant production of privileges, mandates and other written instruments by the peripatetic court was one of the most significant achievements of German medieval governance, keeping the recipients in touch with the king as protector of all rights in the realm. Normally there was a chancellor at court who directed the work of the clerics, and their intimacy with the royal politics of the day served as training for the reward often granted, a bishopric. So prestigious was the chancery that the late Carolingian practice of designating archbishops as honorary chancellors was readopted by Otto the Great. From 965 the archbishop of Mainz was normally recognised as archchancellor of the German kingdom. From 1031 the same honour was extended to the archbishops of Cologne as arch-chancellors of Italy. The arch-chancellorship for Burgundy passed from the metropolitans of Besançon in the eleventh century to Vienne in the twelfth[67] and then to Trier in the thirteenth.

German Kingship and the Administration of Justice

The king was the supreme magistrate of his realms, raising the controversial question of the extent to which the German rulers could be regarded as legislators or creators of law, an idea somewhat abrasive to the medieval mind with its conception of law as more or less a divinely constituted and unchanging quantity. More straightforward to understand is the function of the royal court as the judicial guardian of rights in particular and of justice in general. Since the German crown did not operate a system of assizes or specialised subordinate courts, the cases we are informed about concern the high and mighty, the bishops, other prelates, and secular magnates who could expect a hearing at the itinerant royal court. Early in Conrad I's reign, for example, we learn that Bishop Erchanbald of Eichstätt had come to court with a plea for royal protection for such property of his see as was currently under threat. The king held a court meeting or *placitum* at Ulm to hear the evidence, attended by three bishops and nine counts. When the correct list of properties had been established, it was confirmed by the *placitum* and recorded in a diploma issued a little later.[68] Several diplomas of Otto the Great refer to the redistribution of rights or property by royal authority, but after due examination in a public court and after judgement by competent magistrates.[69] A good example concerns the royal estate at Zizers conferred by the king upon the bishopric of Chur in 955 and then confirmed in 956, the original diplomas still surviving. But one of the Raetian magnates not identifiable except as Arnaldus son of Odalric later claimed Zizers for himself. At Constance in 972 the ruler therefore set up a panel of inquiry to decide the issue in his presence. Fourteen named *optimi* or noblemen of Raetia were elected to swear to whom the property justly belonged.

Before the emperor, ten counts and other noblemen present, the *optimi* swore that Zizers had belonged to the emperor 'and therefore he had had the unfettered authority to do whatever he pleased with it.'[70] There is no record of a penalty inflicted upon Arnaldus.

For the same year, 972, we possess the record of a variation to this juridical method. The bishops of Augsburg and Constance and the duke of Swabia came to the emperor at Strasbourg to plead that the Swabian abbey of Ottobeuern ought to be excused from its secular obligations, the military and political *servitia* owed to the Empire. The emperor replied that he would not decide the claim himself as judge, but abide by the decision of the magnates present. They advised that it would be fair to abstract some of the abbey's property into royal hands, so that it could then be enfeoffed to Duke Burchard of Swabia and his successors on condition that they fulfilled the abbey's obligations themselves. The possessions and revenues to be transferred were then cited.[71]

Another important function of the royal court in its judicial aspect was to act as the forum for trial by combat. Bishop Thietmar of Merseburg's chronicle preserves a detailed example of the procedures, in a case of serious political misdemeanour.[72] In 979 Count Gero of Alsleben was arrested by Archbishop Adalbert of Magdeburg and Margrave Dietrich of the North March on a charge brought by a Saxon called Waldo, and the case then came to Otto II's court. Weak points in the story are that we know nothing more of Waldo's background, nor of the actual accusation. But it was serious enough for the emperor to summon the princes of East Francia to Magdeburg for the duel of Gero and Waldo, which was staged upon an island in the River Elbe. Although Waldo sustained two neck wounds, he was able to strike so heavy a blow to Gero's head that, upon inquiry, the count admitted that he had no strength left to continue the fight. Waldo then left the site and disarmed, but as he refreshed himself he dropped down dead of his wounds. It was nevertheless decided by decree of the judges over the case that Gero had lost the duel and was therefore guilty. The emperor ordered him to be decapitated at sundown in spite of protests by Duke Otto of Bavaria and Count Berthold of Schweinfurt that the charges were too thin to warrant the death penalty. The story was long remembered, and many years later Count Gero's innocence was still being maintained.

Such trials by the ordeal of battle were held in high regard as a judicial method as late as the twelfth century and were not forbidden by papal decree until 1234. According to Widukind of Corvey, disputes broke out amongst the Westphalians about what was the correct law on the descent and division of property among male heirs in a lineage. In 938 Otto I held a court-day at Steele near Essen, when it was at first proposed to submit the problem to arbitrators.[73] 'But the king followed better counsel, not wishing noblemen and the elders of the people to be put at risk from dishonourable usage, and ordered the matter to be decided by combat.' This primitive and irrational way of defending the status and self-interest of magnates provides a useful comment upon tenth-century attitudes.

Kingship and Law-making

Historians of medieval German law and law-making generally hold to an interpretation whereby the very concept of royal legislation was extremely restricted before the gradual revival of Roman jurispruden-tial ideas about imperial law-giving in the twelfth century. To medieval notions the law was essentially a form of divinely sanctioned custom reverently handed down the generations.[74] All that was needed was for courts of law, including the royal court, to find out what was right by consultation, memory and discussion in each case in dispute, and to pronounce accordingly. This outline fits what we would consider 'civil' cases. Crimes were also the subject of public concern, of course, but until the rise of the *Landfrieden*, to which we will return, the pursuit of violent wrongdoers was as much a matter for the offended kindred as for public authority. Rulers nevertheless exhibited an inclination to legislate, and as we have seen, the Germanic kings codified law for the various *gentes*, inspired by Roman models. The extensive material of a legislative nature put out by the Carolingians under headings or *capitula* – hence the modern term 'capitulary' for such sources – also came close to royal and imperial law-making in the classical or post-1100 senses.[75]

Capitulary legislation was influenced by the ecclesiastical practice of issuing binding injunctions through provincial councils and synods, and the method was strongly supported by the Carolingian rulers who often presided over church councils themselves as Christ's vicars. This practice was continued by the Ottonian and Salian kings, providing some structural models for the practice of legislation. In 948, for example, Otto I and King Louis IV of France sat with a crowd of bishops in the palace at Ingelheim and issued synodal decrees under twelve headings, on political as well as ecclesiastical affairs. From 951 the two surviving canons of the Synod of Frankfurt, on the abduction of women and the status of monasteries, are clearly royal legislative acts passed with the consent of the counts, bishops and others present.[76] As active head of the Church in its actual organisation, the German ruler kept up the tradition of holding synods. Early in his reign Henry II summoned such synods to Dortmund in 1005 and to Frankfurt in 1007, at which the bishopric of Bamberg was constituted. Conrad II met thirty bishops and abbots at another Frankfurt synod in 1027. As we have seen, one of the most spectacular was held jointly by Emperor Henry III and Pope Leo IX at Mainz in 1049, where they harangued about forty bishops on the importance of their ecclesiastical reform programme.[77] Although his supporters and panegyrists considered Henry IV just as pious and worthy as his synod-holding predecessors, the Roman reform movement then tried to end royal influence over synods where possible, although imperial ambitions to use such meetings were to cause problems well into the twelfth century. In any case Henry IV rather overplayed his hand at his synods, using Worms in 1076 and Brixen in 1080 to try to sack Pope Gregory VII.

Synods preserved positive notions of legislation north of the Alps. Then the German rulers and their advisers were exposed to Roman traditions of jurisprudence once stronger links with Italy were set up in the 960s, although it is a controversial subject. The capitulary on judicial trials by combat issued by Otto the Great and Otto II at Verona in 967 certainly reads like a legislative edict.[78] The language is not easy to press for certainty about law-making intention, but early in the twelfth century Cosmas of Prague preserved an interesting report on the subject in his chronicle. In 1040 Henry III is supposed to have informed the Czechs that in practice every German king added to the laws. If they were strong kings, they could be high-handed and even disregard laws which did not suit them.[79] In a revealing phrase, the law 'has a nose of wax, and a king has a long and iron hand with which to twist it as he pleases.' In other words, the king was to some extent the lord of laws, and perhaps many more were written down than the surviving record attests. For 1044 it is recorded that Henry III conferred either Bavarian law or German law upon the Hungarians at their own request.[80] The sources refer to *lex* or *scita*, law or ordinances, and it is tempting to assume that the transmission could not have been achieved without writing them down in a codified form now lost. But it has to be admitted that the event may simply refer to a single peace-declaration which might have been recited verbally.

Legislation by Diploma and Custumal

Several productions of the royal chancery contain what looks like a direct approach to legislation, however incorrect such a description may be technically. In a privilege issued to the merchants of Magdeburg in 975, Otto II repeated his father's general prohibition against the destruction of bridges in Germany, and forbade any other obstruction to traffic.[81] Since so many of the diplomas deal with the privileges and ongoing endowment of the Church, at times the clergy's concern for correct social conduct also shows through, and reflects the interest in proper Christian hierarchies known from the synods. In two enactments from the end of Henry II's reign, we learn that the violence associated with aristocratic feuds was not confined to the upper crust but that homicide and grievous assault as well as damage to tenements and violent housebreaking were commonly carried out by the dependents of the German abbots and bishops. The cases upon which Henry II issued diplomas were for the *familiae* or dependents of the bishopric of Worms against those of the abbey of Lorsch (December 1023), and for the dependents of Fulda Abbey against those of Hersfeld (March 1024). The diplomas are related and use the terms *decretum* and *constitutio* for what Henry II commands, but these are not unusual words for royal decisions recorded in diplomas.[82] It is in the content that the legislative style becomes apparent; for the crimes outlined above, physical penalties including branding and scalping as well as heavy fines were to be imposed.

Just at this time, Bishop Burchard I of Worms, a close associate of the emperor, issued his own custumal which endeavoured, among other things, to prevent abuse of the same sort within his own *familia*, so this corroborates in a remarkably accurate way the content of the emperor's diploma of December 1023. But modern commentators do not agree on whether or not the imperial diploma was based upon the bishop's regulations, although it is recognised that the scribe for the diploma was a cleric of the bishop's household, not a chancery clerk. Again, it was not uncommon to borrow local expertise in this manner. The Worms custumal was a piece of private legislation for application within one lordship, and dealt with many aspects: possessions, marriages and inheritances of the dependents, urban and rural, and the conduct of court cases, fines and compositions. But it also included material similar to the imperial diploma, in this case violent acts between members of the one *familia*; forcible entry of houses, abduction, causing bodily harm, robbery, and above all homicide. Bishop

Burchard complained that his serfs were murdering one another at the rate of thirty-five a year. The custumal imposed penalties similar to those in Henry II's charter; scalping of skin and hair, branding with a burning iron, and payment of composition money.[83]

A number of such custumals for estates and lordships belonging to the jurisdiction of the crown and the Church have survived, and somewhat like the synodal proceedings which kept alive the current of legislation, some custumals approach the formality of codification in the style of Burchard of Worms's compilation. A notable example was contained in the diploma issued in 1035 by Conrad II for the large abbey founded about a decade earlier upon his property at Limburg an der Haardt. The diploma outlined the obligations of the dependent population residing in the abbot's villages and manors, 'in case the *familia* should forget as time passes their obligations, and in their pride against the abbot they might neglect to deliver what is due ...'. In fairness, the abbots were also warned not to ask for more in labour services and renders in cash and kind than the diploma certified, an interesting comment upon the relationship between lord and peasant at the time of a newly expanding economy in Germany. The source also treats of the various secular offices needed by a large monastic household and manorial establishment. The details about appointing, employing and rewarding the abbot's men are laid down. This portion of the text has always aroused great interest because it allows for the promotion of an abbot's man to the status of a beneficed *miles*, possibly translatable as knight. Could this be technical evidence for the establishment of *ministeriales* in Germany?[84]

The Twelfth Century: The Rise of the Landfrieden

In the event, it was not so much the revival of the study of Roman law which attracted the German rulers back onto a course of systematic legislation as the introduction of *Landfrieden* or peace-keeping associations at the end of the eleventh century. Before the promulgation of the *Constitutio Criminalis Carolina* in 1532, the *Landfriede* established itself as the type of royal legislation in Germany *par excellence*. Such peace-keeping associations with their ecclesiastically sanctioned truces – again an echo of the synodal contribution to medieval legislative activity – are well known from France, but it is still an open question as to how far the French *Treuga Dei* may have served as models for German *Landfrieden*. After all, the function of the king as supreme magistrate of the realm and guardian of peace and justice for all orders of society goes back to the Germanic image of kingship, and it was much developed in the Carolingian capitularies. As we saw in Part I, the attainment of secure peace was just beyond the grasp of political authority in medieval Germany, so peace-keeping declarations were actually made more practical by specifying their scope and duration. An early example dates from Henry II's time. Visiting Merseburg in 1012, the king is reported by Bishop Thietmar to have agreed a five-year mutual peace between the Saxon magnates, but by 1014 it had broken apart under pressure from feuds by one of the bishop's own cousins, Margrave Werner of the North March.[85] According to Hermann of Reichenau, Henry III went a stage further in 1043, preaching peace to the Swabians gathered at Constance and then confirming it by edict. The chronicler claims that this was the most efficacious imposition of peace for centuries.[86] At the least his words testify to the political discernment of the Salian dynasty in its concern for finding effective methods of peace keeping. The German crown was on the threshold of taking up the *Landfriede* as the practical response to its regal duty of guarding peace, justice and order.

The disturbances of Henry IV's reign rendered the need for a programme of *Landfrieden* all the more pressing but at the same time more difficult to achieve. At first Henry IV left it to the bishops to impose diocesan peace legislation where they could, and records survive for the sees of Liège in 1082, Cologne in 1083 and Mainz and Bamberg in 1085. Technically they were *Treuga Dei*, holy truces in line with the diocesan peace movement in France,[87] but from their content their function as incipient *Landfrieden* is plain to see.[88] The details given in the Cologne source about the restricted days in the calendar, the delicts forbidden, and the types of weapon banned at those times give by inference a grim picture of the crimes most feared: murder, arson, robbery and assault. What the source also reveals is the practical difficulty of policing the restrictions, a problem which dogs the history of the German *Landfrieden* for the next four hundred years. If a castle is under attack during the safe periods, then the defenders may nevertheless fire back, and

if it should be necessary for someone to leave our bishopric within the stated times of this peace . . . and go where this peace is not recognised, then he may carry arms as long as he harms no one, unless he is attacked and has to defend himself.[89]

One way in which greater effectiveness was being sought was to deny to free men and to the nobles the opportunity to compound for their misdeeds by paying composition money, or by relying upon the oaths of their friends and kindred in the old style. Instead, they were to be banished and their property taken over by their heirs, thus giving the previous support-group some incentive to uphold the sentences. The legislation also endeavoured to break up the cycle of feuds by forbidding any resumption of plundering the villages and houses of enemies once the restricted days were over. A *Landfriede* organised in Saxony at about the same time as the Cologne ordinance shows how the hue and cry was really the only effective method for dealing with the widescale violence expected during feuds: everyone was to seize arms and pursue the wrongdoers.[90] Carrying arms for this purpose was protected by the peace, as the contingents set out and returned home.

The sudden increase in German material relating to peace-keeping associations at the end of the eleventh century is partly explained by the horror at widespread destruction caused by the War of Investitures. Henry IV's enemies, who had much the better of the argument in the polemical literature, blamed the ruler as the persecutor of the Church and the bane of the Empire. But his supporters, especially the author of the *Vita Heinrici IV. Imperatoris*, ascribed to him in some detail the traditional royal concern for providing peace, justice and order. The explicit evidence for his involvement with the *Landfrieden* comes late in the reign, probably because there was little point in proclaiming a royal *Landfriede* before he had made peace with his south German enemies, notably the Welf and Zähringen dynasties, in the 1090s. In relation to the 1103 *Landfriede*, the author of the *Vita* accurately recorded that one reason for current disorder was the greater size and effectiveness of the military retinues which were being enfeoffed by the secular and ecclesiastical magnates. Eventually Henry IV was able to launch a *Landfriede* with the help of the princes assembled at Mainz in 1103, so that, according to a turn of phrase in the *Vita*, 'while others avenged their injuries with injuries, the Emperor avenged his with peace.'[91]

The text of the *Landfriede* has not survived, but a cleric at Augsburg preserved an extremely vivid account of what it was about. As a prelude to the great era of royal peace legislation, the rugged style, brutal content and textual brevity of the Augsburg source certainly conveys a sombre sense of immediacy to the programme of peace keeping.[92] Its context is politically important because the three ducal dynasties of southern Germany whose feuds had shattered the peace at least since 1079 subscribed to it:

> The year of our Lord's incarnation 1103. Emperor Henry established and ordained peace at Mainz by his own hand, and the archbishops and bishops confirmed it likewise. The king's son swore to it and the leading men of the entire realm, dukes, margraves, counts and many others. Duke Welf (of Bavaria) and Duke Berthold (of Zähringen) and Duke Frederick (of Swabia) swore to this peace until Whitsun and for four years thereafter. They swore, I declare, peace to the Church, clergy and monks, and to the laity, to merchants, to women lest they be abducted, and to the Jews.
>
> The oath ran as follows. No one shall violently enter anyone's house nor devastate it by fire, and no one shall kidnap anyone for money, nor wound, nor beat up nor kill them. And if anyone should do this, then he shall lose his eyes or a hand. If someone protects him, he shall suffer the same penalty. If he flees to a castle, it shall be destroyed in a three-day siege by those who have sworn to the peace. If anyone tries to evade such judgement, his lord shall confiscate his fief if he has one, and his kindred shall take away his patrimony for themselves. If anyone steals to the value of five shillings or more, he shall lose his eyes or a hand. If he commits a robbery worth less than five shillings, he shall have his hair torn from his head and be scourged and shall restore the theft. And if he should commit this sort of robbery or theft three times, then he shall lose his eyes or a hand. If your enemy should run into you on the open road, you may injure him if you can. If he flees into a house or some other building, he must remain unharmed.
>
> The king's friends employed this oath for their defence, and it did no good to his enemies.

Henry IV's immediate successors are known to have issued *Landfrieden*, but the texts have not survived until Frederick Barbarossa's detailed peace legislation from the very first year of his reign, which was sent out in many copies.[93] According to the prologue, it was valid in all parts of the Empire. The source attends in detail to the crimes of homicide, grievous bodily harm, assault and theft; to disputes about fiefs; to fixing fair prices for grain in each region – to exceed them identified the culprits as peace-breakers; to the right to carry arms in self-defence; to disputes between knights and peasants, a social problem now much in evidence in the chronicle literature as well. The ruling on theft resembled the 1103 *Landfriede* in that the penalties were governed by the five-shilling threshold. Below it, the punishment was a severe scourging; above it, hanging. The *Landfrieden* were instrumental in diffusing the death penalty as a response to the perceived problem of violent crime.

Frederick Barbarossa's first *Landfriede* was of great significance to the future of German local jurisdictions, because it addressed the necessity of making the legislation effective in the various localities where, as the prologue stressed, the people were in need of defence for their rights and where peace had been desired for a long time. This does not necessarily imply criticism of the bishops, dukes, counts, and margraves to whom the *Landfriede* was sent, nor of the king's uncle and predecessor Conrad III. It probably reflects what both men had discovered when they returned from the Second Crusade, an increase in local violence which was in any case one result of many years of provincial feuds which marked the reigns of Lothar III and Conrad III. At least the new king heeded his own injunctions. For 1154 a Swabian annalist reported that 'to uphold the peace, many were hanged by King Frederick.'[94]

Landfrieden were sworn associations to enforce the peace and to pursue and punish malefactors. What Frederick Barbarossa intended in the *Landfriede* of 1152 and confirmed in subsequent legislation was that the jurisdictions exercised by the dukes, bishops, margraves and counts of Germany should carry out the work. This was a practical solution and indeed the only one in a large kingdom which could not be covered by regular royal assizes. Obviously this had a political effect upon the regional distribution of power in Germany in that the princes' local jurisdiction was enhanced by the prestigious task of enforcing the *Landfrieden*. The 1152 source goes into detail about the function of the local courts as administrators of the *Landfriede*: carrying out capital sentences, confiscating property, imposing fines in cash, pursuing criminous clerks, hearing oaths in property disputes and in several other matters. This provided a sound foundation for active magistracy. The princes were able to use such powers to build up the typical *Landgerichte* or regional jurisdictions of the thirteenth century.[95] The crown gained a point in that the *Landfrieden* enjoyed some hope of being respected in the localities, but this was always at hazard. In the 1180s, for example, Frederick Barbarossa issued new peace legislation designed to prevent arson during feuds. But later on Provost Burchard of Ursberg commented about it that the emperor

> arranged peace over the land and ordered it to be recorded in letters which the Germans up to the present time call *fridebrief*, that is, letters of peace, nor do they use any other laws. But they do not carry them out properly, being such a savage and ungovernable people.[96]

Frederick II as Legislator for Germany

In the Freising biography of Frederick Barbarossa, Rahewin noted that the ruler 'let no days pass in idleness, thinking those lost on which he had not made some enactment to the advantage of the empire for the preservation of law and justice among all peoples',[97] adapting a phrase or two from Suetonius about the virtuous emperor Titus to the ideals of medieval kingship. Something similar could be claimed for Barbarossa's grandson Frederick II, whose *Landfriede* proclaimed at Mainz in 1235 seemed to sum up the legislative aspirations of the dynasty. For over two decades before this, Frederick II and his son Henry VII had issued several detailed enactments about the respective rights of the crown and its officials, the jurisdictions of the secular princes, and the possessions and privileges of the Church. Seen in the long term, they confirm and update the material relationship of the king and the princes stretching back several centuries, and it is no longer tenable to regard them as concessions extracted by the princes from the court.[98] The crown and its officials were, on the contrary, serious competitors with the landowners in the localities, and the legislation explicitly sought to remove the material and theoretical causes for complaint against the court.

The chief purpose of Frederick II's *acta* was therefore to define and to adjust the rights of three powerful parties, the royal dynasty, the German Church, and the secular princes into a mutual exercise of regional political authority fitted to the circumstances of thirteenth-century Germany. So the details were concerned with the operation of law-courts and magistrates; the control of towns; the obligations of the unfree social orders and their policing; the status of fiefs; the correct uses of ecclesiastical advocacy; the regulation of tolls, markets, mints, roads and fortifications; and several other issues.[99] It can be discerned that such a wide net would reach out to all the inhabitants of medieval Germany.

Several historians have drawn attention to the diverse genres in which written law was on the increase. In the preamble to the Mainz *Landfriede*, Frederick II pointed out that throughout Germany cases and disputes had been settled 'by customs handed down of old and by unwritten law' but now recommended that written regulations expressed in specific chapters would be much more efficacious.[100] Of course the Mainz *Landfriede* was not the first piece of royal legislation to employ the method, but it does reveal a perception of how the tradition of law was passing from the oral to the written in Germany. The marked preference for oral law had relied upon the social belief that proper justice and true judgement were best upheld by numerous witnesses, who saw the prescribed rituals and heard in the vernacular what was happening at the *placita* or court meetings.[101] In 1235 Frederick II endeavoured to encourage written law by promulgating the *Landfriede* in German as well as Latin, and it is possible that the former was the first version. In any case it made a stir which was remembered for a long time. The Cologne chronicler reported that 'the peace was sworn, old laws were stabilised, new laws were established and written down on parchment in German, *Teutonico sermone*, and they were thus promulgated to everyone'.[102]

Frederick II's formidable contribution to royal legislation set a standard which was sustained, especially in the proclamation of *Landfrieden*, by his successors.[103] Growing interest in written law characterised by Eike von Repgow's private compilation of the 1220s, the *Sachsenspiegel* with its wide circulation and its derivative texts,[104] by no means stopped at the royal court. It contributed to the increasing complexity of political authority in the regions of Germany under the princes, the bishops and the cities, a phenomenon which was recorded in writing. In 1254, hardly a generation later than the Mainz *Landfriede*, the Rhineland towns issued their own *Landfriede*, its significance enhanced by the large number of bishops and secular princes who also subscribed to it.[105] In the sphere of German political ideas in the thirteenth and fourteenth centuries, the *Landfriede* in all its variety had an enormously creative influence. The new town leagues were given their sinews by the *Landfrieden*; the princes seized upon them in order to justify their ambition for territorial rule, the dukes of Bavaria providing an early and well-documented example; and it has long been recognised that the association of communities which eventuated in the Swiss Confederation was based upon a *Landfriede* issued in 1291, in all likelihood the renewal of a previous royal *Landfriede*.[106]

The Material Resources of Kingship

In medieval Germany the itinerant royal court developed comple-
mentary sources of material sustenance. Chiefly they were the renders
from the varied resources of the royal fisc, followed by support from the
episcopal and abbatial churches which the court took in the form of
hospitality upon its journeys as well as payments in kind – and cash in
some cases. In addition, the richer churches placed their military
retinues at the disposal of the crown, as we have seen. In 1149 Abbot
Wibald of Corvey wrote to the bishop of Hildesheim to explain,
amongst other things, that the Church must be generous with its
obligation to royal service, in military support, in performing political
duty at court, and in providing the king with hospitality.[107]

The royal fisc rested upon the Carolingian landowning foundation
extended by the Liudolfing contribution after 919 and the Salian after
1024. When the ascertainable items of the fisc are mapped, then these
inheritances show up an impressive extent in Saxony in the tenth
century and in the Rhineland in the eleventh.[108] This is why the
chronicler of Petershausen Abbey in Swabia noticed that Saxony,
being so rich in royal estates, 'was assigned to be the emperor's
kitchen'. This picturesque definition had to change when Henry IV
lost control of Saxony in the 1070s, although his successors still
retained important possessions in Eastphalia, Thuringia and the
marches. Reflecting upon the early twelfth century, Bishop Otto of
Freising had, in a well-known phrase, shifted the *maxima vis regni*, 'the
greatest resource of the realm', to the Rhineland,[109] and this is what
the Staufen inherited from the Salians. The new dynasty was attuned
to the importance of maintaining and expanding the fisc, a process
followed in detail in several modern works.[110]

Modernising attempts to broaden the scope of royal taxation beyond
the fisc are recorded from the reigns of Henry IV and Henry V, but
they aroused great hostility because they were not grounded in the
institutional heritage of the German realm.[111] Otto of Freising asserts
that Henry V was advised by his father-in-law Henry I of England to
raise a tax, and given the much more advanced tax structure in
England, this does sound plausible. Back in 1084 Henry IV had
endeavoured to raise an unpopular tax which did not, in the event,
reach beyond Regensburg and other royal towns, inviting comparison
with the 1241 levy which was also confined to the towns.

As the manifold military, judicial and sacral functions of itinerant
kingship unfolded during the annual cycles of the court's journeys,[112]

so the royal fisc and ecclesiastical resources were employed to pay for them. Recent studies by Eckhard Müller-Mertens and his pupils, and by the American historian John Bernhardt, have sharpened perceptions about how intimately the journeys were related to material resources as well as to political aims.[113] For example, they have shown how for Otto the Great's time the court travelled between three core areas of rich fiscal concentration, that is, eastern Saxony, the Franconian Rhineland, and lower Lotharingia, with the regions between them serving as transit zones with carefully designated resources of their own earmarked for the court's use.

The Royal Palaces and Other Residences Used

At its disposal the court had palaces and manors of its own, the residences of bishops and abbots and, on occasion, the seats of secular noblemen and noblewomen. The numerous palaces of the German royal dynasties have long been the subject of intensive investigation in relation to their topography and archaeology; the *iter* of the court and all the political work associated with it; and in their impact upon the economic, urban and military structure of local society.[114] The outline of the great Carolingian complex at Aachen is still plain to see, and its principal secular building, much altered, has served since the fourteenth century as the town hall. Again and again Aachen was singled out in generous royal privileges and other sources as the German realm's most prestigious palace, mainly because its magnificent octagonal chapel was normally the site of the king's inauguration by unction and coronation. As we have seen, successive kings favoured different palaces for various military or religious or personal reasons, and we know that certain sites were chosen as hunting lodges.

Economic advantage played a large part in the development of royal residences, Frankfurt, Magdeburg and Dortmund providing obvious examples already in the tenth century. In the sources, Nuremberg first emerges in 1050.[115] It grew fast as a town under the protection of the new castle-residence of the Salians, and was one of the more frequently visited palaces of their Staufen successors. Charters for the towns of Hagenau and Gelnhausen, which were founded in the shadow of the royal palaces there, have survived from the twelfth century. The effect of the economy upon the palaces has been demonstrated by the excavations at Tilleda, originally an Ottonian palace, reported by the German archaeologist Günter Fehring:[116]

The palace Tilleda reveals itself to be a complex at which most of its elements – palace proper, chapel, supply-buildings, manufacturing settlement – were all concentrated on the Pfingstberg and were all protected by a fortification composed of several enclosures. Only the needs of the agricultural estate and the marketplace of the Staufen period demanded a move down into the valley.

And just at this point in its history, we know from the *Tafelgüterver-zeichnis* that Tilleda was still one of the great royal manors providing sustenance for the court. At Quedlinburg too, the first royal residence was the hilltop castle converted in 936 into the nunnery serving King Henry I's tomb-site, continuing to function as a stopping-place for the itinerant court as well. But as economic circumstances grew more propitious, the royal manor in the valley was developed as the residence by the end of the tenth century, served by its own collegiate church.[117]

To underline the splendour and legitimacy of their rule, the Staufen kings rebuilt or repaired palaces of their Carolingian and Salian predecessors such as Nijmegen, Kaiserswerth and Ingelheim. As symbols of descent from such illustrious dynasties, and where justice and peace were proclaimed over the realm, such palaces meant so much to Frederick Barbarossa that when he was marching to the East on the Third Crusade, he wrote home to Henry VI warning him not to neglect finishing off the building programmes.[118] The Staufen were in any case building new palaces of their own, a signal of economic expansion, such as Hagenau, Eger, Wimpfen and Ulm. There are some surviving descriptions of what was achieved. In his continuation of the *Gesta Frederici*, Rahewin reports that at Kaiserslautern Frederick I

built a royal palace of red stone and adorned it quite lavishly. On one side he surrounded it with a very strong wall, the other side is enclosed by a lake-like fishpond, which contains for the delectation of the eyes and the palate all delicacies of fish and fowl. An adjoining park offers nourishment to a wealth of stags and deer. The royal splendor of all these things and their abundance, which is greater than one could describe, strikes all who see it with amazement.[119]

Like the episcopal and abbatial residences which the court regularly shared with the ecclesiastical incumbents upon the king's perambulation, the royal palaces served to display the honour and the glory of the ruler to the aristocracy and episcopate upon which secular governance so heavily relied. In reference to the crown-wearing ceremonies already noted, Frederick Barbarossa's chancery observed of him that 'we wear a crown and diadem of glory, namely at Christmas, at Easter and at Pentecost'.[120] The chronicles and other sources often record the whereabouts of the German king at such feasts of the Church, because his liturgical glorification coincided with the eternal glory of the everlasting king, Christ in Heaven. For the purpose, the Ottonians are known to have favoured celebrating Easter at Quedlinburg, Ingelheim and Aachen. Then the pattern was altered by Henry II to include Merseburg and Bamberg.[121]

Not much remains to be seen of the palaces, although the two-storey chapels at Aachen, Nuremberg and Eger have survived and the castle ruins of Gelnhausen and Wimpfen make a fine impression. According to Godfrey of Viterbo, there was a good library in the palace at Hagenau full of the classical and Christian authors; history, law, philosophy, poetry and medicine were represented. In his *Liber ad honorem Augusti*, Peter of Eboli recorded the cycle of murals with which Henry VI decorated one of his palaces; these depicted scenes from the Bible and events from the Third Crusade.[122] The palace in question is likely to have been in Italy, but the reference provides more evidence for the impressive impact which the royal residences made upon their visitors.

The Church and Its Renders to the Royal Court

The royal *iter* taking in residence at various palaces was a feature of governance carefully integrated with the contribution proferred by or extracted from the Church. Hardly any other aspect of royal rule in the medieval centuries in Germany has attracted so much scholarly attention as the relationship between the crown and the clergy. Here we need to survey only one of its facets, the use which the itinerant court made of ecclesiastical resources in conjunction with its own wealth drawn from the fisc, the whole technically comprehended by the eleventh century under the Latin term *servitium*.[123]

According to Wipo, Archbishop Aribo of Mainz proclaimed to Conrad II that 'you are the Vicar of Christ', and Abbot Ekbert of Tegernsee told Henry III that he was 'head of the Church'.[124] In such circumstances it is not perhaps surprising that the royal court regarded some of the resources of the Church as a justifiable perquisite of the crown. In a classic study published in 1872, the Austrian scholar Julius Ficker established that in medieval Germany the property of the Church was treated in law and in practice virtually as an asset at the disposal of the king himself.[125] This fruitful idea helps to explain why the royal dynasties were keen to endow the Church, and why the bishops and abbots thought it right to offer the *servitia* in exchange. As we shall see, this word was also used of the renders from royal estates, and from other assets such as forests and towns, to the court.

The ecclesiastical *servitia* are poorly documented. We know that in addition to offering hospitality to the itinerant court, *servitium* could refer to political and military service as well. For the see of Hildesheim a diploma from Henry II in 1013 mentions how the bishop might be needed on campaign with his retinue, or for giving advice and consent at court, or to undertake journeys, for which we know that diplomatic, missionary and synodal work involved the bishops. In the course of the eleventh century, ecclesiastical *servitia* focused upon specific economic support for the court. In the time of Henry IV, the items required from the rich Alsatian nunnery of Remiremont were listed, although the source as it stands has been considerably reworked.[126] The demands, which were large, referred to visits by the royal court to the episcopal residences at Toul and Metz. Eighty measures of grain for baking and 400 of oats for the horses (including 100 for the abbess's own horses during their cartage) were to be sent, as well as twenty head of cattle and nearly seventy pigs. Also to be made available in quantity were fish, poultry, eggs, milk, cheese, wine, mead, dishes, beakers and charcoal, as well as wax for making into candles and, as a luxury item, pepper. Some of the abbey's officials responsible for assembling this *servitium* were listed: the treasurer, the foresters, and the masters of the Remiremont mint.

It was also possible for the court to levy its returns in cash, but again the sources are irritatingly fragmentary. Twelfth-century royal diplomas for Worms confirmed that the crown received as part of the bishopric's *servitium* a cut from the urban tolls, and Frederick II's treaty with the German bishops confirmed in 1220 shows that when the court took up residence in a cathedral town, then the profits from the tolls and the mint were appropriated to the crown's use for eight days before the official 'day' or convention of princes and for eight days afterwards, a custom in force since the 1150s at the latest. In charters issued in 1208 and 1209, Otto IV remitted such rights relevant to royal visits to Magdeburg as a concession to gain political support from an important archbishopric.[127] Cash payments were explicitly mentioned in sources on the first-rank abbeys of Stablo and Lorsch. In 1137 Lothar III confirmed that Stablo paid thirty marks when the court stayed at Stablo itself, and twenty for a visit to Aachen. A similar cash-payment from Lorsch Abbey, which appears by contrast to have been an annual levy, was remitted by Conrad III in 1147.[128]

The peculiar status of ecclesiastical property in Germany and its use by the crown was justified by the effective protection which the crown provided for the Church, including the repeated grants of judicial immunity from neighbouring secular jurisdictions; by the theory of *regalia*, that the best part of ecclesiastical temporalities were in any case fiefs of the crown; and by older notions of *Eigenkirchenrecht*,[129] the exercise of proprietary right by laymen, usually of royal or noble status, over specific churches and their appurtenances. In other words, the king was advocate of the German Church, the regulator of its secular affairs.

The consequent demand for *servitia* was, nevertheless, questioned from time to time. A late eleventh-century source claims that when Henry II, on his way to Regensburg some time before 1015, demanded sustenance for his court from Bishop Megingaud of Eichstätt, he was refused with expostulations, although bolts of cloth from the episcopal storerooms were prudently sent as some kind of substitute.[130] The account is probably not reliable as to detail, but the outline is sound enough. For 1063 Lampert of Hersfeld, another rather biased source, reported that the system of *servitia* was being much abused during the regency for Henry IV, the archbishops not only handing out monastic property to their supporters but also exploiting the monasteries for the royal *servitia* to the last degree. Lampert also claims that at court in Bamberg late in 1075, the election to the abbacy of Fulda was turned by the candidates into a squalid auction of the abbey's assets: the bidders were offering mountains of gold, or rich grants from the monastic lands, or a huge increase in Fulda's *servitia* to the crown. To his credit the king was disgusted, and snatching a monk from Hersfeld who happened to be at court on business for his own abbey, appointed him abbot of Fulda. No doubt the story is exaggerated, but it shows the crown's interest in preserving a realistic estimate of what could be demanded of the Church. This had already been demonstrated by Henry IV in 1073 when he regulated and reduced the *servitia* demanded from Obermünster and Niedermünster in Regensburg, two of the richest nunneries in Germany.[131]

The Status of Royal and Ecclesiastical Property

It is not perhaps surprising that the theory and practice of *regalia*, *servitia* and the king's secular governorship of the imperial Church should have given rise to disputes about property. Conrad II, for example, fell out with Bishop Egilbert of Freising about the ownership of the castle and monastery of Moosburg in Bavaria. Did they belong to the crown or to Freising? This became something of a test case when the emperor summoned a number of Bavarian noblemen to court at Regensburg in 1027 to ascertain generally what possessions in Bavaria belonged by right to the throne, including towns in the Bavarian marches, and the Bavarian abbeys. Unfortunately for Conrad II, Count Adalbero of Ebersberg and other nobles who then held a court-day at Tittenkofen on the Moosburg dispute came to the conclusion that under Bavarian law, the property belonged to Freising.[132]

It is perfectly credible that the crown's own handling of ecclesiastical lands could cause muddles of this nature. In order to endow the new royal monastery of Memleben in 979, Otto II required Hersfeld Abbey to give up property suitable for the purpose, offering other assets in exchange, including the royal manor of Moffendorf in the Rhineland 'from our property'. By 1015 Henry II had decided to reverse this arrangement, and Moffendorf returned to his possession. In 1020 he gave it to the collegiate foundation of St Mary at Aachen, explaining that the manor belonged to him by particular property right and did not pertain to the kingdom. Somehow we have here an early adumbration of the distinction between the personal property of the German king and the assets belonging to the kingdom. In any case Moffendorf had twice been a royal possession and twice an ecclesiastical property within forty-two years, and it was fortunate for the parties that good records in the form of explanatory imperial diplomas were preserved.[133]

The idea of distinguishing the personal from the crown property at the disposal of a king was alien to the German tradition, although Conrad II was, according to Wipo, acquainted with something like it when he reprimanded the Pavians for destroying the royal palace at Pavia, the symbol of an unwanted regime, upon Henry II's death in 1024.[134] 'Whom have we offended?' exclaimed the Pavians:

'We were faithful and honored our Emperor . . . until the end of his life. Since we had no king after he died, we will not be accused legally of having destroyed the house of our king.' The King said in opposition, 'I know that you have not destroyed the house of your king, since you had none at that time, but you cannot deny that you have rent asunder a regal house. Even if the king died, the kingdom remained, just as the ship whose steersman falls remains. They were state, not private, buildings; they were under another law, not yours.'

Charters conferring royal possessions upon the bishopric of Speyer dating from Henry IV's minority also point to the notion that the crown owned hereditary, personal property as well as assets pertaining to the royal fisc, but how the categories were supposed to be distinguished is not at all clear.[135] In 1125 such issues came to a fight. Upon the election of Lothar III, Duke Frederick II of Swabia and his brother Conrad claimed the entire Salian inheritance as nearest heirs by blood to Emperor Henry V. Lothar III claimed it as royal property. According to the Annalist of Disibodenberg, the princes adjudicated in Lothar III's favour at court in Regensburg late in 1125 that royal property should preferably be subjected to the current regime of a German king and not pertain to his actual person. It was a long time before the Staufen brothers would accept such a ruling, but it appears to have prevailed in the twelfth century. For example, Duke Frederick's son Frederick Barbarossa received Badenweiler Castle in Swabia in 1158 as personal property from Duke Henry the Lion of Saxony, who received three royal castles in Saxony in exchange. This diminution of the royal fisc the emperor made up by donating Colditz Castle, which was in his hands personally, having been purchased from Count Rapoto of Abenberg.[136]

Although the German Church obviously provided enormous resources for the crown's use, we are inadequately informed about their worth when balanced against the returns from the royal fisc. The ecclesiastical *servitia* are thought to have reached their peak in the eleventh century. Upset by the War of Investitures, the *pax* of Worms confirmed service to the crown on the basis of the bishops' temporalities. Measured by the statistic of hospitality to the court in the cathedral towns, the royal fisc then outstripped the contribution of the Church in the reigns of Henry VI and Frederick II, before the collapse of Staufen rule and the loss of most of its fisc confirmed the towns as the mainstay of royal support – apart from the dynastic lands of the successive royal dynasties – for the rest of the Middle Ages.

The Twelfth-Century Land Register of the King of the Romans

From the twelfth century there survives the first substantial source about the fiscal resources of the German crown before the tax-list of 1241, the *Tafelgüterverzeichnis* or register of household lands pertaining to the king of the Romans, preserved in a manuscript from Aachen.[137] It is a memorandum by an unidentified official about some of the royal assets in Germany and Lombardy, and what they were expected to provide for the *mensa* or 'table' of the king of the Romans, by the twelfth century the usual title given to a German ruler before his Roman coronation as an emperor. We do not know which of these kings is meant; Henry V from 1098 to 1111, Lothar III from 1125 to 1133, Conrad III from 1138 to 1152, Frederick Barbarossa from 1152 to 1155, or Henry VI from 1169 to 1191. In any case the German scholar Wolfgang Metz believed that the source as it stands was constructed in at least three phases, and if this is so then more than one king may be relevant to the outcome.

Although it is quite short, the register is difficult to interpret and its purpose has never achieved a consensus as to an explanation in modern scholarship. It is certainly not a complete list of crown land, much of which was enfeoffed, or even of fisc currently exploitable. The manors, towns and castles were arranged in groups under the ancient headings of Saxony, Franconia along the Rhine (but also including Lotharingia), Bavaria and Lombardy. Were Swabia and Alsace left out because the crown lands there had informally been added to the duchy of Swabia as a species of royal appanage? If this is so, then a date after the accession of the Swabian Staufen dynasty (1138) is appropriate.

On the other hand the Saxon *servitia* outstrip all the others put together, leading to a supposition that the register was drawn up for Lothar III when the royal court was predominantly Saxon. But it has been pointed out that as a peripatetic king like all the others, Lothar III spent hardly more than a year of his reign in Saxony. There are further difficulties of analysis. The 405 *servitia* owed by Saxony alone would have been high for any royal court. In words reminiscent of the source for Remiremont Abbey, 'we also inform you of what a royal *servitium* in Saxony consists: thirty large pigs, three cows, five suckling pigs, fifty hens, fifty eggs, ninety cheeses, ten geese, five barrels of beer, five pounds of pepper, ten pounds of wax, wine from cellars all over Saxony.' So the provisioning outlined in the source, it has been suggested, refers to sustaining a whole army, or perhaps to the maintenance of the royal palaces all the year round. Another consideration is for how long these assets were being set aside for the king in question. That its drafting preceded the first Italian expedition of a king, most likely Lothar III's beginning in 1132 or Frederick Barbarossa's beginning in 1154, is suggested by an expression used of the Lombard possessions; 'How much they give no one can relate or find out unless we first come to Lombardy.'

For the economic history of royal governance the register is of great interest, because the renders from German fisc are in kind. With slight variation in the figures, the *servitia* of Franconia and Lotharingia consist of the same products provided by the Saxon manors, and the Bavarian *servitia* are 'as large as those of Franconia'. But some of the Lombard renders are in cash. Of the twenty-eight manors, castles and towns named, nine paid cash totalling 5600 marks. It supports the view that the more advanced economy of Lombardy was attractive to a revenue-seeking crown in the twelfth century, with more cash based upon commerce and manufacture in circulation than in Germany. But it must be remembered that minting coinage by the crown, the bishops, and the secular princes was on the increase in Germany as well, and could be tapped in the form of tolls. The crown tolls were becoming extremely lucrative, yet none are mentioned in the *Tafelgüterverzeichnis*. This is something of a mystery, because sixteen of the properties recorded are known to have housed royal toll-stations in the twelfth century.

The *Tafelgüterverzeichnis* should remind us that the German crown lacked a general system of taxation, relying instead upon renders from its fisc, the towns and the Church. It is trying that so little documentation about royal revenues has survived, but this is characteristic of a peripatetic court. It is difficult to argue *ex silentio* about cash flow into the royal treasury, although we know that it happened. When he was regent, Archbishop Anno II of Cologne arranged to divert a ninth of it annually into his own coffers for the benefit of his monastic foundations, the source making it explicit that cash revenues were what was meant.[138]

Royal Wealth and Revenues after the Tafelgüterverzeichnis

It was certainly easier to perceive northern Italy as a readier source of royal income in cash than Germany, and usually this is taken to have provided strong motivation for Frederick Barbarossa's programme of resumptions announced at Roncaglia in 1158. In the biography of the emperor, Rahewin mentioned that in addition to lucrative rights such as the tolls familiar in Germany, the Lombards owed the crown 'the payment of an annual tax, not only on the land, but also on their own persons'. This complete contrast with Germany was confirmed by Vittore Colorni's remarkable discovery in a manuscript in the Bibliothèque Nationale in Paris of the lost Roncaglia decrees which he published in 1966; the relevant phrase runs *Tributum dabatur pro capite, tributum dabatur pro agro,* – 'tax should be paid per head, tax should be paid by the field'. Rahewin goes on to say that the emperor was generous in remitting such payments, and yet 'there accrued to the public revenues annually thirty thousand talents'.[139] Whatever this astronomical sum is supposed to mean in real terms, we can see why the German court was keen to impose its will upon Lombardy, and fought the communes for so long. By treaty in 1183 Frederick Barbarossa and Henry VI were still guaranteed some payments by the Lombard League.

In Germany itself the evidence for cash income from the crown lands improves in the thirteenth century, as we saw in the case of the 1241 tax-list imposed upon towns. In 1216 the procuration of extensive royal estates in the lower Rhineland was entrusted to the imperial *ministerialis* Gerhard of Sinzig, and from 1242 there survives an account rendered for it to the royal court by his son and successor: 272½ marks' income, 306 marks' expenditure, the latter chiefly for supporting the Staufen cause under arms in the current civil war with the Rhenish archbishops.[140] In another case, one of the great royal estates featured in the *Tafelgüterverzeichnis*, Neuburg in Bavaria, was entrusted in 1197 to the imperial marshal of Pappenheim for its administration. In the *Tafelgüterverzeichnis* it owed two *servitia* to the king. In the first half of the thirteenth century a cadastral survey was drawn up for it, and a fifteenth-century copy of it was discovered in the Pappenheim archives by Wilhelm Kraft in 1925. His analysis shows that although Neuburg still produced renders in kind – grain, pigs, poultry, cheeses – its principal returns were reckoned in cash totalling £353.[141] But the division of the spoils between the royal court and the feoffee has never been clarified.

Records from the royal lordships of Pfullendorf, Kirchheimbolanden and Goslar have also survived,[142] but superficially the most promising is the survey or *Reichssalbüchlein* drawn up about 1300 for Nuremberg and the adjacent crown lands,[143] which had been so phenomenally developed during the Salian and Staufen eras. Incomes in cash and kind from many *officia* or administrative districts were recorded, with named towns, markets, forests, castles and lands. But since most of the assets had long before been pledged or enfeoffed to the crown's debtors, the *Reichssalbüchlein* is more like a ghost holding out a vain hope of resumptions, and not a realistic account at all. Only the short section on Nuremberg itself, which always provided handsome subventions to the court, sounds convincing: £2000 from the citizens, £2000 from the Jews, £200 from the tolls, £100 from the magistrate's court, £500 from the mint. As servile dependents of the royal court, Jews could be squeezed out of proportion to their actual numbers.

Great scholarly effort has gone into pressing the sources to find out how the German royal court, its perambulation, and its military campaigns were sustained. Obviously the ruler, his deputies and their advisers understood that extensive resources had to be exploited on some sort of planned annual basis, a headache at the best of times. No wonder that men such as Duke Bernhard III of Saxony and Duke Berthold V of Zähringen declined the expensive honour of royal election in 1197 and 1198. This is why Philip of Swabia claimed in a letter sent to Pope Innocent III in 1206 that the German princes had urged him to accept election in 1198, declaring 'that no other prince was capable of sustaining the burdens of Empire or could worthily match the imperial dignity in wealth'.[144] But we should note that conceptions of wealth which underlined royal power connected the economic with decisive psychological, theocratic and dynastic authority which Philip of Swabia was confident he possessed as well. The letter goes on:

Amongst all the princes of the Empire there is none richer, more powerful or more glorious than ourselves. For we have very ample and widespread possessions, we have very many castles, strongly fortified and impregnable. [Arnold of Lübeck reckoned up a total of 350, possibly an underestimate.][145] We have so many *ministeriales* that we can scarcely comprehend them in any certain number. [Modern scholarship computes about 500 families at this time.] We have much money in gold and silver, and many precious stones. We have under our control the Holy Cross [Conrad II's great processional cross of the Empire is meant here], the Lance, the crown, the imperial vestments and all the insignia of the Empire. God has blessed us with much property and he increases our house with power and fame.

Evidently the pope was impressed. With some reluctance he decided to abandon his support for Otto IV and began to negotiate a treaty with King Philip.[146] The plan fell through when the latter was assassinated in 1208, as we have seen in Part II.

Governance, Royal Permabulation and Their Consequences

The resources we have reviewed supported the itinerant court in its military, political and religious duties, if not the length and breadth of the German, Burgundian and Lombard kingdoms, then in those *Basislandschaften*, the heartlands of royal property, presence and power, and in the *Durchzugsgebiete*, transit zones, discerned by the school of Eckhard Müller-Mertens.[147] What happened upon the perambulation makes up so substantial a part of Germany's political history before 1300 that another book would have to be written to cover it. But as an annual cycle, the *iter* made so great an impact upon royal governance that some further comment is pertinent.

Although the chancery which travelled with the court was constantly turning out diplomas, mandates and other written instruments, the principal impact of royal governance, in the absence of general taxation or assizes, appears to have been made by personal contact. Time and again the sources report meetings on the road and in private houses; gatherings at the royal palaces, episcopal residences and in abbeys; and the more formal court-days as well as the crown wearings at the great feasts of the Church. In other words, the royal presence was itself an instrument of authority, which is not surprising given the formidable military, theocratic, judicial and economic status of a figure who stood at the apex of the aristocracy, an image of Christ on earth, and the protector of the powerful and the poor alike, all outlined so plainly in Wipo's biography of Conrad II. A reference, also from the eleventh century, reveals that the bishops respectfully rose to their feet whenever their ruler came into the chamber. Bishop Megingaud of Eichstätt, a known eccentric, refused to do so, claiming that he was older than Henry II and a cousin to boot.[148] But the emperor so widely acclaimed for his dignity and sanctity was not above teasing the bishops in return. Bishop Meinwerk of Paderborn's Latin was shaky, so he had to read out mass more or less at sight. As a joke the emperor secretly had a couple of syllables erased from the bishop's missal so that he would read out a prayer, not for the servants of God but for his mules – *pro mulis et mulabus* instead of *pro famulis et famulabus*.[149]

The origins of parliament represent a minefield in modern historiography, but the notion that royal court meetings to seek advice and consent provided one basis in German parliamentary history is still alive. One of the German scholars most concerned with this problem, Peter Moraw, holds that *Reichstag* is not an appropriate term before the greater formalisation of the institution in the 1490s,[150] emphasising instead the variable times and places of the politically potent 'days' upon which the ruler met his bishops and lay princes and, later on, representatives of towns and knights.

The way in which court meetings were set up is aptly demonstrated by a circular from Henry IV inviting the princes to a colloquium at Mainz, the letter surviving in its version to Bishop Rupert of Bamberg (1075–1102).[151] There is a suspicion that it was a chancery exercise never actually sent out, but that in no way detracts from its value for showing how the ruler and his advisers conceived of court-days. The source recites what a king expected of the German princes in the way of political participation:

> All the faithful princes of our realm will participate in this assembly and besides them all those whose good faith or provident counsel is shown advantageous to us. We ask you very cordially to come to it, since never could such difficult affairs of state and the problem of the divided Church be dispatched without your consummate wisdom, excellent counsel, and good faith.

Since we are in the depths of the War of Investitures, the issues for discussion were, not surprisingly, the immense peril in which the whole Church was asserted to be adrift; the dissensions of Saxony; and the more specific problems of the diocese of Metz which, like so many others in the German kingdom, was divided between the Gregorians and the imperialists.

From the time of the Frankish kings onwards, numerous reports have survived about what went on at such assemblies. To take the reign of Frederick Barbarossa as an example, the tone of the meetings obviously varied according to current needs, preoccupations and purposes, although it is not necessarily helpful to distinguish political, festive, religious, dynastic, juridical and diplomatic motives from each other at the court assemblies. All this can be discerned at the Christmas court held at Aachen in December 1165 and January

1166 during which Charlemagne was canonised. The cult of Charlemagne as a possible saint was a genuine one, but the event was also of significance as part of the political strategy to outface the Alexandrine party in the current papal schism. The aura of Charlemagne as saint and emperor added weight to the imperial cause, particularly since the Staufen themselves claimed descent from Charlemagne through the Salians. Aachen, the tomb-site of Charlemagne, was in any case the place of Barbarossa's induction as a king, and it was now proclaimed the capital of the German kingdom, with the palace chapel and town being granted new privileges.[152]

A more specifically political purpose was fulfilled by the court-day at Regensburg on 17 September 1156, when the rival claims to the duchy of Bavaria were finally settled. As we have seen, Margrave Henry Jasomirgott was promoted to duke of Austria and Duke Henry the Lion of Saxony was confirmed as duke of Bavaria. The agreement was the result of years of negotiations, and as Bishop Otto of Freising reports, the emperor 'prized this more highly than the successes of all his other undertakings: the fact that, without the shedding of blood, he was able to bring to friendly relations princes of the realm so mighty and so closely related to himself.'[153] At Worms that year the main business of the Christmas court was judicial in tone. The bishop of Freising preserved the report that Archbishop Arnold of Mainz and Count Palatine Hermann of Stahleck with their accomplices were brought to trial for their incessant feuding.

> Now an old custom has gained the status of a law among the Franks and the Swabians, that whenever a noble, a *ministerialis*, or a peasant (*colonus*) has been found guilty by his judge of such offenses, before he is punished by sentence of death the noble is obliged to carry a dog, the *ministerialis* a saddle, the peasant (*rusticus*) the wheel of a plow, from one county into the next in token of his shame. The emperor, observing this custom, compelled that count palatine, a great prince of the realm, together with ten counts, his accomplices, to carry dogs the distance of a German mile.[154]

But the capital sentences were not carried out. Also predominantly judicial in tendency were the conventions held at Weissenburg (Alsace) in February 1179 to proclaim a *Landfriede* in the Rhineland, and at Würzburg in January 1180 to deprive Henry the Lion of his fiefs, the duchies of Bavaria and Saxony, almost certainly *sub feodali iure*, under feudal law.[155]

The Würzburg court of June 1156 was a festival in which the emperor 'celebrated in royal state, with many princes assisting, his marriage with Beatrice, the daughter of Count Rainald'. This was Rainald III of Mâcon, count of Burgundy, and the bridegroom took the trouble to issue privileges for the monasteries in Burgundy patronised by the Mâcon dynasty.[156] But the famed festival of Whitsun 1184 held at Mainz was undoubtedly the grandest such affair in the whole reign. Attended by more than seventy princes of the Empire and their retinues, it opened with a crown-wearing ceremony by the emperor, empress and Henry VI, followed by a huge banquet and then the knighting of King Henry and his brother, Duke Frederick V of Swabia.[157] If the emperor's charter of 18 January 1158 about crown-wearings in Germany and Bohemia can be taken at face value,[158] then any court held at Christmas, Easter or Whitsun would normally have begun with a crown-wearing ceremony when the *laudes regiae* would have been intoned. Even more seriously religious in tone was the meeting summoned to Mainz in March 1188 and designated in advance *curia Ihesu Christi*, 'the court of Jesus Christ'.[159] It proclaimed Germany's adherence to the Third Crusade and Frederick Barbarossa undertook its military command himself.

However well planned and managed, the royal *iter* was prone to perils and frustrations. Obviously the risks were far greater when the king was travelling on campaign, but there could be unexpected turns even in times of peace. When Henry III returned as emperor from his successful Italian expedition of 1046–7, he went to Saxony to stay with Archbishop Adalbert of Bremen. This diocese was well off the usual track of royal itineraries and the archbishop's enemies, the Billung family, perceived the visit as a threat to their own position. According to Adam of Bremen, Duke Bernhard II of Saxony's brother, Count Thietmar Billung, therefore planned to ambush the emperor on the road between Bremen and Lesum, but the archbishop got wind of it in time.[160] The count was arrested and then killed in the subsequent judicial duel.

Another hazard was posed by the inadequacy of medieval building technique. In 870 King Louis of East Francia was staying at the royal manor in Flamersheim west of Bonn on the way to Meersen to meet his half-brother Charles the Bald for the purpose of partitioning Lotharingia between them. When that part of the building in which he was staying collapsed, his limbs were badly injured. He managed nevertheless to get to Meersen and kept up a brave face in case Charles should try to take advantage of his dangerous physical state and cheat him. After the conference, Louis retired to Aachen to recover at the royal palace with its natural warm baths.[161]

Even more dramatic was Henry III's escape from death when Persenbeug Castle fell down in 1045. Invited on a state visit to Hungary, the king was sailing down the Danube and stopped off at Persenbeug in Austria to visit, at her request, the chatelaine. This was Countess Richlinde of Ebersberg, who wanted the king to settle her recently deceased husband's opulent estate.[162] When the company was conversing in an upper room of the castle, the floor gave way and they all collapsed into the bath-house in the basement. Count Welf III came to no harm, and Henry III escaped with no more than a contusion of the arm. Abbot Altmann of Ebersberg, Bishop Bruno of Würzburg and the countess had to be pulled from the rubble, and subsequently died of their injuries. The king carried on with his journey to Hungary *animo anxius*, 'with a troubled soul'.

Elective Monarchy in Medieval Germany

Kingship in medieval Germany was itinerant in practice and sacral in theory, supposedly commissioned by divine command. But the right to sacred kingship was politicised by the belief that the celestial will was discerned through election by the ecclesiastical and secular princes as representatives of the *gentes*. It was also possible to elect the ruler's designated son during the father's lifetime,[163] thus reconciling electoral right with dynastic succession. We have already noted how electoral right was often submerged by dynastic loyalty in the Frankish and German Empires and how Henry VI endeavoured, without success, to establish explicit hereditary right in 1196: '. . . the emperor wanted to confirm with the princes a new and unheard of decree in the Roman realm, that just as in France or the other kingdoms, kings should succeed him by hereditary right in the Roman realm'.[164]

In the thirteenth century, electoral methods were revolutionised with the emergence in the 1250s of a tiny college of seven princely electors who boldly took permanent responsibility for representing the general electoral right of the entire Church and aristocracy in Germany.[165] Formalised in the elaborate 'Golden Bull' issued by Emperor Charles IV in 1356,[166] this arrangement lasted more or less unchanged – apart from the addition of two more electors in the seventeenth century – until the last imperial election in 1792. We will return to the specifically thirteenth-century phase shortly.

The electoral technique provided Germany with highly charged political opportunities. Arnulf of Carinthia exploited them when he replaced Emperor Charles III in East Francia in 887, as we have seen. German historiography has always enjoyed a searching debate about the meaning and impact of the elections of Conrad I in 911, Henry I and Arnulf of Bavaria in 919, and Otto I in 936 and their relevance to the emergence of medieval Germany from the debacle of the Carolingian political experience.[167] In this context it is worth quoting Widukind of Corvey about Otto the Great's election, since he supplies the basic considerations facing the East Frankish Church and aristocracy in their electoral capacity: the existence of an already prestigious royal house although it was new; the designatory power of the ruler, made plain in Otto's favour in 927 or 929; and the ancient right of the magnates who actually turned up at Aachen in 936 for Otto's election and installation as their king:[168]

> When Henry, the father of his country and the greatest and best of kings, had died, the Franconians and Saxons elected as their ruler his son Otto, already designated as king by his father. It was ordered that the site of the collective election was to be the palace of Aachen.

In the subsequent reigns the power of established royal dynasties, the capacity for designation and election within a ruler's lifetime, and aristocratic reaction towards more competitive elections kept the issue of choosing kings extremely warm as a political question in the German realm. In 1002 Henry II experienced unexpected difficulty in having his claim to the thrones of Germany and Italy accepted against frightening rivals, Ekkehard of Meissen and Arduin of Ivrea. With sombre eloquence Wipo's dominant report of the election of 1024 pitches the electoral debate between Conrad II and his cousin into the very centre of German aristocratic and ecclesiastical perceptions of rule by kings and emperors at that period.[169] Henry IV had a bad time of it, because the electoral method was employed four times with the serious intention of replacing him with another king: Rudolf of Rheinfelden in 1077, Hermann of Salm in 1081, and the king's sons Conrad in 1093 and Henry V in 1106; the last coup succeeded.

Such elections might appear to have been the more dangerous because, as Bruno of Magdeburg reported in his *Book of the Saxon*

War,[170] it was decided during Rudolf of Rheinfelden's election at Forchheim in 1077

> that royal power, *regia potestas*, should pass to no one by heredity as was the custom hitherto, but that the king's son, however worthy he might be, should rather go on to be king by spontaneous election, not by line of succession.

If he were judged not worthy, or if the *populus* did not want him, then an unfettered choice should be made. It can be perceived that such principles added up to an attack upon Henry IV because he was considered unworthy by the papalists, but they do not diverge so very far from what had happened to Otto the Great in 936 either – a worthy son desired by the *populus* and advanced by spontaneous election. The fact that Henry IV's enemies chose his sons as anti-kings in 1093 and 1106 reveals the intensity with which dynastic right recommended itself to the minds and traditions of a conservative body such as the churchmen and aristocrats of Germany and Italy.

This helps to explain why the electoral method was not consciously perceived as a threat by the rulers of twelfth-century Germany in spite of its political potential for prelates and princes to make trouble. After the election of 1152 Bishop Otto of Freising asserted that 'this is the very apex of the law of the Roman empire, namely, that kings are chosen not by lineal descent but through election by the princes,'[171] the means by which his nephew Frederick Barbarossa had, to the bishop's satisfaction, just reached the throne. Yet the dynasty had failed to achieve election at its first attempt in 1125, when Barbarossa's father was passed over in favour of Lothar III, and a serious effort was made to remove it by another election, when Otto IV was promoted as rival king in 1198. But as we saw in Part II, Frederick Barbarossa himself endorsed what Otto of Freising had had to say. After the contretemps with the papal legates at Besançon in 1157 when it was suggested that the Empire might be no more than a fief from the papacy, the imperial circular to the bishops reiterated that kingdom and Empire were granted by God alone, His will made manifest by the electoral process carried out by the Church and aristocracy, as in 1152.

The electoral schism of 1198 and the extraordinary claims of Pope Innocent III's *Venerabilem* in 1202 kept the question of royal elections at the forefront of German politics. But perhaps the most significant development for the future of the electoral process was the transition of electoral right in the thirteenth century from the Church and aristocracy as a whole to a representative college of just seven electors instead. Why did this happen?

It should be noted that in the scholarly literature there is no agreement about this contentious issue. Yet it is obvious that no German king had ever been elected by the whole eligible body; only a representative few would actually have made the journey to the place of election, traditionally upon Franconian soil, to make known the wishes of their own *gens* or to listen to the debate and then come to a decision, as Wipo claimed for the election of 1024. So it was not extraordinary that Archbishop Adalbert I of Mainz could sell the idea of a representative college of forty electors, ten from each *gens* (Franconia joining with Lotharingia in this case), in 1125, as we saw in the Introduction.

Although Adalbert of Mainz would probably have preferred the margrave of Austria to the duke of Saxony as the next king,[172] the political usefulness of such *ad hoc* colleges to archbishops who could the more easily manipulate the result was twice more demonstrated in the twelfth century. When Lothar III died late in 1137, the see of Mainz was vacant and the new archbishop of Cologne was not yet consecrated, so Archbishop Albero of Trier used the opportunity, with the assistance of legatine authority, to have Conrad III elected by a small assembly at Coblenz, a town in his own possession, in 1138. More destructive was Archbishop Adolf I of Cologne's attempt to seize the presidency of royal elections from the see of Mainz in 1198, as we saw in Part II, because it resulted in civil war between two royal candidates until 1208.

We know that small assemblies were responsible for the election of Frederick II at Nuremberg in 1211 and of Conrad IV at Vienna in 1237. In the meantime, Eike von Repgow had dropped a bombshell in his *Sachsenspiegel*:[173]

> In electing the emperor, the bishop of Trier should be the first, Mainz the second, and Cologne the third. Of the laity, the first to choose is the palatine of the Rhine, the Empire's seneschal; the second the marshal, the duke of Saxony; the third the chamberlain, the margrave of Brandenburg. The butler of the Empire, the king of Bohemia, has no electoral powers because he is not a German.

This extraordinary statement could hardly be derived from current practice, since the re-election of Otto IV at Halberstadt in 1208, the re-election of Frederick II at Frankfurt in 1212, and the election of Frederick's son Henry VII, also at Frankfurt, in 1220 appear to have involved large gatherings of eligible princes. But the fantasy of a lawyer was actually employed for the double election of 1257, corrected to include the king of Bohemia's rights. Adopted again for Rudolf of Habsburg's election in 1273, it became standard practice,[174] but without Eike's curious bid for the primacy of Trier over Mainz's accepted seniority.

The theory propounded in the *Sachsenspiegel* was repeated in a slightly different form by Albert of Stade in his *Annales Stadenses* for 1240, on the occasion of Gregory IX's call for a new German king to replace the recently excommunicated Frederick II.[175] Reinmar von Zweter, practitioner of didactic verse, also recorded the idea, revising it to assert the king of Bohemia's proper right to vote. At present, one historiographical tradition suggests that the theory of a small college of electors was ultimately a response to the crisis of 1198 when royal elections seemed to get out of hand. But the problem remains that subsequent elite assemblies did not prevent schisms either: anti-kings elected in 1246 and 1247, Henry Raspe of Thuringia and William of Holland respectively; then two kings elected in 1257, Alfonso X of Castile and Richard of Cornwall.

Another attractive theory, revived by Egon Boshof and refined by Heinz Thomas,[176] concentrates upon the senior offices of the Empire which figure so prominently in the statements of Eike, Albert and Reinmar. The three archbishops named were also arch-chancellors of the German, Italian and Burgundian kingdoms, and the four secular princes were supposed to correspond to the honourable court offices of butler, seneschal, marshal and chamberlain, although the actual duties were carried out by eminent families of imperial *ministeriales*. In reality the equation of electoral right with three arch-chancellorships and four court offices was fanciful if not bizarre. According to the theory, it finds its roots in Cologne's need to justify the smallest credible electoral college, in order to validate its threadbare machination which had put forward Otto IV in 1198. Contextually there is much to be said for this explanation, but it says nothing about why the rest of the eligible electorate, the vast majority of German prelates and secular princes, would ever want to accept it.

Another explanation is sociological in colour, suggesting the restriction of electoral right to those magnates who were politically the most prestigious. During the twelfth century the German princes were becoming more clearly differentiated between an upper tier of first-rate bishops, dukes and margraves, the *principes imperii* close to the crown and known to modern scholarship as the *Reichsfürstenstand*,[177] and the mass of prelates and aristocrats whose authority would always be localised. But the problem with this interpretation is the absurd exclusion by Eike, Reinmar and Albert of far too many front-rank princes: the archbishops of Bremen, Magdeburg and Salzburg and a handful of the richest suffragans and abbots; the dukes of Austria, Brabant, Brunswick, Carinthia, Lotharingia and Merania; the margraves of Baden and Meissen; and the landgraves of Thuringia who were also entitled counts palatine of Saxony since 1180. In this respect the eleven princes assembled at Vienna who elected Conrad IV in 1237 made up just as convincing a college as Eike von Repgow's choice in the *Sachsenspiegel*: the archbishops of Mainz, Salzburg and Trier; the bishops of Bamberg, Regensburg, Freising and Passau, in whose diocese Vienna lay; Duke Otto II of Bavaria, who was also count palatine of the Rhine, the king of Bohemia, the landgrave of Thuringia, and the duke of Carinthia.[178] What the 1237 election also reveals is that the collegiate method recommended itself to the court, and was not therefore simply a ploy invented by the Cologne party in 1198 and then adopted by the papalists in 1246 to get rid of what Pope Innocent III had already described in *Venerabilem* as *gens persecutorum* – 'the race of oppressors'. Frederick II's legitimisation of a college of electors as a contribution to the institutional history of German elective kingship deserves wider recognition.

Elective kingship in medieval Germany did not add up to rule by contract. Well-conducted elections were not in themselves a sign of political weakness on the part of the royal dynasties, and simply recognised the obvious realities of needing princely advice and consent because, as Wipo put it for Conrad II's election in 1024, the princes who elected were *vires et viscera regni*, 'the vigour and inner strength of the realm'.[179] As the British historian John Gillingham has recently pointed out, the persistence of the elective system did not threaten political coherence and continuity in medieval Germany. He argues for various political advantages which Germany enjoyed as a result of elective kingship, even after the recognition of the monopoly of seven electors in 1273 and later.[180] The elective system also matched theories of the Empire as a corporate body with the king as head balanced by the princes as limbs. This organological approach was well known to the royal court, which logically regarded rebellion as a disease, *morbus intestinus*.[181]

Conclusion: Tasks of Governance in Medieval Germany

What description of the medieval German polity would be taxonomically convincing in our present state of knowledge? To find in the sources some equivalent of 'state' and 'nation' is not easy, but the labels 'kingdom' and 'Empire' are well grounded: *regnum* of the East Franks from the ninth century, *regnum Teutonicorum* from the eleventh, and Henry VII addressed as *rex Alamannie* by his father's chancery in 1231.[1] *Romanum imperium* was in literary use, as in Gerbert of Aurillac's letters or the *Vita Heinrici Quarti*. It was fitfully in chancery usage in the eleventh century, and habitually in Frederick Barbarossa's diplomas. But what sort of kingdom and Empire are being advertised in tandem? Some reverence for Frankish tradition; the immediate diplomatic geometry of the Papacy, the East Frankish kingdom, and the Lombard royal inheritance; and the capacity of Otto the Great for political innovation – all these motivated the restoration of the neo-Roman western Empire in 962.

The German imperial age inaugurated in 962 traded to some extent upon Roman and Frankish memories. Adam of Bremen declared that Henry III was the ninetieth Roman emperor since Caesar Augustus, and a diploma composed in all likelihood by Gottschalk of Aachen for Henry IV in the fateful year 1076 asserts that, of all the predecessors, it was Charlemagne who was the most diligent in founding and endowing churches and in extending religion. This is taken to be the true cause of his colossal prestige, and the current ruler wishes to follow his meritorious example in honouring the Church.[2] Such inspiration culminated in the canonisation of Charlemagne at Aachen in 1165. As we saw, the German rulers expected to be crowned as emperors in

Rome. For various reasons Conrad III never made it, but many sources credit him with the title in any case.

As German kings, these men had to be reasonably proficient military commanders, if not invariably victorious in battle. They had to be knowledgeable and upright magistrates, a training for which they would already have received as noblemen with jurisdictions of their own in the case of new or unexpected rulers such as Conrad I, Henry I, Henry II, Conrad II, Lothar III, Conrad III, Frederick Barbarossa, and Philip of Swabia, while Otto IV gained some notion of statecraft as trainee count of Poitou. German kings had to be capable political managers of the magnates in the regions, the intractable puzzles of conflicting interests so often frustrating even the most formidable of rulers such as Otto the Great, Conrad II, and Frederick Barbarossa. As we have seen, the chronicles are full of pained comment upon the phenomenon, and it arises in the *Vita* of Abbot John of Gorze in an illuminating way.

Otto I's contemporary, Caliph Abdalrahman III of Cordova (912–61), could not understand, as a successful despot himself, why Otto I tolerated regional autonomy, thus misunderstanding the fundamental nature of barbarian, Frankish and German kingship, which could only function as an exercise in political cooperation with the Church and the secular aristocracy. From the *Vita* we hear of a conversation between John of Gorze, Otto's envoy, and the caliph about the relative strengths of Germany and al-Andalus.[3] John ventured to boast of the power and the glory of Otto's realm, based principally upon its military forces. Slightly nettled, the caliph pointed out that Otto the Great did not retain power for himself, but permitted his circle to exercise their own power. 'Thus he divides the regions of the kingdom between them, as if to make them the more faithful and subjected to him,' the caliph scornfully remarked. 'But this is far from the case, since pride and rebellion, *superbia et rebellio*, are forthwith nurtured and equipped.' The caliph is certainly right about the *superbia* of the medieval German magnates. Then he cites what he sees as the consequences; the perfidy of Duke Liudolf of Swabia since 953 and the devastating raids of the Magyars upon East Francia in 954 and 955. Abdalrahman III thus regarded royal power as of one kind, with Otto failing to act up to the ideal. But he had correctly raised the great issue of power-sharing in the medieval German polity, that inheritance from the Frankish past which we have closely examined. In the Cordovan caliphate there was, theoretically, no regional autonomy, although it was to come soon enough. In Germany it was inevitable.

German rulers had to be pious souls committed to the welfare of the Church, sensitive to the difference between the material element, bishoprics and the like which kings dominated as legal protector or *Vicarius Christi* or advocate or feudal lord, and the spiritual agenda over which they might themselves preside at synods and councils. Henry II and Henry III were famed for their skills in the royal business of overseeing ecclesiastical affairs; Henry IV and Henry V were roundly condemned for their meddling. Even the illiterate Conrad II scored good marks, at least according to Wipo: 'For although he was ignorant of letters, nevertheless he prudently instructed every cleric not only lovingly and courteously in public, but also with fitting discipline in secret.'[4]

It would be rash to regard neo-Roman imperial aspirations as politically superfluous to what German kings could have achieved in any case.[5] But apart from the *expeditio Romana* for the purpose of imperial coronation at the hands of the pope, there existed no imperial institutions of rule separable from those of German and Italian kingship, with the possible exception of a handful of edicts inserted into the *Corpus Iuris civilis*.[6] The principal instrument of government was the itinerant royal household, supported by its chapel and chancery, the political and military services offered by the prelates and secular nobles, physical hospitality from the bishops and abbots, and the *servitia* of the royal fisc. Bereft of any regular tax system or an organisation of subordinate courts, the performance of the crown is all the more remarkable in that the realms of the Empire were so diverse, and given that the *gentes*, the peoples of Germany descending from the East Frankish past, were not malleable into a 'Holy Roman Empire of the German Nation' before the fifteenth century.[7]

These considerations justify, in my view, a coherent interpretation of medieval German politics under three separable headings – peoples, Empire, kingship – without even touching upon the actual workings of the territorial, urban and princely politics at the local level about which I have written in my books *Princes and Territories in Medieval Germany* and *Count and Bishop in Medieval Germany*. It would also be dangerous to suppose that the peasants who made up the mass of the German population in the Middle Ages were without political capacity. Their contribution to the massive programmes of internal and external colonisation between the eleventh and the thirteenth centuries testifies to this, and we know of many instances where the lords deliberately relied upon the judgement of their agriculturists about the better development of their mutual interests and possessions.[8]

The above headings are separable but not separate; the exercise of neo-Roman *imperium* and the functions of kingship had a profound effect upon the ingrained regionalism of medieval Germany all the same. For example, in German medieval kingship, the close ties of the crown with the Church, standardised royal grants of immunity and other benefits to the bishoprics, and the ceaseless perambulation of the court resulted in a certain political convergence. But these energetic methods never solved the political problem of the royal eye needing to see to everything in so large an empire, a difficulty faced by Frederick II when he appointed a chief justiciar for Germany in 1235 on the grounds that he could not preside in person, *personaliter presidere non possumus*. And why not? 'The government of the Empire and the affairs of diverse lands and regions cause such cares as have always to be put right by our diligence.' In other words, the ruler could not be everywhere at once, a point repeated more naïvely to the Styrians when the duchy was provided with a captain-general in 1248. The cares of office required the ruler's presence in so many regions that 'We cannot personally reside continuously in the duchy of Styria.'[9]

The royal *iter* was bound to make inroads upon provincial autonomy of the type discussed by the caliph of Cordova and the future abbot of Gorze, but without the overturn of institutions such as *ducatus* and the kaleidoscope of other regional jurisdictions,[10] it is difficult to see how German kingship could ever have prevailed over local political power implicit in the Carolingian settlement. Modern scholarship proposes some jargon to elucidate this. The court operated at its most efficacious in 'core areas' or *Basislandschaften*, where it was rich in resources and residences. During the *iter* it passed through well-established 'transit zones' or *Durchzugsgebiete*.[11] Its influence was at a discount in regions not visited by custom, although magnates from there would visit the court and come back with diplomas, titles and other grants. This is why Henry III's unexpected visit to Bremen in 1047 came as an unpleasant surprise to the Saxon nobility, as we saw in Part III. The structure of 'core areas' might well change – for example, with Henry IV's effective expulsion from Saxony in 1076 or with Frederick Barbarossa's development of the royal fisc from 1167 – but the fall of the Staufen in the mid-thirteenth century and the loss to the crown of most of their lands restricted the scope of the *iter* and the core areas, as the German scholar Thomas Martin pointed out in 1977.[12] One consequence was that certain large regions were rendered permanently 'distant from the crown', to employ an idea expounded by Peter Moraw and others. All this is useful for understanding why royal governance, however successful upon its own terms, was not really designed to overcome Germany's ingrained regionalism as one of its political purposes.

Another reason for the relatively restricted impact of kingship in medieval Germany was the sheer difficulty of ruling a large Empire put together by successful military campaigns, but without modern institutions. No one denied that kingly office was a thankless task demanding much diligence and virtue. Tracts were sometimes written to assist kings in their trials. Wipo's biography of Conrad II can partly be construed as a 'princely mirror' for his son and successor Henry III, and so can Benzo of Alba's *Epygrama* presented to Henry IV in the 1080s, exalting the glory of the Empire.[13] The basic duty of kingship was to defend right order in Christendom as the faithful persevered, under the spiritual guidance of the Church, towards the culmination of history at the Day of the Lord. This is partly why Henry IV and Frederick II aroused such hatred and recrimination; the Papacy proclaimed that they had betrayed the very order they had been elected to defend,[14] and reacted by excommunicating them permanently, from 1080 and 1239 respectively. As we have seen, Gregory VII, in his famous open letter to Bishop Hermann of Metz, even attacked the very institution of kingship, basing his ideas upon some remarks of St Augustine.[15] But this summary dismissal of divinely commissioned kingship did not get very far. The Church had nothing to put in place of kingly governance, and what popes really needed were kings obedient to the aims of the reform movement.

Henry IV's biographer, sometimes thought to be Bishop Erlung of Würzburg (1105–21),[16] defended the opposite view. In a complicated text sensitive to the ideological needs of the Gregorians as well, the author returns several times to the ruler's proclamation of *pax et iustitia*, peace and justice, the slogan so often used in medieval times to justify all imperial and royal governance. The biographer claims that after the disorders during the regency of 1062 to 1065, Henry IV strove to restore *pax et iustitia* at the very outset of his personal rule. For the Mainz *Landfriede* of 1103, the author uses the same words, *pax et iustitia revocabat*, 'he summoned peace and justice again'. Then, in a literary flourish, justice and peace depart from the Roman Empire upon the emperor's death in 1106.[17]

At its simplest, therefore, German kingship did not entertain a programme extending much beyond providing peace and justice in general, as the *Landfrieden* were so often to assert, and protection for the Church in particular, to which the *arengae* of so many royal diplomas testify. In terms of salvation history, this was already quite a lot. Here are two examples from the chancery: 'Since we cultivate justice and peace, it is our wish that the Church of God should tranquilly possess what has legitimately been transferred to her' – thus Lothar III; and 'The office of imperial majesty is to provide peace and justice in the affairs of the Empire, according to instituted law and canonical decree' – thus Frederick Barbarossa.[18]

It was the perceived duty of the ruler to fight for the ideal if necessary. In an extraordinary diplomatic manifesto reminiscent of the days of Louis the Pious, Henry IV declared in 1091 that he was inspired both by the grace of the Holy Spirit and by the ruination of the Roman Empire in his own day to undertake by warfare the defence and restoration of proper order, just when liegeman and traitor, friend and foe, had to be winnowed like the wheat from the chaff. With more than a hint to the Gregorians, Henry appeals to apostolic injunctions, from St Paul and St Peter, to the effect that kings rightly wield the power of the sword as God's retribution upon malefactors.[19]

Whatever weighting one might choose to give to Frankish and German kingship with its bedfellow, the neo-Roman imperial ideal, as politically unifying forces, it is surely the social, legal, economic, linguistic and political dynamics of diversity which strike the observer as typical of Germany in the Middle Ages. Such agency can first be discerned in the ethnogenesis of the *gentes*, a subject academically in the melting-pot, reinforced by the latinised law codes, a bountiful source-base ripe for reappraisal. *Gens* and *lex* survived the cruel experience of Frankish conquest, since its leaders did not deliberately mean to dismantle regional identities. Represented again in the tenth century by the revived *ducatus*, at least in the military and peace keeping spheres, the legacy of ethnicity ensured a quite extreme form of regionalism which had to be reconciled with the ambitions and requirements of *regnum* and *imperium* as conducted by the successive imperial dynasties. But in normal times, *ducatus* and the royal court were in any case aligned in their mutual interests.

In its classic form, ducal authority quite rapidly fragmented in the decades after 1076. Economic expansion was in any case transforming the regions at the same time, by means of external and internal colonisation based upon the demographic increment. This was matched by the extremely significant phenomenon of urban growth and the establishment of new commercial connections and the multiplication of markets, tolls and mints as profitable new sources of wealth.[20] Previous patterns could therefore change quite rapidly in medieval Germany, enhancing regional diversity: the geopolitical space of the *gens* underlined by its dialects; the *ducatus* re-established about 900 with its tendency to multiplication from 1098; the structure of dioceses, recruited to the tasks of peace keeping by the *Treuga Dei*, the *ducatus*, and the *Landfriede* from the eleventh century. Another enormously potential source of enforced regionalism was the rise of revised local jurisdiction in the hands of the secular princes and the Church. For a long time it was thought that the vigour of such territorial jurisdictions was based upon the usurpation of royal authority and the decay of comital jurisdiction as introduced by the Carolingians. But in many remarkable studies by historians such as Hans Hirsch, Otto von Dungern, Walter Schlesinger, and Otto Brunner, twentieth-century scholarship ascertained that the new jurisdiction was allodial, autogenous and advocatial in nature.[21] Its regional character had an assured future.

The jurisdictionally modernising tendency of the royal *Landfrieden* after 1103 was in part designed to take the duties to *pax et iustitia*, peace and justice, exercised by the crown into partnership with local powers; dukes, bishops, margraves, and counts, and later on, with knights and townsmen as well. This fertile idea had a great future, yet from the start there was uncertainty about whether to declare peace over the whole Empire in hope, as Henry IV attempted in 1103, or in prudence to confine *Landfrieden* to regions like the *ducatus*, as in Saxony (1084), Bavaria (1094) and Swabia (before 1108).[22] Emperor Frederick Barbarossa tried both. One of the first acts of his reign was to set up a universal *Landfriede*, but later legislation was more circumspect, confined to a single region (1179) or to a single delict, incendiarism during feuds (1186–88).[23] The debate about the desirability of universal or local *Landfrieden* went on; for example, a Saxon *Landfriede* in 1221, the Mainz *Reichslandfriede* of 1235, then the Bavarian *Landfriede* of 1244, and so on.

Peace keeping was perceived as so strong a political desideratum in the feud-ridden circumstances of medieval Germany that there was strong convergence in using *ducatus*, diocese, and *Landfriede* for similar purposes. In the eleventh century the incumbents of the dioceses of Bremen, Aquileia and Würzburg evidently regarded their temporal authority as ducal power, and in the twelfth century the archbishops of Cologne were confirmed in ducal powers both west (1151) and east of the Rhine (1180).[24] Other bishops to whom ducal powers were ascribed included Magdeburg, Brixen, Münster and Liège.[25] To make the point, the bishop of Liège dressed up one day as a duke while attending the Fourth Lateran Council in 1215, much to the astonishment of the other delegates. But the best-known example concerns the see of Würzburg because the detailed imperial charter of 1168 has survived.[26] The title, jurisdiction, subordinate courts and magistrates were listed, with authority to enforce the peace:

> ... full power to do justice throughout the bishopric and duchy of Würzburg, and in all the counties situated in that bishopric and duchy, about robbery and arson, about allods and fiefs, about vassals, with the infliction of capital punishment.

Landfriede, diocese and *ducatus* may have had convergent aims in the legal sphere, but the growth of the urban economy, the programmes of agricultural and manorial colonisation, and the establishment of aristocratic and ecclesiastical territorial jurisdictions actually multiplied the legal diversity of medieval Germany. For example, the town laws of Magdeburg, Lübeck, Nuremberg, and Vienna which were creations of the twelfth century were models for civic laws throughout the colonial East, and in Poland and Hungary as well.[27] The rise of territorial lordship also created diversity in that the princes established regional codes or *Landrechte* based upon local custom, although it was a long time before they moved from the oral to the written stage.[28] As Emperor Frederick II pointed out at Mainz in 1235, 'throughout the whole of Germany the people live according to customs handed down of old and according to unwritten law, for their court cases and their personal affairs ...'.[29] In 1231 the royal court had recognised that if a prince, called in the source *dominus terre* or 'lord of the land', wished to introduce regulations or new laws, *constituciones vel nova iura*, then it could only be done with the prior consent of the leading men, the *meliores et maiores terre*.[30] This extraordinary statement is not a testimony to the inability of the royal court to centralise legislation in Germany, but to its determination to effectualise *pax et iusticia* through very necessary delegation of legal powers to the princes within their own lands or *terrae*.

As the German legal historian Friedrich Merzbacher has pointed out, the convergence of political intention implied by the *Landfrieden* just resulted in divergent definitions in the various regions of Germany:[31]

> In Bavaria the competence of the ducal and comital criminal jurisdictions was paraphrased by the formula of the so-called 'three causes' worthy of death, or the blood causes of theft, rape, and

homicide; in Franconia by the 'four high judgements' or chief matters for condemnation, being murder or homicide, robbery or theft, rape and incendiarism, or 'Whatever strikes neck and hand, stone and bone'; and in Saxony by the 'chief breaches', being murder, rape, and fatal or disabling wounds.

And so, when the duchies began to fall apart from the 1070s, there came a creative era of jurisdictional reform using comital authority, the *ducatus*, ecclesiastical advocacy, the *Landfrieden*, and other legal enactments from the royal court.[32] Significant examples of reform such as the *ducatus* for Cologne (1151–80) and Würzburg (1168), the *Landfrieden* for Rhenish Franconia (1179), Saxony (1221) and Bavaria (1244), and the town laws of Nuremberg and Lübeck confirmed in 1219 and 1226 respectively, have already indicated that juridical evolution in Germany was regional in scope. The list can fruitfully be extended.

To the medieval turn of mind, governance or *regimen*, and the authority to administer justice, *iurisdictio*, were virtually indistinguishable. Their exalted status was to some extent contaminated by using them as nutcrackers to extract taxes and corvées, but theoretically these mundane resources were based upon inferior sets of property rights. In Germany the twelfth and thirteenth centuries marked the introduction of many revised enterprises in *regimen* and *iurisdictio* at the local level which served to enforce the legacy of regionalism implied by the diverse ethnicity, the dialect variation, and the multiple legal heritage of the past.

The combination of *iurisdictio* and *regimen*, sometimes called *principatus*, was by no means reserved exclusively for royal governance. In 1186 Margrave Otto of Meissen asserted that he exercised *principatus* over the march of Meissen in order to provide prompt and effective *pax et iusticia*; in 1255 ducal governance over Bavaria was described as *principatus*; and in 1124 the *Pegau Annals* recorded the powers of the margraves of Lusatia as *principatus quoque ac monarchia*, 'governance and sole rule'.[33] In other words, regional power sharing between the crown and the aristocracy as a legacy from the Frankish and Ottonian eras was being updated into reformed jurisdiction under the influence of territorial lordship, colonisation and the *Landfrieden*.

The twelfth and thirteenth centuries provide several telling examples of this process, in which the political abilities of the magnates also played a part. In 1131 Lothar III bestowed the title of landgrave of Thuringia upon Louis I, and in 1134 the title of margrave of the North

March (later Brandenburg) upon Albert the Bear, count of Ballenstedt. In 1156 Frederick Barbarossa conferred the title of count
palatine of the Rhine upon his half-brother, Conrad of Staufen. The
titles of margrave, landgrave and count palatine contained the
jurisdictional implications of comital power, which was itself in a state
of flux as so many new allodial counties were being established by the
enriched aristocratic dynasties of Germany.[34] So it was up to the
grantees to make something of the jurisdiction, and in the three cases
mentioned the result was a new principality, an autonomous regional
regimen. The landgraves of Thuringia inherited the high court at
Mittelhausen with capital powers, but the main foundation for their
success was provided by their vast lands stretching across the middle of
Germany from the Rhine to the Saale. When the dynasty failed in
1247, Thuringia was, as we have seen, partitioned between the rival
houses of Brabant and Meissen in 1263, the Brabantine portion
eventually accepted by the royal court as a genuine *principatus*, the
landgraviate of Hesse.[35] This simply extended the twelfth-century
definition of Thuringia as a *principatus*.[36]

Similar drives, comital right, land holdings and military power,
permitted Albert the Bear to found the princely jurisdiction known as
Brandenburg and which he called *dicio*,[37] dominion or authority. In
1150 he succeeded the childless Slav prince Pribislav of Brandenburg
by treaty, and in 1157 drove out his only serious rival, Prince Jaxa of
Köpenick. Thereafter the forces of colonisation, the foundation of
towns, the institutions of the Church, and the enfeoffment of knights
created a new German margraviate for Albert's dynasty, the Ascanians. Conrad of Staufen's career was less spectacular, yet he succeeded in creating a lasting palatine county of the Rhine. The grant
consisted of the lordship of Stahleck inherited from the count palatine
of Lotharingia, Hermann of Stahleck, who was Conrad's uncle by
marriage. But the establishment was greatly extended by imperial
grants out of the Salian and Staufen estates in the Rhineland, and of
extremely valuable advocacies over possessions of the churches of
Worms, Speyer and Lorsch. From these ingredients the new count
palatine forged a lasting territorial jurisdiction, which passed in 1214
to the ducal house of Bavaria.[38]

Another jurisdiction modernised in 1156 was the march of Austria,
which was promoted into a duchy by Frederick Barbarossa, *in ducatum
commutavimus*.[39] It was stated that 'no greater or lesser person shall
presume to exercise any justice, *iusticia*, within the government, *regimen*,
of this duchy without consent or permission of the duke'. This is

usually taken to mean that the Bavarian churches and aristocrats who owned lands in Austria might still exercise their jurisdictions, but the subordination of territory and jurisdiction to the overall ducal *regimen* is plain to see. This eventuated in the establishment of the Austrian *Landrecht* during the reign of Duke Leopold VI (1198–1230), confirmed by Emperor Frederick II in 1237.[40] Although Austria and Styria were confiscated by the crown between 1236 and 1240, the emperor did not attempt to abolish local jurisdiction in favour of some chimera of centralised juridical authority. On the contrary, the regional customs of Styria and Austria were confirmed because they were practical. Austria's integrity as an autonomous jurisdiction founded in 976 and upgraded in 1156 is particularly well documented in the thirteenth century through the confirmations of its *Landfrieden*.[41]

But not all the intended reforms to regional jurisdiction worked out as their architects proposed. In a major reorganisation planned for the low countries, Frederick Barbarossa commissioned the bishop of Utrecht and the count of Holland to exercise *bannus et potestas iudicandi*, juridical rule and power of judgement, over the best part of Frisia through appointed deputies.[42] The Frisians would have none of it. In subsequent military operations to enforce territorial supremacy, the bishop of Utrecht was killed in battle in 1227 and the count of Holland in 1256. The Frisians did not finally give up their juridical autonomy until the sixteenth century.

In another case, the duchy of Brunswick-Lüneburg created in 1235, it was the largest allodial inheritance in Germany which became the basis of a new jurisdiction and region. When Henry the Lion lost his duchies of Bavaria and Saxony in 1180, his descendants retained their huge family inheritance in central Saxony and informally, the title of duke. This *de facto* position of local authority Emperor Frederick II regularised in 1235.[43] The castle of Lüneburg was the proprietal centre of the dynastic lands, and with its subordinate castles, lands and vassals it was converted into an imperial fief with the addition of the town of Brunswick which the emperor generously bought back from Otto of Lüneburg's cousins and then donated to the duchy. The new *ducatus* was declared heritable in both lines, and it was assigned the imperial tithes of Goslar into the bargain. So now there were three dukedoms in Saxony: the archbishop of Cologne's in Westphalia, the Ascanian dynasty's in the east and Brunswick-Lüneburg in the centre, this one forming the nucleus of the later electorate of Hanover eventually absorbed by Prussia in 1866 but surviving today as *Land* Niedersachsen.

Perhaps as much as a third of the land in medieval Germany belonged to the Church, and its prelates were not backward in facing up to the challenge of secular rivals. To ensure the autonomy of the ecclesiastical endowment, it proved necessary to use military, spiritual and jurisdictional methods. Of the last mentioned we may take just one example; the archbishopric of Salzburg was a large, mountainous principality constructed in the thirteenth century out of forest grants stretching back to the eighth,[44] several comital inheritances purchased or seized, and a series of other rights made good by a vigorous incumbent, Archbishop Eberhard II (1200–46). The essential act was to ensure recognition of the jurisdiction, and this was achieved by Archbishop Frederick II through a royal charter in 1278:

> You have received complete and unfettered authority in your districts and territories to judge civil and criminal cases in the manner of our greater princes. For we recognise you to be one of the highest princes of the Roman Empire, and we wish no one to question that *merum imperium*, full juridical authority, is subjoined to your principality, through which you have the right to punish wrongdoers with the powers of capital sentences. . . .[45]

In spite of such diplomas for Austria in 1156, Würzburg in 1168, Brunswick in 1235 and Salzburg in 1278, the crown was not necessarily prejudiced in favour of princely power against townsmen and peasants perceived as locally effective in the peace-keeping process. This is demonstrated from surviving grants to the Alpine communities of Swabia, placing them under immediate royal protection: Uri in 1231, Schwyz in 1240, and Unterwalden in 1309. It is thought that a league of these communities may have existed in the thirteenth century to protect roads, pastures and the peace generally. Some such *Landfriede* was confirmed in 1291, and this is taken nowadays to have been the original constitutive act founding the Swiss Confederation.[46]

So the dynamics of internal and external colonisation compounded by jurisdictional adaptations reliant to a great extent upon the *Landfrieden* created new foundations for the continued regionalism of medieval Germany. Some of the regions just considered – Thuringia, Hesse, Brandenburg, the Rhine-Palatinate, Austria, Frisia, Salzburg and the Swiss Confederation – still exist as regional or sovereign governments in operation today.

This ongoing regionalism of medieval Germany can be illustrated in another way; from dialect history. Investigation supports the

identification of languages based upon the *gentes*: Bavarian, Alemannic, Franconian (in four sub-sections) and Old Low German (Saxon),
with Frisian as a separate tongue. Then, in spite of the possibly
unifying potential of Middle High German as a great creation of the
twelfth century,[47] its irrelevance to spoken tongues became apparent
as Germany colonised towards the East: twelve identifiable dialects
(1150–1250) expanded to eighteen (1250–1500).[48]

We can see that the evolution of dialects, the expansion of the urban
and rural economies, the reforms to jurisdiction, and the rise of
territorial lordship continued to sustain the power of regionalism
based originally upon the subdivision of the German realm between
the *gentes*. At the same time, the symbolic, political and religious
importance of kingship, though occasionally devalued in such crises as
the Gregorian revolution or during Gregory IX's and Innocent IV's
attacks upon Frederick II's status, was accepted as a representation of
social unity. The western Roman Empire functioned alongside the
Christian Church, which it was supposed to protect as an apparatus
necessary for the eventual salvation of mankind. In its classic form,
German kingship was a terrestrial vicariate for Christ the King, as
Archbishop Aribo of Mainz pointed out to Conrad II in 1024.[49] As
Christ ruled in Heaven so the emperor reigned on earth, and from his
faithful princes, almost always the principal political concern of the
court, there was constituted a sole imperial framework, or *imperii corpus*,
as Frederick II phrased it in 1235.[50] If regionalism was one reality in
medieval German society, then German kingship and the neo-Roman
Empire provided plentiful unifying metaphors as guidelines for the
conduct of the court. The political history of medieval Germany thus
exhibits an extended dialogue between regional dynamics and the
convergent or unifying ideal of the king reigning under divine
providence which also extended the neo-Roman imperial crown and
sceptre to the incumbent.[51] As the great cycle of human history turned
inexorably towards the Apocalypse, 'the excellence and virtue of
imperial majesty in the government of the Empire' never neglected
the practical aims of medieval kingship either:

> The office of Our Majesty is entrusted to us by God to maintain to
> everyone what is his by right, and to remedy injury through
> rendering judgement and by the mercy of imperial authority.[52]

A meritorious ideal indeed.

Abbreviations

AQ Ausgewählte Quellen zur deutschen Geschichte des Mittelalters. Freiherr vom Stein Gedächtnisausgabe.

Bauer and Rau, *Quellen* A. Bauer and R. Rau (eds), *Quellen zur Geschichte der sächsischen Kaiserzeit*, AQ vol. VIII (Darmstadt, 1977).

HRG *Handwörterbuch zur Deutschen Rechtsgeschichte.*

LMA *Lexikon des Mittelalters.*

MGH Monumenta Germaniae Historica.

Trillmich, *Quellen* W. Trillmich (ed.), *Quellen des 9. und 11. Jahrhunderts zur Geschichte der Hamburgischen Kirche und des Reiches*, AQ vol. XI (Darmstadt, 1978).

Notes

Introduction: German Political Identity in the Middle Ages

1. A. Schmidt and F-J. Schmale (eds), *Ottonis episcopi Frisingensis et Rahewini. Gesta Frederici seu rectius Cronica*, AQ vol. XVII (Darmstadt, 1974) p. 208.
2. G. H. Pertz and F. Kurze (eds) *Annales regni Francorum*, MGH Scriptores rerum Germanicarum vol. VI (Hanover, 1895) p. 80. See H. Thomas, 'Der Ursprung des Wortes Theodiscus', *Historische Zeitschrift*, CCXLVII (1988), 295–331.
3. L. Halphen (ed.), *Eginhard. Vie de Charlemagne*, Les Classiques de l'Histoire de France au Moyen Age, 3rd edn (Paris, 1947) pp. 82–4. In 'Die volkssprachige Überlieferung der Karolingerzeit aus der Sicht des Historikers', *Deutsches Archiv* XXXIX (1983), 104–30, Dieter Geuenich would like to shift the significance of the vernacular language programme to ninth-century East Francia.
4. K. F. Werner, 'Deutschland' in LMA vol. III, cols 781–9; S. Reynolds, *Kingdoms and Communities in Western Europe, 900–1300* (Oxford, 1984) pp. 289–97; T. Reuter, *Germany in the Early Middle Ages c. 800–1056* (London and New York, 1991) pp. 51–4.
5. *Nithardi Historiarum*, MGH Scriptores vol. II, pp. 665–6; in translation in B. W. Scholz, *Carolingian Chronicles. Royal Frankish Annals and Nithard's Histories* (Ann Arbor, 1970) pp. 161–3.
6. MGH Constitutiones vol. I, no. 1, pp. 1–2 (921).
7. Bauer and Rau, *Quellen*, p. 556.
8. W. Trillmich (ed.), *Thietmar von Merseburg. Chronik*, AQ vol. IX (Darmstadt, 1974) pp. 6, 170, 220, 290.
9. Trillmich, *Quellen*, pp. 566–74; so did the imperial chancery, e.g. MGH Diplomata Otto III, no. 324, p. 752 (999).

10. A. Schmidt (ed.), *Lampert von Hersfeld. Annalen*, AQ vol. XIII (Darmstadt, 1957) index at *Teutonici, T(h)eutonicus*, p. 446.

11. Following the interpretation of Heinz Thomas in 'Julius Caesar und die Deutschen. Zu Ursprung und Gehalt eines deutschen Geschichtsbewusstseins in der Zeit Gregors VII. und Heinrichs IV.', in S. Weinfurter (ed.), *Die Salier und das Reich*, vol. III (Sigmaringen, 1991) pp. 265–73.

12. MGH Diplomata Henry III, no. 239, p. 320.

13. E. Caspar (ed.), *Das Register Gregors VII.*, MGH Epistolae selectae vol. II, part i, 2nd edn (Berlin, 1955) pp. 314–15.

14. *Annales Iuvavenses Maximi*, MGH Scriptores vol. XXX, p. 742.

15. See F. L. Borchardt, *German Antiquity in Renaissance Myth* (Baltimore and London, 1971) p. 178.

16. MGH Diplomata Otto I, no. 62, p. 144 (944); Otto II, no. 165, p. 185 (977); Otto III, no. 261, p. 678 (997).

17. H. Kallfelz (ed.), *Lebensbeschreibungen einiger Bischöfe des 10.–12. Jahrhunderts*, AQ vol. XXII (Darmstadt, 1972) p. 320.

18. Kallfelz, *Lebensbeschreibungen*, p. 398.

19. F-J. Schmale and I. Schmale-Ott (eds), *Frutolfs und Ekkehards Chroniken und die Anonyme Kaiserchronik*, AQ vol. XV (Darmstadt, 1972) p. 140.

20. MGH Diplomata Conrad III, no. 81, p. 144; MGH Constitutiones vol. I, no. 138, p. 192.

21. Schmidt and Schmale, *Ottonis Gesta*, index under Teutonicum regnum, p. 756.

22. J. F. Niermeyer, *Mediae Latinitatis Lexicon Minus* (Leiden, 1976), p. 1027.

23. H. Stoob (ed.), *Helmold von Bosau. Slawenchronik*, AQ vol. XIX (Darmstadt, 1973) p. 216; MGH Diplomata Conrad III, no. 69, p. 123 (1142).

24. Schmidt and Schmale, *Ottonis Gesta*, p. 146.

25. Schmidt and Schmale, *Ottonis Gesta*, pp. 304, 348 (based on Num. 11, 23) 356.

26. MGH Diplomata Frederick I, no. 153, p. 263 (1156).

27. H. Grundmann and H. Heimpel (eds), *Die Schriften des Alexander von Roes*, MGH Deutsches Mittelalter vol. IV (Weimar, 1949) p. 54.

28. T. Reuter (ed.), *The Annals of Fulda. Ninth-Century Histories, Volume II*, Manchester Medieval Sources Series (Manchester and New York, 1992) pp. 71, 84, 90.

29. Reuter, *Annals of Fulda*, pp. 91–2.

30. Bauer and Rau, *Quellen*, pp. 134, 178, 180; Trillmich, *Thietmar. Chronik*, pp. 42, 50; Trillmich, *Quellen*, pp. 364, 434.
31. Trillmich, *Quellen*, p. 536.
32. Schmale and Schmale-Ott, *Frutolfs und Ekkehards Chroniken*, p. 298.
33. Schmidt and Schmale, *Ottonis Gesta*, pp. 152, 376, 208.
34. Grundmann and Heimpel, *Schriften des Alexander von Roes*, pp. 50, 90.
35. For example, MGH Diplomata Lothar III, no. 101, p. 163 (1136) and Conrad III, no. 81, p. 144 (1142).
36. Schmidt, *Lampert. Annalen*, pp. 378, 386 (1076).
37. Thomas, 'Julius Caesar und die Deutschen', pp. 251–4.
38. M. Roediger (ed.), *Das Annolied*, MGH Deutsche Chroniken vol. I, part 2 (Hanover, 1895) pp. 63–145. There is a huge literature on the *Annolied*. In English see B. Arnold, 'From Warfare on Earth to Eternal Paradise: Archbishop Anno II of Cologne, the History of the Western Empire in the *Annolied*, and the Salvation of Mankind', *Viator* XXIII (1992) 95–113.
39. K. A. Eckhardt (ed.), *Sachsenspiegel Landrecht*, MGH Fontes iuris Germanici antiqui, new series vol. I, part 1, 2nd edn (Göttingen, 1955) pp. 230–1 and the materials cited there.
40. Eckhardt, *Sachsenspiegel Landrecht*, p. 238.
41. Schmale and Schmale-Ott, *Frutolfs und Ekkehards Chroniken*, p. 352 (1121).
42. *Narratio de Electione Lotharii*, MGH Scriptores vol. XII, pp. 509–12.
43. Trillmich, *Quellen*, pp. 556–8.
44. E. Müller-Mertens, *Regnum Teutonicum. Aufkommen und Verbreitung der deutschen Reichs- und Königsauffassung im früheren Mittelalter*, Forschungen zur Mittelalterlichen Geschichte vol. XV (Vienna, Cologne and Graz, 1970) pp. 316–27, 384–93.

Part I: The Peoples and Provinces of Medieval Germany

1. Quoted by K. F. Werner, 'Les Nations et le sentiment national dans l'Europe médiévale', *Revue Historique*, CCXLIV (1970) 291; MGH Diplomata Otto III, no. 197, p. 605 and no. 208, p. 619 (996).
2. C. C. Mierow (ed.), *The Gothic History of Jordanes*, Speculum Historiale edition (Cambridge and New York, 1966) p. 132. See

NOTES

197

R. Christlein and P. Fried, 'Bayern' in LMA vol. I, cols. 1696–1704.

3. See discussion by Kurt Reindel in *Handbuch der bayerischen Geschichte*, vol. I *Das alte Bayern*, ed. M. Spindler, 3rd edn (Munich, 1975) pp. 75–92.
4. Report by T. L. Markey on W. Mayerthaler's theories in F. M. Clover and R. S. Humphries (eds), *Tradition and Innovation in Late Antiquity* (Madison and London, 1989) pp. 63–4, 70–1. For work on Bavarian ethnogenesis, see the *Denkschriften* series (phil.-hist. Klasse) published by the Österreichische Akademie der Wissenschaften (Vienna), vols CXLV (1980), CLXXIX–XXX (1985), CCI and CCIV (1990), eds F. Daim, H. Friesinger, W. Pohl, A. Schwarcz and H. Wolfram.
5. E. von Schwind (ed.), *Lex Baiwariorum*, MGH Leges nationum Germanicarum vol. V, part 2 (Hanover, 1926) pp. 312–15.
6. W. Störmer, 'Agilolfinger', in LMA vol. I, cols 207–8. See the important arguments of Jörg Jarnut in his *Agilolfingerstudien. Untersuchungen zur Geschichte einer adeligen Familie im 6. und 7. Jahrhundert*, Monographien zur Geschichte des Mittelalters vol. XXXII (Stuttgart, 1986).
7. R. Scheyhing, 'Dux' in HRG vol. I, cols 792–3 and H. Werle, 'Herzog, Herzogtum' in vol. II, cols 119–20. See A. R. Lewis, 'Dukes in the *regnum Francorum*, 550–751', *Speculum*, LI (1976) 381–410.
8. A. Kraus, 'Marginalien zur ältesten Geschichte des bayerischen Nordgaus', *Jahrbuch für fränkische Landesforschung*, XXXIV-V (1975) 163–84.
9. T. R. Mommsen (ed.), *Eugippii vita Severini*, MGH Scriptores rerum Germanicarum vol. XXVI (Berlin, 1898); G. P. Fehring, *The Archaeology of Medieval Germany: An Introduction*, transl. R. Samson, Studies in Archaeology (London and New York, 1991) pp. 73–5; F. Lotter, *Severinus von Noricum. Legende und historische Wirklichkeit. Untersuchungen zur Phase des Übergangs von spätantiken zu mittelalterlichen Denk- und Lebensformen*, Monographien zur Geschichte des Mittelalters vol. XII (Stuttgart, 1976).
10. T. Schieffer, *Winfrid-Bonifatius und die christliche Grundlegung Europas*, new edn (Darmstadt, 1980) pp. 92–5, 181–5.
11. Discussed by H. Siems, with extensive bibliography, in 'Lex Baiuvariorum' in HRG vol. II, cols 1887–1901.
12. Von Schwind, *Lex Baiwariorum*, pp. 302–3.
13. H. Schlosser, 'Decreta Tassilonis' in HRG vol. I, cols 665–6.

14. I. Wood, *The Merovingian Kingdoms 450–751* (London and New York, 1994) p. 162.

15. Pertz and Kurze, *Annales regni Francorum*, pp. 14–17; J. Fried, *Der Weg in die Geschichte. Die Ursprünge Deutschlands bis 1024*, Propyläen Geschichte Deutschlands vol. I (Berlin, 1994) p. 243.

16. Halphen, *Eginhard*, p. 34.

17. MGH Diplomata Charlemagne, no. 162, pp. 219–20.

18. A. Boretius (ed.), *Capitularia regum Francorum*, MGH Legum sectio II, vol. I (Hanover, 1883) no. 68, pp. 157–8 (801–13).

19. Boretius, *Capitularia* i, no. 136 (ch. 2) p. 271.

20. C. R. Bowlus, *Franks, Moravians, and Magyars. The Struggle for the Middle Danube, 788–907*, Middle Ages Series (Philadelphia, 1995) and the literature cited there.

21. MGH Diplomata Louis the German, nos. 1–12, pp. 1–14 (829–33). See K. Reindel in Spindler, *Handbuch der bayerischen Geschichte* vol. I, p. 173, note 5.

22. The intrigues are described in detail in Reuter, *Annals of Fulda*, pp. 15–18.

23. See Paul Kehr in MGH Diplomata Arnolf, pp. xi–xii.

24. See K. Reindel in Spindler, *Handbuch der bayerischen Geschichte* vol. I, p. 206.

25. As in MGH Diplomata Louis the Child, no. 9, p. 110 and no. 12, p. 114 (901).

26. H. Faussner, *Zum Regnum Bavariae Herzog Arnulfs (907–938)*, Sitzungsberichte der Österreichischen Akademie der Wissenschaften, phil.-hist. Klasse, vol. CCCCXXVI (Vienna, 1984).

27. The essential monograph is Wilhelm Störmer's *Früher Adel. Studien zur politischen Führungsschicht im fränkisch-deutschen Reich vom 8. bis 11. Jahrhundert*, Monographien zur Geschichte des Mittelalters vol. VI, 2 parts (Stuttgart, 1973).

28. MGH Diplomata Otto I, no. 423, pp. 577–8 (972).

29. J. Engel (ed.), *Grosser Historischer Weltatlas*, vol. II, *Mittelalter* (Munich, 1970) p. 111.

30. J. M. Wallace-Hadrill, *The Fourth Book of the Chronicle of Fredegar*, Medieval Classics (London, 1960), pp. 39–40, 56–8; H-D. Kahl, 'Conversio Bagoariorum et Carantanorum' in LMA vol. III, col. 208.

31. H. Wolfram, 'The Shaping of the Early Medieval Principality as a Type of Non-royal Rulership', *Viator*, II (1971) 33–51.

NOTES 199

32. On Carinthia/Carantania see H. Baltl, 'Karantanien' in HRG vol. II, cols 629–34 and H. Dopsch, 'Kärnten' in LMA vol. V, cols 1002–8.
33. F. Staab (ed.), *Zur Kontinuität zwischen Antike und Mittelalter am Oberrhein*, Oberrheinische Studien vol. II (Sigmaringen, 1994); J. Matthews, *The Roman Empire of Ammianus* (London, 1989) pp. 306–18; T. Zotz and H. Ament, 'Alamannen, Alemannen' in LMA vol. I, cols 263–6.
34. For example, *Annales Argentinenses*, MGH Scriptores vol. XVII, p. 89 (1191).
35. T. Zotz, 'Cannstadt, Gerichtstag von' in LMA vol. II, cols 1436–7.
36. K. Lehmann and K. A. Eckhardt, *Leges Alamannorum*, MGH Leges nationum Germanicarum vol. V, part 1, 2nd edn (Hanover, 1966).
37. C. Schott, 'Lex Alamannorum' in HRG vol. II, cols. 1879–86.
38. H. Siems, 'Lex Baiuvariorum' in HRG vol. II, col. 1893.
39. For example, W. Horn and E. Born, *The Plan of St. Gall*, 3 vols (Berkeley, Los Angeles and London, 1979).
40. E. Meyer-Marthaler, 'Churrätien' in LMA vol. II, cols 2060–1 and 'Lex Romana Curiensis' in HRG vol. II, cols 1935–40.
41. O. P. Clavadetscher, 'Die Einführung der Grafschaftsverfassung in Rätien und die Klageschriften Bischof Viktors III. von Chur,' *Zeitschrift der Savigny-Stiftung für Rechtsgeschichte. Kanonistische Abteilung*, LXX (1953) 46–111.
42. See H. K. Schulze, *Die Grafschaftsverfassung der Karolingerzeit in den Gebieten östlich des Rheins*, Schriften zur Verfassungsgeschichte, vol. XIX (Berlin, 1973).
43. Since 'Swabia' begins to prevail over 'Alemannia' in tenth-century sources, I have adopted the transition here.
44. For the evolution of the Swabian duchy, H. Maurer, *Der Herzog von Schwaben. Grundlagen, Wirkungen und Wesen seiner Herrschaft in ottonischer, salischer und staufischer Zeit* (Sigmaringen, 1978).
45. E. James, *The Origins of France. From Clovis to the Capetians 500–1000*, New Studies in Medieval History (London and Basingstoke, 1982) pp. 26–32; P. J. Geary, *Before France and Germany. The Creation and Transformation of the Merovingian World* (New York and Oxford, 1988) pp. 77–86; M. Todd, *The Early Germans*, The Peoples of Europe (Oxford and Cambridge, Mass., 1992) pp. 192–207.

46. H. H. Anton, 'Franken, Frankenreich' in LMA vol. IV, cols 695–99.
47. Further discussion in Wood, *Merovingian Kingdoms*, pp. 33–8.
48. B. S. Bachrach, *Merovingian Military Organization 481–751* (Minneapolis, 1972) pp. 3–35.
49. R. Butzen, *Die Merowinger östlich des mittleren Rheins. Studien zur Erfassung durch Königtum und Adel im 6. sowie 7. Jahrhundert*, Mainfränkische Studien vol. XXXVIII (Würzburg, 1987).
50. MGH Diplomata Henry III, no. 303, p. 412.
51. In 'Grundlegung: Die Eingliederung Thüringens in das merowingische Frankenreich' in Spindler, *Handbuch der bayerischen Geschichte* vol. III/1, p. 18.
52. Schieffer, *Winfrid-Bonifatius*, pp. 120–256.
53. A. Wendehorst, *Das Bistum Würzburg*, part I, *Die Bischofsreihe bis 1254*, Germania Sacra, New Series, Die Bistümer der Kirchenprovinz Mainz vol. I (Berlin, 1962) pp. 15–16.
54. On Franconia at this time, K. Bosl, *Franken um 800. Strukturanalyse einer fränkischen Königsprovinz*, 2nd edn (Munich, 1969).
55. Halphen, *Eginhard*, pp. 50, 90.
56. Wood, *Merovingian Kingdoms*, p. 104.
57. R. Schmidt-Wiegand, 'Lex Salica' in HRG vol. III, cols 1949–62. There are two recent translations into English: T. J. Rivers, *Laws of the Salian and Ripuarian Franks* (New York, 1986) and K. F. Drew, *The Laws of the Salian Franks*, Middle Ages Series (Philadelphia, 1991).
58. Transl. by Wood, *Merovingian Kingdoms*, p. 116.
59. Reuter, *Annals of Fulda*, pp. 55, 112.
60. See MGH Diplomata Arnolf, no. 174, pp. 263–4 (899), where possessions are restored.
61. Bauer and Rau, *Quellen*, pp. 48–50.
62. W. Kienast, *Der Herzogstitel in Frankreich und Deutschland (9. bis 12. Jahrhundert)* (Munich and Vienna, 1968), pp. 316, 446. See D. C. Jackman, *The Konradiner. A Study in Genealogical Methodology*, Ius Commune Sonderhefte. Studien zur Europäischen Rechtsgeschichte, vol. XLVII (Frankfurt am Main, 1990).
63. Bauer and Rau, *Quellen*, pp. 56–8.
64. Bauer and Rau, *Quellen*, pp. 92–4.
65. Explained by K. J. Leyser in *Rule and Conflict in an Early Medieval Society. Ottonian Saxony* (London, 1979) pp. 9–22 and by Reuter, *Germany*, pp. 148–54.

66. P. Riché, *The Carolingians. A Family who forged Europe*, transl. M. I. Allen, Middle Ages Series (Philadelphia, 1993) pp. 160–9 has all the details.

67. B. Schneidmüller, 'Regnum und ducatus. Identität und Integration in der lotharingischen Geschichte des 9. bis 11. Jahrhunderts', *Rheinische Vierteljahrsblätter*, LI (1987) 81–114.

68. N. Parisse, 'Giselbert' in LMA vol. IV, col. 1466.

69. D. P. Blok and H. Hinz, 'Friesen, Friesland' in LMA vol. IV, cols 970–3.

70. H. Siems, 'Lex Frisionum' in HRG, vol. II, cols 1916–22; K. A. and A. Eckhardt (eds), *Lex Frisionum*, MGH Fontes iuris Germanici antiqui vol. XII (Hanover, 1982).

71. W. Levison (ed.), *Vitae sancti Bonifatii archiepiscopi Moguntini*, MGH Scriptores rerum Germanicarum vol. LVII (Hanover and Leipzig, 1905) p. 47.

72. H. Wolfram, *History of the Goths*, transl. T. J. Dunlap (Berkeley, Los Angeles and London, 1988) pp. 19–171.

73. On the controversies, N. Higham, *Rome, Britain and the Anglo-Saxons* (London, 1992) esp. pp. 209–36.

74. K. Jordan and W. Lammers, 'Sachsen' in HRG vol. IV, col. 1224.

75. R. Schmidt-Wiegand, 'Lex Saxonum' in HRG vol. II, cols 1962–5.

76. See the classic work of Reinhard Wenskus in *Stammesbildung und Verfassung. Das Werden der frühmittelalterlichen gentes* (Cologne and Graz, 1961) pp. 541–51.

77. This has sometimes been dismissed as a literary invention, but see G. Spreckelmeyer, 'Marklo (an der Weser)' in LMA vol. VI, col. 306.

78. Halphen, *Eginhard*, pp. 22–6.

79. Reuter, *Annals of Fulda*, p. 21 and note 6; E. J. Goldberg, 'Popular Revolt, Dynastic Politics, and Aristocratic Factionalism in the Early Middle Ages: the Saxon *Stellinga* Reconsidered', *Speculum*, LXX (1995) 467–501.

80. Boretius, *Capitularia regum Francorum* i, no. 26, pp. 68–70 (now 785) and no. 27, pp. 71–2 (797); translations by H. R. Loyn and J. Percival in *The Reign of Charlemagne. Documents on Carolingian Government and Administration*, Documents of Medieval History vol. II (London, 1975), nos. 11–12, pp. 51–6.

81. Boretius, *Capitularia regum Francorum* i, p. 71, note 3.

82. R. Schmidt-Wiegand, 'Lex Ribuaria' in HRG vol. i, cols 1923–7. The additions are translated by Loyn and Percival, *Reign of Charlemagne*, no. 19, pp. 85–6.

83. MGH Diplomata Arnolf, no. 155, pp. 235–6 (897).

84. MGH Diplomata Louis the German, no. 93, p. 135 (858) already has *in ducatu Saxonico*.

85. Bauer and Rau, *Quellen*, pp. 44–6, 48.

86. Kienast, *Herzogstitel*, pp. 445–6.

87. Bauer and Rau, *Quellen*, p. 62.

88. K. J. Leyser, 'Henry I and the Beginnings of the Saxon Empire', *English Historical Review*, LXXXIII (1968) 1–32.

89. MGH Diplomata Otto II, no. 112, pp. 126–7; Trillmich, *Thietmar. Chronik*, pp. 74, 104.

90. Bauer and Rau, *Quellen*, p. 92.

91. Kienast, *Herzogstitel*, pp. 326–9.

92. Bauer and Rau, *Quellen*, pp. 152–6.

93. W. Schlesinger, *Die Entstehung der Landesherrschaft. Untersuchungen vorwiegend nach mitteldeutschen Quellen*, Sächsische Forschungen zur Geschichte vol. i, new edn (Darmstadt, 1973) pp. 16–38; Schmale, 'Grundlegung', pp. 3–17; H. Weddige, *Heldensage und Stammessage. Iring und der Untergang des Thüringerreiches in Historiographie und heroischer Dichtung*, Hermaea. Germanistische Forschungen, New Series, vol. LXI (Tübingen, 1989) pp. 5–11.

94. Schlesinger, *Entstehung*, pp. 21, 155.

95. Wallace-Hadrill, *Chronicle of Fredegar*, pp. 73–4.

96. Wood, *Merovingian Kingdoms*, pp. 162–4,

97. G. Streich, 'Erfurt' in LMA vol. III, cols 2131–2; the possible dates are 741/43 to 746/54.

98. On this era, Schlesinger, *Entstehung*, pp. 50–83.

99. R. Schmidt-Wiegand, 'Lex Thuringorum' in HRG vol. II, cols 1965–6.

100. Bauer and Rau, *Quellen*, p. 44.

101. Bauer and Rau, *Quellen*, p. 78.

102. Bauer and Rau, *Quellen*, pp. 84–90.

103. Leyser, *Rule and Conflict*, pp. 9–47.

104. J. Laudage in his 'Hausrecht und Thronfolge. Überlegungen zur Königserhebungen Ottos des Grossen und zu den Aufständen Thankmars, Heinrichs und Liudolfs', *Historisches Jahrbuch* CXII (1992) 23–71. In 'Nochmals zur *benedictio Ottonis in regem*: 927 oder 929?', *Archiv für Diplomatik*, XL (1994) 79–84, Gunther Wolf prefers 927 as the date.

105. Bauer and Rau, *Quellen*, p. 152; see K. J. Leyser, 'The Battle at the Lech, 955. A Study in Tenth-Century Warfare', History L (1965) 1–25.

106. MGH Constitutiones vol. I, no. 436, pp. 632–3; K. F. Werner, 'Heeresorganisation und Kriegführung im deutschen Königreich des 10. und 11. Jahrhundert' in *Ordinamenti militari in Occidente nell'alto Medioevo*, Settimane di Studio del Centro Italiano di Studi sull'alto Medioevo vol. XV (Spoleto, 1968) 791–843.

107. Reuter, *Germany*, pp. 148–59, 199–208.

108. G. Tellenbach, 'Vom karolingischen Reichsadel zum deutschen Reichsfürstenstand' in T. Mayer (ed.), *Adel und Bauern im deutschen Staat des Mittelalters*, new edn (Darmstadt, 1976) pp. 22–73, transl. T. Reuter, 'From the Carolingian Imperial Nobility to the German Estate of Imperial Princes' in *The Medieval Nobility. Studies on the Ruling Classes of France and Germany* (Amsterdam, etc., 1978) pp. 203–42.

109. There are several studies; see H. C. Faussner, *Königliches Designationsrecht und herzögliches Geblutsrecht. Zum Königtum und Herzogtum in Baiern im Hochmittelalter*, Sitzungsberichte. Österreichische Akademie der Wissenschaften, phil.-hist. Klasse vol. CCCCXXIX (Vienna, 1984).

110. H. Werle, 'Herzog, Herzogtum' in HRG vol. II, cols 119–27 and H.-W. Goetz, 'Herzog, Herzogtum' in LMA vol. IV, cols 2189–93.

111. H. Lieberich, 'Ranshofener Gesetze' in HRG vol. IV, cols 151–2.

112. Trillmich, *Quellen*, pp. 332, 336, 378–82, 388–90; see H.-W. Goetz, 'Das Herzogtum im Spiegel der salierzeitlichen Geschichtsschreibung' in Weinfurter, *Die Salier und das Reich* i, pp. 259–62 and P. Johanek, 'Die Erzbischöfe von Hamburg-Bremen und ihre Kirche im Reich der Salierzeit' in ii, pp. 79–112.

113. G. Althoff, 'Die Billunger in der Salierzeit' in Weinfurter, *Die Salier und das Reich* i, pp. 309–29.

114. G. Althoff, 'Das Bett des Königs in Magdeburg. Zu Thietmar II, 28' in H. Maurer and H. Patze (ed.), *Festschrift für Berent Schwineköper zu seinem siebzigsten Geburtstag* (Sigmaringen, 1982) pp. 141–53.

115. Trillmich, *Quellen*, pp. 574–6.

116. On the basis of MGH Diplomata Conrad II, no. 144, p. 195 (1030) Frederick has been identified as count in the Ries.

117. The translation is from T. E. Mommsen and K. F. Morrison (eds), *Imperial Lives and Letters of the Eleventh Century*, Records of

Civilization. Sources and Studies vol. LXVII (New York and London, 1962) p. 82.

118. Trillmich, *Quellen*, p. 582; on the politics of feud in the eleventh century, see now T. Reuter, 'Unruhestiftung, Fehde, Rebellion, Widerstand: Gewalt und Frieden in der Politik der Salierzeit' in Weinfurter, *Die Salier und das Reich* iii, pp. 297–325.

119. H. Keller, *Zwischen regionaler Begrenzung und universalem Horizont. Deutschland im Imperium der Salier und Staufer 1024–1250*, Propyläen Geschichte Deutschlands, vol. II (Berlin, 1986) p. 86.

120. Leyser, *Rule and Conflict*, p. 20.

121. Kallfelz, *Lebensbeschreibungen*, pp. 196–212.

122. Tellenbach, 'Vom karolingischen Reichsadel', p. 205.

123. Kallfelz, *Lebensbeschreibungen*, pp. 242–4.

124. Tellenbach, 'Vom karolingischen Reichsadel', pp. 204–7; M. Twellenkamp, 'Das Haus der Luxemburger' in Weinfurter, *Die Salier und das Reich* i, pp. 475–502.

125. P. Leupen, 'Nijmegen' in LMA vol. VI, col. 1149. Godfrey has been renumbered as III; G. Despy, 'Gottfried III. der Bärtige' in LMA vol. IV, col. 1601. See now B. Thissen, 'The Palace of Nijmegen in the Tenth and Early Eleventh Centuries' in A. Davids (ed.), *The Empress Theophano. Byzantium and the West at the Turn of the First Millenium* (Cambridge, 1995) pp. 265–89.

126. See now M. Werner, 'Der Herzog von Lothringen in salischer Zeit' in Weinfurter, *Die Salier und das Reich* i, pp. 367–473.

127. Schmidt and Schmale, *Ottonis Gesta*, p. 276.

128. B. Schmeidler, 'Franconia's Place in the Structure of Mediaeval Germany', transl. G. Barraclough in *Mediaeval Germany 911–1250*, vol. II, *Essays*, Studies in Mediaeval History, 2nd edn (Oxford, 1961) pp. 71–93.

129. A. Gerlich, 'Mainz, Erzbistum und Erzstift' in LMA vol. VI, cols 134–42 and H-J. Becker, 'Primas' in HRG vol. III, cols 1948–50; but Mainz's primacy in the canonical sense was always disputed by the other metropolitan sees of Germany.

130. S. Weinfurter, 'Herrschaftslegitimation und Königsautorität im Wandel: Die Salier und ihr Dom zu Speyer' in Weinfurter, *Die Salier und das Reich* i, pp. 55–96.

131. Bauer and Rau, *Quellen*, p. 156.

132 The results are analysed by Wilhelm Störmer in 'Grundzüge des Adels im hochmittelalterichen Franken' in G. Jenal (ed.), *Herrschaft, Kirche, Kultur. Beiträge zur Geschichte des Mittelalters*,

Monographien zur Geschichte des Mittelalters vol. XXXVII (Stuttgart, 1993) pp. 245–64.

133. MGH Diplomata Henry IV, no. 267, pp. 341–3 (1074), transl. B. H. Hill, *Medieval Monarchy in Action*. *The German Empire from Henry I to Henry IV*, Historical Problems; Studies and Documents vol. XV (London and New York, 1972) no. 48, pp. 235–6.
134. Bauer and Rau, *Quellen*, pp. 144, 148–50.
135. On this phase, W. Störmer, 'Bayern und der bayerische Herzog im 11. Jahrhundert. Fragen der Herzogsgewalt und der königlichen Interessenpolitik' in Weinfurter, *Die Salier und das Reich* i, pp. 503–47.
136. Trillmich, *Thietmar. Chronik*, p. 136.
137. On these tendencies, S. Weinfurter, 'Die Zentralisierung der Herrschaftsgewalt im Reich durch Kaiser Heinrich II.', *Historisches Jahrbuch*, CVI (1986) 241–97 and E. Müller-Mertens, 'Reich und Hauptorte der Salier: Probleme und Fragen' in Weinfurter, *Die Salier und das Reich* i, pp. 139–58.
138. Tellenbach, 'Vom karolingischen Reichsadel', pp. 211–13.
139. MGH Diplomata Otto III, no. 9, pp. 405–6 (985).
140. Trillmich, *Thietmar. Chronik*, p. 220.
141. For example, MGH Diplomata Conrad II, no. 32, p. 35 (1025).
142. See K. Schmid, 'Zum Haus- und Herrschaftsverständnis der Salier' in Weinfurter, *Die Salier und das Reich* i, pp. 30–6. In 1027 Conrad II had deprived Duke Adalbero of claims over the patriarchate of Aquileia, another possible cause of friction; MGH Diplomata Conrad II, no. 92, pp. 125–7.
143. K. J. Leyser, 'The Crisis of Medieval Germany', *Proceedings of the British Academy* LXIX (1983) 409–43.
144. Transl. Arnold, 'From Warfare on Earth', p. 111.
145. F-J. Schmale and I. Schmale-Ott (eds), *Quellen zur Geschichte Kaiser Heinrichs IV.*, AQ vol. XII (Berlin, 1963) p. 244.
146. Schmidt, *Lampert. Annalen*, pp. 288–94.
147. Schmale and Schmale-Ott, *Quellen*, pp. 174–6.
148. Maurer, *Der Herzog von Schwaben*, pp. 218–26, and in English, B. Arnold, *Princes and Territories in Medieval Germany* (Cambridge, 1991) pp. 95–6.
149. Schmale and Schmale-Ott, *Frutolfs und Ekkehards Chroniken*, p. 316; Trillmich, *Quellen*, p. 384.
150. See K. J. Leyser, 'From Saxon Freedoms to the Freedom of Saxony: The Crisis of the Eleventh Century' in T. Reuter (ed.), *Communications and Power in Medieval Europe. The Gregorian Revolu-*

tion and Beyond (London and Rio Grande, 1994), pp. 51–67; W. Petke, 'Zur Herzogserhebung Lothars von Süpplingenburg im Jahre 1106', *Deutsches Archiv*, XLVI (1990) 60–84.

151. Translated by C. C. Mierow, *The Deeds of Frederick Barbarossa by Otto of Freising and his continuator, Rahewin*, Records of Civilization. Sources and Studies vol. XLIX (New York, 1953) p. 45.

152. R. Bartlett, *The Making of Europe. Conquest, Colonization and Cultural Change 950–1350* (London etc., 1993) pp. 60–84.

153. Possibly the custumal was revised before it was recorded in the *Codex Udalrici* in 1125; P. Jaffé (ed.), *Monumenta Bambergensia*, Bibliotheca rerum Germanicarum vol. V (Berlin, 1869) pp. 51–2.

154. MGH Diplomata Lothar III, no. 105, pp. 168–70 (1136); MGH Diplomata Frederick I, no. 91, pp. 151–3 (1154) and nos. 222 and 242, pp. 4–5, 34–6 (1158); MGH Constitutiones vol. I, no. 447, pp. 661–3 and G. Theuerkauf, 'Constitutio de expeditio Romana' in HRG vol. I, cols 634–6. On the rules for retinues of *ministeriales*, B. Arnold, *German Knighthood 1050–1300* (Oxford, 1985) pp. 76–99.

155. Schmale and Schmale-Ott, *Frutolfs und Ekkehards Chroniken*, pp. 204, 272; MGH Diplomata Lothar III, no. 34, p. 57.

156. For an account in English, see B. Arnold, *Count and Bishop in Medieval Germany. A Study of Regional Power 1100–1350*, Middle Ages Series (Philadelphia, 1991) pp. 24–43.

157. Arnold, *Princes and Territories*, pp. 88–111.

158. On the usage of fief in Germany see now S. Reynolds, *Fiefs and Vassals. The Medieval Evidence Reinterpreted* (Oxford, 1994) pp. 396–474.

159. On the Hirschberg case, Arnold, *Count and Bishop*, pp. 111–52.

160. K. Jordan, *Henry the Lion. A Biography*, transl. P. S. Falla (Oxford, 1986), pp. 89–106, 160–82.

161. G. Heinrich, 'Askanier' in LMA vol. I, cols 1109–12.

162. MGH Constitutiones vol. II, no. 197, pp. 263–5.

163. Stoob, *Helmold von Bosau, Slawenchronik*; transl. F. J. Tschan, *The Chronicle of the Slavs by Helmold, Priest of Bosau*, Records of Civilization. Sources and Studies vol. XXI (New York, 1935).

164. See W-H. Struck, 'Nassau' in HRG vol. III, cols 850–60.

165. MGH Diplomata Frederick I, no. 151, pp. 255–60 (1156).

166. On Styria at this time, K. Lechner, *Die Babenberger. Markgrafen und Herzoge von Österreich 976–1246*, Veröffentlichungen des Instituts für Österreichische Geschichtsforschung vol. XXIII (Vienna, Cologne and Graz, 1976) pp. 173–81.

167. A. Kraus, 'Das Herzogtum der Wittelsbacher: Die Grundlegung des Landes Bayern' and F. Prinz, 'Die bayerischen Dynastengeschlechter des Hochmittelalters' in H. Glaser (ed.), *Die Zeit der frühen Herzöge. Von Otto I. zu Ludwig dem Bayern*, Beiträge zur Bayerischen Geschichte und Kunst 1180–1350 (Munich and Zurich, 1980) vol. I, part 1, pp. 165–200, 253–67.
168. MGH Constitutiones vol. II, no. 427, pp. 570–9.
169. *Genealogia Ottonis II. ducis Bavariae* and *Chounradi Schirensis Chronicon* in MGH Scriptores vol. XVII, pp. 377–8, 621.
170. Goetz, 'Das Herzogtum' in Weinfurter, *Die Salier und das Reich* i, pp. 268–71.
171. Arnold, *Princes and Territories*, pp. 61–73, 152–85.
172. 'Sachsenrecht im Übergang von der Lex Saxonum zum Sachsenspiegel' in Weinfurter, *Die Salier und das Reich* iii, pp. 415–23.
173. Otto Brunner's classic account of the *Land* is now in translation by H. Kaminsky and J. Van Horn Melton as *Land and Lordship. Structures of Governance in Medieval Austria*, Middle Ages Series (Philadelphia, 1992).
174. MGH Constitutiones vol. II, no. 285, pp. 401–2 (1224), no. 304, pp. 418–20 and no. 305, p. 420 (1231).

Part II: Germany and its Neo-Roman Empire

1. Bauer and Rau, *Quellen*, p. 178; explained by J. A. Brundage, 'Widukind of Corvey and the "Non-Roman" Imperial Idea', *Mediaeval Studies*, XXII (1960) 15–26.
2. MGH Diplomata Otto I, nos. 318–29, pp. 432–44 (966); C. Erdmann, 'Das ottonische Reich als Imperium Romanum', *Deutsches Archiv*, VI (1943) 412–41.
3. H. Beumann, 'Nomen imperatoris. Studien zur Kaiseridee Karls des Grossen', *Historische Zeitschrift*, CLXXXV (1958) 515–49; J. L. Nelson, 'The Lord's Anointed and the People's Choice: Carolingian Royal Ritual' in D. Cannadine and S. Price (eds), *Rituals of Royalty. Power and Ceremonial in Traditional Societies*, Past and Present publications (Cambridge, etc. 1987) pp. 137–80 and 'Kingship and Empire in the Carolingian World' in R. McKitterick (ed.), *Carolingian Culture: Emulation and Innovation* (Cambridge, 1994) pp. 52–87.
4. *Annales Laureshamenses*, MGH Scriptores vol. I, p. 38.
5. T. Reuter, 'Plunder and Tribute in the Carolingian Empire', *Transactions of the Royal Historical Society*, Fifth Series XXXV (1985) 75–94.

6. Reynolds, *Fiefs and Vassals*, pp. 75–114.
7. J. Fleckenstein, 'Maifeld' in LMA vol. VI, col. 113. But the studies of Bernard Bachrach urge caution about overestimating Frankish military reforms: *Armies and Politics in the Early Medieval West*, Variorum Collected Studies Series (Aldershot and Brookfield, 1993) parts IX, XII–XIV.
8. Halphen, *Eginhard*, p. 42.
9. J. N. D. Kelly, *The Oxford Dictionary Of Popes* (Oxford and New York, 1986) pp. 89–92; since 1961 Stephen III has been renumbered II.
10. T. F. X. Noble, 'Pippinische Schenkung' in LMA vol. VI, cols 2171–2.
11. H. Fuhrmann (ed.), *Das Constitutum Constantini*, MGH Fontes iuris Germanici antiqui, vol. X (Hanover, 1968).
12. Translation from R. Folz, *The Concept of Empire in Western Europe from the Fifth to the Fourteenth Century*, transl. S. A. Ogilvie (London, 1969) pp. 178–9.
13. T. F. X. Noble, *The Republic of St Peter. The Birth of the Papal State, 680–825*, The Middle Ages (Philadelphia, 1984) esp. pp. 138–83, 256–91.
14. Folz, *Concept of Empire*, pp. 13–15.
15. Translation by L. Thorpe from *Einhard and Notker the Stammerer. Two Lives of Charlemagne* (Harmondsworth, 1969) p. 93.
16. The classic is by Robert Folz, *Le Souvenir et la Légende de Charlemagne dans l'Empire germanique médiévale*, Publications de l'Université de Dijon vol. VII (Paris, 1950).
17. Folz, *Concept of Empire*, pp. 180–1 (799 source); E. Dümmler (ed.), *Epistolae Karolini Aevi*, vol. II, MGH Epistolae vol. VI (Berlin, 1895) no. 148, p. 241 (798).
18. Halphen, *Eginhard*, p. 80; Pertz and Kurze, *Annales regni Francorum*, p. 112; Loyn and Percival, *Reign of Charlemagne*, p. 26; H. Turtledove (ed.), *The Chronicle of Theophanes*, The Middle Ages (Philadelphia, 1982), p. 155.
19. Politically, that is; see E.-D. Hehl, '798 – ein erstes Zitat aus der Konstantinischen Schenkung', *Deutsches Archiv*, XLVII (1991) 1–17.
20. Folz, *Concept of Empire*, p. 181.
21. Loyn and Percival, *Reign of Charlemagne*, p. 118.
22. Boretius, *Capitularia regum Francorum* vol. I, no. 161, pp. 322–4; see Noble, *Republic of St Peter*, pp. 308–22.

23. See the several relevant papers in P. Godman and R. Collins (eds), *Charlemagne's Heir. New Perspectives on the Reign of Louis the Pious (814–840)* (Oxford, 1990).

24. Folz, *Concept of Empire*, p. 182.

25. On this phase, see P. Llewellyn, *Rome in the Dark Ages* (London, 1971) pp. 286–315.

26. *Kaiser, Rom und Renovatio. Studien zur Geschichte des römischen Erneuerungsgedankens vom Ende des karolingischen Reiches bis zum Investiturstreit*, 3rd edn (Darmstadt, 1975) pp. 44–67.

27. Bauer and Rau, *Quellen*, pp. 496–8.

28. Schramm, *Kaiser, Rom und Renovatio*, pp. 79–82.

29. Bauer and Rau, *Quellen*, p. 76.

30. Bauer and Rau, *Quellen*, p. 158.

31. H. Beumann, 'Imperator Romanorum, rex gentium. Zu Widukind III 76' in N. Kamp and J. Wollasch (eds), *Tradition als historische Kraft* (Berlin and New York, 1982) pp. 214–30.

32. Report preserved in *Annalista Saxo*, MGH Scriptores vol. VI, p. 616.

33. Schramm, *Kaiser, Rom und Renovatio*, pp. 68–70.

34. Bauer and Rau, *Quellen*, pp. 216, 498.

35. MGH Diplomata Otto I, no. 235, pp. 322–7, transl. Hill, *Medieval Monarchy*, pp. 149–52; see H. Zimmermann, 'Privilegium Ottonianum' in HRG vol. III, cols 2025–7.

36. From Hill, *Medieval Monarchy in Action*, p. 121 (transl. M. B. Bergman, 1942).

37. F. A. Wright (ed.), *The Works of Liudprand of Cremona*, Broadway Medieval Library (London, 1930) p. 217.

38. G. Zucchetti (ed.), *Il Chronicon di Benedetto monaco di S. Andrea del Sorate*, Fonti per la storia d'Italia (Rome, 1920) p. 186; Schramm, *Kaiser, Rom und Renovatio*, pp. 64–7.

39. Wright, *Works of Liudprand*, pp. 237, 249; on this phase see K. J. Leyser, 'The Tenth Century in Byzantine–Western Relationships' in D. Baker (ed.), *Relations between East and West in the Middle Ages* (Edinburgh, 1973) pp. 29–63.

40. A. von Euw and P. Schreiner (eds), *Kaiserin Theophanu: Begegnung des Ostens und Westens um die Wende des ersten Jahrtausends*, 2 vols (Cologne, 1991); Davids (ed.), *The Empress Theophano*.

41. Trillmich, *Thietmar. Chronik*, pp. 106–8.

42. H. Enzensberger, 'Capo Colonne, Schlacht von' in LMA vol. II, col. 1484.

43. Schramm, *Kaiser, Rom und Renovatio*, pp. 116–18, 155–6.
44. K. Strecker (ed.), *Die lateinischen Dichter des deutschen Mittelalters*, MGH Poetae Latini Medii Aevi vol. V (Dublin and Zürich, 1970) p. 480; Schramm, *Kaiser, Rom und Renovatio*, pp. 119–31 and R. Pauler, *Das Regnum Italiae in ottonischer Zeit. Markgrafen, Grafen und Bischöfe als politische Kräfte*, Bibliothek des Deutschen Historischen Instituts in Rom vol. LIV (Tübingen, 1982) pp. 33–45.
45. J. Fried, *Otto III. und Boleslaw Chrobry. Widmungsbild des Aachener Evangeliars, der 'Akt von Gnesen' und das frühe polnische und ungarische Königtum* (Stuttgart, 1989); E. Eickhoff, 'Basilianer und Ottonen', *Historisches Jahrbuch*, CXIV (1994) 10–46; K. Görich, *Otto III., Romanus, Saxonicus et Italicus. Kaiserliche Rompolitik und sächsische Historiographie*, Historische Forschungen, vol. XVIII (Sigmaringen, 1993).
46. *Annales Quedlinburgenses*, MGH Scriptores vol. III, p. 77.
47. Folz, *Concept of Empire*, p. 185.
48. F. J. Tschan, *Saint Bernward of Hildesheim*, vol. I, *His Life and Times*, Publications in Mediaeval Studies vol. VI (Notre Dame, 1942) p. 110.
49. Reuter, *Germany in the Early Middle Ages*, p. 171.
50. Trillmich, *Thietmar. Chronik*, p. 352.
51. MGH Diplomata Henry II, no. 427, pp. 542–8 (1020).
52. Mommsen and Morrison, *Imperial Lives and Letters*, pp. 3–51; H. Mayr-Harting, *Ottonian Book Illumination. An Historical Study*, Part I, *Themes* (London and New York, 1991) pp. 57–68.
53. Schmid, 'Zum Haus- und Herrschaftsverständnis der Salier' and Weinfurter, 'Herrschaftslegitimation und Königsautorität' in Weinfurter, *Die Salier und das Reich* i, pp. 21–54, 55–96.
54. M. Schulze-Dörrlamm, *Die Kaiserkrone Konrads II. (1024–1039): Eine archäologische Untersuchung zu Alter und Herkunft der Reichskrone*, Römisch-Germanisches Zentralmuseum. Monographien vol. XXIII (Sigmaringen, 1992).
55. MGH Diplomata Conrad II, no. 198, p. 263 (1033).
56. Schramm, *Kaiser, Rom und Renovatio*, pp. 203–4, 227.
57. Trillmich, *Quellen*, pp. 558–60, 664–8, 570–2, 598–606; on the problem see G. Tabacco, *The Struggle for Power in Medieval Italy. Structures of Political Rule*, transl. R. B. Jensen, Cambridge Medieval Textbooks (Cambridge etc., 1989) esp. pp. 144–236.
58. Mommsen and Morrison, *Imperial Lives and Letters*, p. 72.

59. For a cogent review of these issues, see U-R. Blumenthal, *The Investiture Controversy. Church and Monarchy from the Ninth to the Twelfth Century*, The Middle Ages (Philadelphia, 1988) pp. 64–134.
60. Trillmich, *Quellen*, p. 690 (ed. Buchner).
61. 'Lay Investiture and its Relation to the Conflict of Empire and Papacy', *Proceedings of the British Academy*, XXV (1939) 217–47.
62. E. Emerton (ed.), *The Correspondence of Pope Gregory VII. Selected Letters from the Registrum*, Records of Civilization. Sources and Studies (New York, 1932), p. 87.
63. Mommsen and Morrison, *Imperial Lives and Letters*, pp. 146–9.
64. Caspar, *Das Register Gregors VII.*, pp. 201–8.
65. Mommsen and Morrison, *Imperial Lives and Letters*, pp. 150–1; T. Struve, 'Gottschalk von Aachen' in LMA vol. IV, cols 1610–11.
66. See I. S. Robinson, *Authority and Resistance in the Investiture Contest. The Polemical Literature of the late Eleventh Century* (Manchester and New York, 1978) and the sources in the indispensible MGH edition, E. Dümmler *et al.* (eds), *Libelli de Lite imperatorum et pontificium saeculis XI. et XII. conscripti*, 3 vols (Hanover, 1891–97).
67. Emerton, *Correspondence of Pope Gregory VII*, pp. 149–52.
68. Quoted in T. Struve, 'Die Wende des 11. Jahrhunderts. Symptome eines Epochenwandels im Spiegel der Geschichtsschreibung', *Historisches Jahrbuch*, CXII (1992) 352, 354.
69. Texts in MGH Constitutiones vol. I, nos 107–8, pp. 159–61; see P. Classen, 'Das Wormser Konkordat in der deutschen Verfassungsgeschichte' in J. Fleckenstein (ed.), *Investiturstreit und Reichsverfassung*, Vorträge und Forschungen vol. XVII (Sigmaringen, 1973) pp. 411–60 and R. L. Benson, *The Bishop-Elect, A Study in Medieval Ecclesiastical Office* (Princeton, 1968) pp. 228–50, 303–14.
70. Emerton, *Correspondence of Pope Gregory VII*, pp. 169, 172.
71. Mommsen and Morrison, *Imperial Lives and Letters*, pp. 151–4.
72. E. Bussi, 'Bologna' in HRG vol. I, cols 485–8; A. Söllner, 'Römisches Recht in Deutschland' in HRG vol. IV, cols 1126–8 rightly plays down the actual effect in Germany at this time.
73. MGH Constitutiones, vol. I, no. 167, p. 233 (1158).
74. MGH Diplomata Frederick I, no. 492, p. 416 (1165) and no. 606, p. 92 (1173).

75. MGH Diplomata Frederick I, nos. 284–5, pp. 95–8 (1159); transl. Mierow, *Deeds of Frederick Barbarossa*, pp. 300–1.

76. The classic study is P. Rassow's *Honor Imperii*. *Die neue Politik Friedrich Barbarossas 1152–1159*, new edn (Munich and Darmstadt, 1973).

77. A. Haverkamp (ed.), *Friedrich Barbarossa. Handlungsspielräume und Wirkungsweisen des staufischen Kaisers*, Vorträge und Forschungen, vol. XL (Sigmaringen, 1992) and B. Töpfer, 'Kaiser Friedrich Barbarossa – Grundlinien seiner Politik' in E. Engel and B. Töpfer (eds), *Kaiser Friedrich Barbarossa. Landesausbau – Aspekte seiner Politik – Wirkung*, Forschungen zur Mittelalterlichen Geschichte, vol. XXXVI (Weimar, 1994), pp. 9–30.

78. D. Abulafia, *Frederick II. A Medieval Emperor* (London etc., 1988) pp. 132–407.

79. See my forthcoming chapter 'The Western Empire, 1125–1198' in D. Luscombe and J. Riley-Smith (eds), *New Cambridge Medieval History*, vol. IV, part 2.

80. Schramm, *Kaiser, Rom und Renovatio*, pp. 238–50; C. Morris, *The Papal Monarchy. The Western Church from 1050 to 1250*, Oxford History of the Christian Church (Oxford, 1989) pp. 79–133, 154–73.

81. S. Chodorow, 'Paschal II, Henry V, and the Origins of the Crisis of 1111' in J. R. Sweeney and S. Chodorow (eds) *Popes, Teachers, and Canon Law in the Middle Ages* (Ithaca and London, 1989) pp. 3–25.

82. MGH Diplomata Frederick I, nos 51–2, pp. 86–9 (1153).

83. R. L. Benson, G. Constable and C. D. Lanham (eds), *Renaissance and Renewal in the Twelfth Century* (Oxford, 1982) pp. 299–386.

84. Folz, *Concept of Empire*, pp. 94–7, 192–4.

85. Mierow, *Deeds of Frederick Barbarossa*, pp. 185–6.

86. *Annales Laudenses*, MGH Scriptores vol. XVIII, p. 607.

87. Folz, *Concept of Empire*, p. 102.

88. MGH Constitutiones vol. I, nos 181–90, pp. 251–70 (1159–60) for the dossier.

89. MGH Constitutiones vol. I, nos 259–73, pp. 360–73.

90. J. Sayers, *Innocent III. Leader of Europe 1198–1216*, The Medieval World (London and New York, 1994) p. 197.

91. MGH Diplomata Frederick I, no. 285, p. 97 (1159).

92. P. Csendes, *Heinrich VI.*, Gestalten des Mittelalters und der Renaissance (Darmstadt, 1993) pp. 171–8.

93. F-R. Erkens, *Der Erzbischof von Köln und die deutsche Königswahl.* *Studien zur Kölner Kirchengeschichte, zum Krönungsrecht und zur Verfassung des Reiches,* Studien zur Kölner Kirchengeschichte, vol. XXI (Siegburg, 1987) pp. 17–40; B. U. Hucker, *Kaiser Otto IV.,* MGH Schriften, vol. XXXIV (Hanover, 1990) pp. 22–35.

94. Folz, *Concept of Empire,* pp. 75–89; Morris, *Papal Monarchy,* pp. 117 38.

95. MGH Constitutiones vol. II, no. 398, pp. 505–7 (1202).

96. Caspar, *Das Register Gregors VII.,* vol. I, pp. 201–8.

97. Hucker, *Kaiser Otto IV.,* pp. 95–231.

98. For the best account of this phase in imperial politics, see W. Stürner, *Friedrich II.,* part 1, *Die Königsherrschaft in Sizilien und Deutschland 1194–1220,* Gestalten des Mittelalters und der Renaissance (Darmstadt, 1992) pp. 122–55.

99. In print he is often designated as Henry (VII) to differentiate him from Emperor Henry VII (1308–13). The practice is unhelpful. To my knowledge, Louis IV the Child (900–11) is never muddled with Louis IV the Bavarian (1314–47) and prudent historiography has simply eschewed a reign-number for Rudolf of Rheinfelden (1077–80) turning Rudolf of Habsburg (1273–91) into Rudolf I.

100. MGH Constitutiones vol. II, no. 398, p. 506.

101. For example, P. Partner, *The Lands of St Peter. The Papal State in the Middle Ages and the Early Renaissance* (London, 1972) pp. 229–65.

102. For a warning against too extravagant an approach, see D. Abulafia, 'Kantorowicz and Frederick II', *History,* LXII (1977) 193–210.

103. H. M. Schaller, 'Die Kaiseridee Friedrichs II.' in J. Fleckenstein (ed.), *Probleme um Friedrich II.,* Vorträge und Forschungen vol. XVI (Sigmaringen, 1974) pp. 109–34.

104. MGH Constitutiones vol. II, no. 197, p. 263 (1235).

105. E. Borsook, *Messages in Mosaic. The Royal Programmes of Norman Sicily (1130–1187),* Clarendon Studies in the History of Art (Oxford, 1990).

106. Schaller, 'Kaiseridee', p. 118.

107. MGH Constitutiones vol. II, no. 122, p. 166; H. E. Mayer, *The Crusades,* transl. J. Gillingham, 2nd edn (Oxford, 1988), p. 237.

108. R. M. Kloos, 'Nikolaus von Bari, eine neue Quelle zur Entwicklung der Kaiseridee unter Friedrich II.', *Deutsches Archiv,* XI

(1954–5) 166–90. My rendering uses the Jerusalem Bible for the quotations.

109. Godfrey of Viterbo, *Speculum regum* and *Pantheon*, MGH Scriptores vol. XXII, pp. 21–93, 107–307.

110. Schaller, 'Kaiseridee', p. 125.

111. B. Koehler, 'Goldbulle von Rimini' in HRG vol. I, cols 1737–9; L. Weinrich, *Quellen zur deutschen Verfassungs-, Wirtschafts- und Sozialgeschichte bis 1250*, AQ vol. XXXII (Darmstadt, 1977) no. 104, pp. 404–10.

112. Abulafia, *Frederick II*, pp. 211–12.

113. E. H. Kantorowicz, *The King's Two Bodies. A Study in Mediaeval Political Theology* (Princeton, 1957) pp. 131–2.

114. MGH Constitutiones vol. II, no. 196, pp. 241–2.

115. K. Rodenberg, *Epistolae Saeculi XIII e regestis Pontificum Romanorum*, vol. I, MGH (Berlin, 1883) no. 750, p. 653.

116. H. M. Schaller, 'Die Kanzlei Kaiser Friedrichs II. Ihr Personal und ihr Sprachstil', *Archiv für Diplomatik*, IV (1958) 307–13.

117. R. Vaughan (ed.), *Chronicles of Matthew Paris. Monastic Life in the Thirteenth Century* (Gloucester and New York, 1986) pp. 81–2.

118. MGH Constitutiones vol. II, no. 274, pp. 382–9 (1250).

119. MGH Constitutiones vol. III, no. 77, pp. 64–5 (1275). See now E. Boshof and F-R. Erkens (eds), *Rudolf von Habsburg, 1273–1291. Eine Königsherrschaft zwischen Tradition und Wandel* (Weimar and Vienna, 1993).

120. Grundmann and Heimpel, *Schriften des Alexander von Roes*, pp. 57–8, 76–7.

121. See now A. Black, *Political Thought in Europe, 1250–1450*, Cambridge Medieval Textbooks (Cambridge, 1992) pp. 85–116.

122. Trillmich, *Thietmar. Chronik*, p. 20.

123. Mommsen and Morrison, *Imperial Lives and Letters*, p. 72; on tribute see Reuter, *Germany in the Early Middle Ages*, pp. 165–6, 178–9.

124. K. J. Leyser, 'Ottonian Government', *English Historical Review*, XCVI (1981) 752.

125. B. Kluge, 'Münze und Geld' in *Das Reich der Salier 1024–1125. Katalog zur Ausstellung des Landes Rheinland-Pfalz* (Sigmaringen, 1992) p. 188.

126. MGH Diplomata Frederick I, no. 848, p. 72 (1183); C. Brühl, 'Fodrum (regale)' in HRG vol. II cols 1146–9; W. Metz, *Staufische Güterverzeichnisse. Untersuchungen zur Verfassungs- und*

Wirtschaftsgeschichte des 12. und 13. Jahrhunderts (Berlin, 1964) pp. 6–51.

127. MGH Constitutiones vol. III, pp. 2–4; Metz, *Staufische Güterverzeichnisse*, pp. 98–115.

128. Reuter, *Germany in the Early Middle Ages*, pp. 229–36; A. C. Schlunk, *Königsmacht und Krongut. Die Machtgrundlage des deutschen Königtums im 13. Jahrhundert – und eine neue historische Methode* (Stuttgart, 1988).

129. The texts translated by Bernard McGinn in *Visions of the End. Apocalyptic Traditions in the Middle Ages*, Records of Civilization. Sources and Studies vol. XCVI (New York, 1979) provide a good introduction.

130. G. Fowden, *Empire to Commonwealth. Consequences of Monotheism in Late Antiquity* (Princeton, 1993) pp. 86–93.

131. D. Obolensky, *The Byzantine Commonwealth. Eastern Europe, 500 – 1453*, History of Civilisation (London, 1971) pp. 102–33, 180 – 236; J. M. Hussey, *The Orthodox Church in the Byzantine Empire*, Oxford History of the Christian Church (Oxford, 1986) pp. 90 – 101, 114–19.

132. Hill, *Medieval Monarchy in Action*, p. 185 and H. Nottarp, 'Bamberg' in HRG vol. I, col. 292.

133. Trillmich, *Thietmar. Chronik*, p. 446.

134. R. Landes, 'Lest the Millenium be Fulfilled: Apocalyptic Expectations and the Pattern of Western Chronography 100 – 800 CE' in W. Verbeke, D. Verhelst and A. Welkenhuysen (ed.), *The Use and Abuse of Eschatology in the Middle Ages*, Mediaevalia Lovaniensia, Series 1, Studia XV (Leuven, 1988) pp. 137–211, here 201.

135. Boretius, *Capitularia regum Francorum*, vol. I, no. 22 (ch. 82) p. 62.

136. 'Endzeiterwartung um die Jahrtausendwende', *Deutsches Archiv*, XLV (1989) 381–473.

137. Benzo of Alba, *Ad Heinricum IV Imperatorem Libri VII*, MGH Scriptores vol. XI, pp. 591–681; see Schramm, *Kaiser, Rom und Renovatio*, pp. 258–74.

138. H-D. Kahl, 'Ludus de Antichristo' in LMA vol. V, cols 2169–70.

139. H. M. Schaller, 'Endzeit-Erwartung und Antichrist-Vorstellung in der Politik des 13. Jahrhunderts' in *Festschrift für Hermann Heimpel zum 70. Geburtstag* vol. II, Veröffentlichungen des Max-Planck-Instituts für Geschichte, vol. XXXVI, part 2 (Göttingen, 1972) pp. 924–47.

140. M. Reeves, *The Influence of Prophecy in the Later Middle Ages. A Study in Joachimism* (Oxford, 1969) pp. 306–11; R. E. Lerner, 'Frederick II, Alive, Aloft and Allayed, in Franciscan–Joachite Eschatology' in Verbeke, *et al.* (eds), *Use and Abuse of Eschatology*, pp. 359–84.
141. McGinn, *Visions of the End*, pp. 169, 175.
142. *Hessonis relatio de concilio Remensi*, MGH Libelli de lite, vol. III, pp. 21–8.
143. *Chronica Monasterii Casinensis*, book 4, MGH Scriptores vol. XXXIV, p. 590.
144. H. Böhm (ed.), *Die Gedichte Walthers von der Vogelweide* (Berlin, 1955) pp. 25, 139.
145. Abulafia, *Frederick II*, pp. 408–35.
146. *Sächsische Weltchronik. Erste bairische Fortsetzung*, MGH Deutsche Chroniken vol. II, p. 328.
147. P. G. Ricci (ed.), *Dante Alighieri. Monarchia* (Milan, 1965) pp. 214–17.

Part III: Kingship and Governance in Medieval Germany

1. J. M. Wallace-Hadrill, 'Germanic Kingship and the Romans' in his *Early Germanic Kingship in England and on the Continent* (Oxford, 1971) pp. 1–20.
2. P. S. Barnwell, *Emperor, Prefects and Kings. The Roman West, 395–565* (London, 1992) pp. 71–175.
3. K. Randsborg (ed.), *The Birth of Europe: Archaeology and Social Development in the First Millenium A.D.*, Analecta Romana Instituti Danici, supplement XVI (Rome, 1989).
4. Good discussion in H. Quaritsch (ed.), *Gegenstand und Begriffe der Verfassungsgeschichtsschreibung*, Beihefte zu 'Der Staat'. Zeitschrift für Staatslehre, öffentliches Recht und Verfassungsgeschichte, vol. VI (Berlin, 1983).
5. For example, Wolfram, *History of the Goths*, pp. 211–22, 286–95, 327–32 and Wood, *Merovingian Kingdoms*, pp. 55–70, 102–19, 140–58, 322–44.
6. For such developments, see P. D. King, 'The Barbarian Kingdoms' in Burns, *Cambridge History of Medieval Political Thought*, pp. 123–53, and J. L. Nelson, *Politics and Ritual in Early Medieval Europe* (London and Ronceverte, 1986).
7. Halphen, *Eginhard*, p. 10, transl. Thorpe, *Einhard and Notker*, pp. 55–6; see J. M. Wallace-Hadrill, *The Long-Haired Kings and Other Studies in Frankish History* (London, 1962) pp. 231–48.

8. Good discussion by R. Wenskus in *Sächsischer Stammesadel und fränkischer Reichsadel*, Abhandlungen der Akademie der Wissenschaften in Göttingen, phil.-hist. Klasse, Series 3, vol. XCIII (Göttingen, 1976).
9. T. Reuter, 'The End of Carolingian Military Expansion' in Godman and Collins, *Charlemagne's Heir*, pp. 391–405.
10. F. Prinz, *Klerus und Krieg im früheren Mittelalter. Untersuchungen zur Rolle der Kirche beim Aufbau der Königsherrschaft*, Monographien zur Geschichte des Mittelalters, vol. II (Stuttgart, 1971).
11. MGH Diplomata Arnolf, no. 155, pp. 235–6 (897) and Louis the Child, no. 58, pp. 185–7 (908).
12. Reuter, *Annals of Fulda*, p.95.
13. S. Krüger, *Studien zur sächsischen Grafschaftsverfassung im 9. Jahrhundert*, Studien und Vorarbeiten zum Historischen Atlas Niedersachsens, vol. XIX (Göttingen, 1950).
14. D. Willoweit, 'Immunität' in HRG vol. II, cols 313–30.
15. Boretius and Krause, *Capitularia regum Francorum* vol. II, no. 281, p. 358, In her *Fiefs and Vassals*, pp. 112–13, 402–3, Susan Reynolds raises objections to the more traditional view given here.
16. Reuter, *Annals of Fulda*, pp. 69–75.
17. Reuter, *Annals of Fulda*, p. 115.
18. Boretius and Krause, *Capitularia regum Francorum* vol. II, no. 252, pp. 196–247.
19. On this period see Reuter, *Germany in the Early Middle Ages* pp. 115–37.
20. Boretius and Krause, *Capitularia regum Francorum* vol. II, no. 253, pp. 249–52.
21. E. Kaufmann, 'Königsbann' in HRG vol. II, cols 1023–5; A. Waas, *Herrschaft und Staat im Deutschen Frühmittelalter*, Historische Studien vol. CCCV, 2nd edn (Darmstadt, 1965) pp. 29–106; but J. F. Niermeyer, in *Mediae Latinitatis Lexicon Minus* (Leiden, 1976) pp. 81–4, records the extremely varied usages for *bannus*.
22. H. Fuhrmann, 'Die Synode von Hohenaltheim (916) – quellenkundlich betrachtet', *Deutsches Archiv*, XLIII (1987) 440–68; E-D. Hehl, *Die Konzilien Deutschlands und Reichsitaliens 916–1001*, MGH Concilia vol. VI, part 1 (Hanover, 1987) ch. 23, p. 30.
23. Very useful is H-W. Goetz, 'Der letzte "Karolinger"? Die Regierung Konrads I. im Spiegel seiner Urkunden', *Archiv für Diplomatik*, XXVI (1982) 56–125.

24. The classic analysis is by Helmut Beumann, *Widukind von Korvei. Untersuchungen zur Geschichtsschreibung und Ideengeschichte des 10. Jahrhunderts*, Abhandlungen über Corveyer Geschichtsschreibung, vol. III (Weimar, 1950).

25. Bauer and Rau, *Quellen*, pp. 62–4, 76, 158.

26. For guidance, Reuter, *Germany*, pp. 137–47.

27. C. Erdmann, 'Die Burgenordnung Heinrichs I.', *Deutsches Archiv*, VI (1943) 59–101.

28. Bauer and Rau, *Quellen*, p. 68.

29. G. P. Fehring, *The Archaeology of Medieval Germany: An Introduction*, transl. R. Samson, Studies in Archaeology (London and New York, 1991) p. 12.

30. For example, G. Althoff, *Amicitiae und Pacta. Bündnis, Einung, Politik und Gebetsdenken im beginnenden 10. Jahrhundert*, MGH Schriften, vol. XXXVII (Hanover, 1992) and the literature cited there.

31. Bauer and Rau, *Quellen*, p. 196.

32. Bauer and Rau, *Quellen*, pp. 118, 136.

33. Bauer and Rau, *Quellen*, p. 56.

34. P. E. Schramm and F. Mütherich, *Denkmale der deutschen Könige und Kaiser. Ein Beitrag zur Herrschergeschichte von Karl dem Grossen bis Friedrich II.*, Veröffentlichungen des Zentralinstituts für Kunstgeschichte in München, vol. II (Munich, 1962) pp. 139, 170; Bauer and Rau, *Quellen*, pp. 156, 426–30.

35. In English, see Leyser, *Rule and Conflict*, pp. 9–47; Reuter, *Germany*, pp. 148–54; J. W. Bernhardt, *Itinerant Kingship and Royal Monasteries in Early Medieval Germany, c. 936–1075*, Cambridge Studies in Medieval Life and Thought, Fourth Series (Cambridge, 1993) pp. 16–22.

36. Bauer and Rau, *Quellen*, p. 58.

37. Hehl, *Konzilien*, pp. 57–74, 97–114.

38. Hill, *Medieval Monarchy in Action*, pp. 114–15.

39. On their cultural force, see R. McKitterick, *The Frankish Church and the Carolingian Reforms, 789–895* (London, 1977).

40. P. Jaffé (ed.), *Monumenta Moguntina*, Bibliotheca Rerum Germanicarum, vol. III (Berlin, 1866) p. 348; H. Hoffmann, 'Grafschaften in Bischofshand', *Deutsches Archiv*, XLVI (1990) 375–480.

41. Transl. Leyser, *Medieval Germany and its Neighbours*, p. 139.

42. *The Origins of Courtliness: Civilizing Trends and the Formation of Courtly Ideals 939–1210*, The Middle Ages (Philadelphia, 1985) esp. pp. 19–81.

43. MGH Diplomata Otto I, nos. 1–44, pp. 89–130 (936–41).
44. H. Zielinski, *Der Reichsepiskopat in spätottonischer und salischer Zeit, 1002–1125*, part I (Stuttgart, 1984); T. Reuter, 'The "Imperial Church System" of the Ottonian and Salian Rulers: a Reconsideration', *Journal of Ecclesiastical History*, XXXIII (1982) 347–74.
45. MGH Diplomata Henry II, no. 433, p. 554; Luke 12, 48.
46. Hill, *Medieval Monarchy in Action*, p. 189.
47. H. Mayr-Harting, 'The Church of Magdeburg: its Trade and Its Town in the Tenth and Early Eleventh Centuries' in D. Abulafia, M. Franklin and M. Rubin (eds), *Church and City 1000–1500. Essays in Honour of Christopher Brooke* (Cambridge, 1992) pp. 129–50.
48. MGH Diplomata Otto I, no. 366, pp. 502–3; transl. Hill, *Medieval Monarchy in Action*, p. 162.
49. H. Fichtenau, *Arenga. Spätantike und Mittelalter im Spiegel von Urkundenformeln*, Mitteilungen des Instituts für Österreichische Geschichtsforschung, Ergänzungsband XVIII (Graz and Cologne, 1957); down to 1197 they have been collected by F. Hausmann and A. Gawlik, *Arengenverzeichnis zu den Königs- und Kaiserurkunden von den Merowingern bis Heinrich VI.*, MGH Hilfsmittel, vol. IX (Munich, 1987).
50. Brun of Querfurt, *Vita Sancti Adalberti*, MGH Scriptores, vol. IV, p. 596.
51. MGH Diplomata Henry II, no. 143, pp. 169–72 (1007), transl. Hill, *Medieval Monarchy in Action*, pp. 185–7; see K. Schwarz and F. Geldner, 'Bamberg' in LMA vol. I, cols 1394–1401.
52. They are attested in MGH Diplomata Conrad II, nos 206 A & B, pp. 279–81 (1034) and later sources.
53. See J. Dahlhaus, 'Zu den Anfängen von Pfalz und Stiften in Goslar' in Weinfurter, *Die Salier und das Reich* ii, pp. 403–5.
54. H-W. Klewitz, *Die Festkrönungen der deutschen Könige*, Libelli, vol. CXXXIII (Darmstadt, 1966) first published in 1939.
55. Böhm, *Gedichte Walthers*, pp. 22–4.
56. M. Groten, 'Von der Gebetsverbrüderung zum Königskanonikat. Zu Vorgeschichte und Entwicklung des Königskanonikate an den Dom- und Stiftskirchen des deutschen Reiches', *Historisches Jahrbuch*, CIII (1983) 1–34.
57. On this transition, see now J. Laudage, 'Reich und Kirche in der Salierzeit', *Historisches Jahrbuch*, CXIV (1994) 427–44.
58. Kallfelz, *Lebensbeschreibungen*, pp. 35–260.
59. Trillmich, *Quellen*, pp. 326–432.

220 NOTES

60. G. Frech, 'Die deutschen Päpste – Kontinuität und Wandel' in Weinfurter, *Die Salier und das Reich* ii, p. 306.

61. Kallfelz, *Lebensbeschreibungen*, pp. 372–440.

62. MGH Constitutiones vol. i, no. 90, pp. 140–2; J. Fried, 'Der Regalienbegriff im 11. und 12. Jahrhundert', *Deutsches Archiv*, xxix (1973) 450–528.

63. Kallfelz, *Lebensbeschreibungen*, pp. 550–616.

64. Schmidt and Schmale, *Gesta Frederici*, p. 288.

65. See especially J. Fleckenstein, *Die Hofkapelle der deutschen Könige*, MGH Schriften, vol. xvi, 2 parts (Stuttgart, 1959–66).

66. The modern foundations of such study were laid by Theodor Sickel and Harry Bresslau.

67. See MGH Diplomata Henry III, no. 239, pp. 318–20 (1049), then Frederick I, no. 184, pp. 308–11 (1157).

68. MGH Diplomata Conrad I, no. 3, pp. 3–4 (912).

69. For example, MGH Diplomata Otto I, no. 207, pp. 285–6 (960).

70. MGH Diplomata Otto I, no. 175, pp. 256–7 (955) and no. 182, pp. 265–6 (956); nos. 419 A and B, pp. 571–4 (972).

71. At MGH Diplomata Otto III, pp. 881–3 (appendix for Otto I, no. 423 A).

72. Trillmich, *Thietmar. Chronik*, p. 94; D. Brennecke, 'Kempfe' in HRG vol. ii, cols 700–1. See R. Bartlett, *Trial by Fire and Water. The Medieval Judicial Ordeal* (Oxford, 1986), pp. 103–26.

73. Bauer and Rau, *Quellen*, pp. 94–6.

74. H. Krause, 'Gesetzgebung' in HRG vol. i, cols 1608–14.

75. W. A. Eckhardt, 'Kapitularien' in HRG vol. ii, cols 623–9; H. Mordek, 'Kapitularien' in LMA vol. v, cols 943–6.

76. Hehl, *Konzilien*, pp. 135–63 (948) and pp. 178–84 (951).

77. MGH Constitutiones vol. i, nos 28–9, pp. 58–61 (1005, 1007); nos 40–2, pp. 85–6 (1027) no. 51, pp. 97–100 (1049).

78. MGH Constitutiones vol. i, no. 13, pp. 27–30.

79. B. Bretholz (ed.), *Die Chronik der Böhmen des Cosmas von Prag*, MGH Scriptores, New Series, vol. ii, 2nd edn (Berlin, 1955) p. 94.

80. Buchner, *Herimanni Augiensis Chronicon* (in Trillmich, *Quellen*) p. 678: *Ungarios petentes lege Baioarica donavit; Annales Altahenses Maiores*, MGH Scriptores, vol. xx, p. 800: *concessit rex scita Teutonica*.

81. MGH Diplomata Otto III, no. 112, pp. 126–7.

82. MGH Diplomata Henry II, nos 501, pp. 639–41 (1023) and 507, pp. 648–50 (1024), the latter transl. Hill, *Medieval Monarchy in Action*, pp. 190–2.

83. MGH Constitutiones, vol. I, no. 438, pp. 640–4, esp. ch. 30; see R. Kaiser and M. Kerner, 'Burchard I., Bischof von Worms' in LMA vol. II, cols 946–51.
84. MGH Diplomata Conrad II, no. 216, pp. 294–6; for comment see Weinfurter, 'Herrschaftslegitimation' in Weinfurter, *Die Salier und das Reich* i, pp. 57–60 and T. Zotz, 'Die Formierung der Ministerialität', ibid. iii, pp. 27–30.
85. Trillmich, *Thietmar. Chronik*, pp. 306, 356–60.
86. Buchner, *Herimanni* in Trillmich, *Quellen*, p. 676.
87. H. Hoffmann, *Gottesfriede und Treuga Dei*, MGH Schriften, vol. XX (Stuttgart, 1964); V. Achter, 'Gottesfrieden' in HRG vol. I, cols 1762–5; R. Kaiser, 'Gottesfrieden' in LMA vol. IV, cols 1587–92.
88. See also Keller, *Zwischen regionaler Begrenzung*, pp. 140–2, 320–1.
89. MGH Constitutiones, vol. I, no. 424, pp. 603–5, taken up almost word for word at Mainz in 1085. E. Kaufmann, 'Landfrieden I (Landfriedensgesetzgebung)' in HRG vol. II cols 1451–65 and H. Holzhauer, 'Landfrieden II (Landfrieden und Landfriedensbruch)' cols 1465–85.
90. MGH Constitutiones, vol. I, no. 426, pp. 608–9 (1084).
91. Schmale and Schmale-Ott, *Quellen*, pp. 438–40; Mommsen and Morrison, *Imperial Lives and Letters*, pp. 120–1.
92. MGH Constitutiones, vol. I, no. 74, pp. 125–6; E. Wadle, 'Heinrich IV. und die deutsche Friedensbewegung' in J. Fleckenstein (ed.), *Investiturstreit und Reichsverfassung*, Vorträge und Forschungen vol. XVII (Sigmaringen, 1973) 141–73.
93. MGH Diplomata Frederick I, no. 25, pp. 39–44 (1152).
94. *Annales Isingrimi Maiores*, MGH Scriptores vol. XVII, p. 313.
95. F. Merzbacher, 'Hochgerichtsbarkeit', 'Landgericht' and 'Landrichter' in HRG vol. II, cols 172–5, 1495–1501, 1545–7.
96. MGH Diplomata Frederick I, no. 988, pp. 273–7 (1186 or 1188); O. Holder-Egger and B. von Simson (eds), *Die Chronik des Propstes Burchard von Ursberg*, MGH Scriptores in usum scholarum vol. XVI, 2nd edn (Hanover and Leipzig, 1916) p. 65.
97. Transl. Mierow, *Deeds of Frederick Barbarossa*, p. 189.
98. W. Goez, 'Fürstenprivilegien Friedrichs II.' in HRG vol. I cols 1358–61.
99. For the content, Arnold, *Princes and Territories*, pp. 202–9.
100. MGH Constitutiones vol. II, no. 196, pp. 241–7; H. Angermeier, 'Landfriedenspolitik und Landfriedensgesetzgebung unter den Staufern' in Fleckenstein, *Probleme um Friedrich II.*, pp. 167–86.

101. D. H. Green, *Medieval Listening and Reading. The Primary Reception of German Literature 800–1300* (Cambridge, 1994) pp. 99–101, 154–6.

102. G. Waitz (ed.), *Chronica regia Coloniensis. Annales maximi Colonienses*, MGH Scriptores in usum scholarum, vol. XVIII (Hanover, 1880) p. 267.

103. H. Angermeier, *Königtum und Landfriede im deutschen Spätmittelalter* (Munich, 1966).

104. H. Schlosser, 'Eike von Repgow' and F. Ebel, 'Sachsenspiegel' in HRG vol. I, cols 896–9 and IV, cols 1228–37; R. Lieberwirth, *Eike von Repchow und der Sachsenspiegel*, Sitzungsberichte der Sächsischen Akademie der Wissenschaften zu Leipzig, phil.-hist. Klasse, vol. CXXII, part 4 (Berlin, 1982).

105. MGH Constitutiones, vol. II, no. 438, pp. 596–602; A. Buschmann, 'Der Rheinische Bund von 1254–1257. Landfriede, Städte, Fürsten und Reichsverfassung im 13. Jahrhundert' in H. Maurer (ed.), *Kommunale Bündnisse Oberitaliens und Oberdeutschlands im Vergleich*, Vorträge und Forschungen vol. XXXIII (Sigmaringen, 1987) pp. 167–212.

106. MGH Constitutiones, vol. II, no. 427, pp. 570–9 (1244); L. Carlen, 'Eidgenossenschaft, Schweizerische' in HRG vol. I, cols 872–6.

107. P. Jaffé (ed.), *Monumenta Corbeiensia*, Bibliotheca Rerum Germanicarum vol. I (Berlin, 1864) no. 150 at p. 239.

108. J. Engel (ed.), *Grosser Historischer Weltatlas*, vol. II, *Mittelalter* (Munich, 1970) pp. 78–9.

109. *Casus Monasterii Petrishusensis* in MGH Scriptores, vol. XX, pp. 645 f; Schmidt and Schmale, *Gesta Frederici*, p. 152.

110. For example, K. J. Leyser, 'Frederick Barbarossa and the Hohenstaufen Polity', *Viator*, XIX (1988) 153–76.

111. R. Schneider, 'Landeserschliessung und Raumerfassung durch salische Herrscher' in Weinfurter, *Die Salier und das Reich* i, pp. 128–30.

112. T. Zotz, 'Carolingian Tradition and Ottonian-Salian Innovation: Comparative Observations on Palatine Policy in the Empire' in A. J. Duggan (ed.), *Kings and Kingship in Medieval Europe*, King's College London Medieval Studies vol. X (London, 1993) pp. 69–100,

113. E. Müller-Mertens, *Die Reichsstruktur im Spiegel der Herrschaftspraxis Ottos des Grossen*, Forschungen zur Mittelalterlichen Geschichte, vol. XXV (Berlin, 1980) and E. Müller-Mertens and W. Huschner, *Reichsintegration im Spiegel der Herrschaftspraxis*

Kaiser Konrads II., Forschungen zur Mittelalterlichen Geschichte, vol. XXXV (Weimar, 1992). For comment on the method, T. F. X. Noble's review of Müller-Merten's 1980 volume in *Speculum* LVI (1981) pp. 634–7; Bernhardt, *Itinerant Kingship*.

114. A. Gauert, 'Königspfalz' in HRG vol. II, cols 1044–55; useful report in English by T. Reuter in *English Historical Review* XCIX (1984) 818–20.

115. MGH Diplomata Henry III, no. 253, p. 337.

116. Fehring, *Archaeology of Medieval Germany*, p. 135.

117. C. Erdmann, 'Burg und Kirche zu Quedlinburg' in his *Ottonische Studien*, ed. H. Beumann (Darmstadt, 1968) pp. 83–106.

118. MGH Diplomata Frederick I, no. 1009, p. 305 (1189).

119. Quoted in J. Bumke, *Courtly Culture. Literature and Society in the High Middle Ages*, transl. T. Dunlap (Berkeley, Los Angeles and Oxford, 1991) p. 125.

120. MGH Diplomata Frederick I, no. 201, p. 337 (1158).

121. G. Beyreuther, 'Die Osterfeier als Akt königlicher Repräsentanz und Herrschaftsausübung unter Heinrich II. (1002–1024)' in D. Altenburg, J. Jarnut and H-H. Steinhoff (eds), *Feste und Feiern im Mittelalter. Paderborner Symposion des Mediävistenverbandes* (Sigmaringen, 1991) pp. 245–53.

122. Bumke, *Courtly Culture*, p. 464; G. B. Siragusa (ed.), *Liber ad Honorem Augusti di Pietro da Eboli*, Fonti per la Storia d'Italia (Rome, 1906) pp. 109–11.

123. The most convenient introduction remains Wolfgang Metz's *Das Servitium Regis. Zur Erforschung der wirtschaftlichen Grundlagen des hochmittelalterlichen deutschen Königtums*, Erträge der Forschung vol. LXXXIX (Darmstadt, 1978).

124. Trillmich, *Quellen*, p. 548 (1024); K. Strecker (ed.), *Die Tegernseer Briefsammlung (Fromund)*, MGH Epistolae selectae vol. III (Berlin, 1925) no. 125, p. 142 (1046–8).

125. J. Ficker, *Über das Eigenthum des Reichs am Reichskirchengute*, reprint (Darmstadt, 1967).

126. C. Brühl, 'Königsgastung' in HRG vol. II, cols 1032–4; MGH Diplomata Henry II, no. 256, pp. 293–301 (1013) and Henry IV, no. 237, pp. 299–301, dated 1070; see D. von Gladiss and A. Gawlik, 'Das servitium regis der Reichsabtei Remiremont', *Deutsches Archiv*, XXX (1974) 216–29.

127. MGH Diplomata Frederick I, no. 853, pp. 82–4 (1184); MGH Constitutiones vol. II, no. 73, ch. 10, p. 90 (1220); Metz, *Servitium Regis*, pp. 104–5.

128. MGH Diplomata Lothar III, no. 119, pp. 190–3 and Conrad III, no. 167, pp. 302–4.

129. See now R. Schieffer, 'Eigenkirche, Eigenkirchenwesen' in LMA vol. III, cols. 1705–8.

130. S. Weinfurter, *Die Geschichte der Eichstätter Bischöfe des Anonymus Haserensis. Edition – Übersetzung – Kommentar*, Eichstätter Studien, New Series, vol. XXIV (Regensburg, 1987) p. 82.

131. Schmidt, *Lampert. Annalen*, pp. 88, 324–6; MGH Diplomata Henry IV, nos 264–5, pp. 339–40 (1073).

132. H. Seibert, 'Libertas und Reichsabtei. Zur Klosterpolitik der salischen Herrscher' in Weinfurter, *Die Salier und das Reich* ii, pp. 518–20; MGH Constitutiones, vol. I, no. 439, pp. 645–6 (1027).

133. MGH Diplomata Otto II, no. 191, pp. 217–19 (979), Henry II, no. 330, pp. 417–18 (1015) and no. 433, pp. 554–5 (1020); on the arrangements, see Bernhardt, *Itinerant Kingship*, pp. 248–52.

134. Mommsen and Morrison, *Imperial Lives and Letters*, p. 73.

135. MGH Diplomata Henry IV, nos. 165–6, pp. 214–5 (1065); M. Herberger, 'Krongut' in HRG vol. II, cols 1217–29.

136. *Annales Sancti Disibodi*, MGH Scriptores vol. XVII, p. 23; MGH Diplomata Frederick I, no. 199, pp. 332–3 (1158); *Arnoldi Chronica Slavorum*, MGH Scriptores vol. XXI, p. 246.

137. C. Brühl and T. Kölzer (ed.), *Das Tafelgüterverzeichnis des römischen Königs (Ms. Bonn S. 1559)* (Cologne and Vienna, 1979); Metz, *Staufischer Güterverzeichnisse*, pp. 6–51 and *Das Servitium Regis*, pp. 21–44.

138. MGH Diplomata Henry IV, no. 104, pp. 137–8 (1063).

139. Mierow, *Deeds of Frederick Barbarossa*, p. 238; V. Colorni, *Le tre leggi perdute di Roncaglia, ritrovate in un manoscritto parigino*, Scritti in memoria di Antonio Giuffrè, vol. I (Milan, 1966); see A. Haverkamp, 'Die Regalien-, Schutz- und Steuerpolitik in Italien unter Friedrich Barbarossa bis zur Entstehung des Lombardenbundes', *Zeitschrift für bayerische Landesgeschichte*, XXIX (1966) 3–156.

140. MGH Constitutiones, vol. II, no. 55, pp. 66–7 (1216) and no. 338, pp. 446–7 (1242); see Metz, *Staufische Güterverzeichnisse*, pp. 116–21.

141. W. Kraft, *Das Urbar der Reichsmarschälle von Pappenheim*, Schriftenreihe zur bayerischen Landesgeschichte vol. III (Munich, 1929).

142. Metz, *Staufische Güterverzeichnisse*, pp. 52–76, 94–7, 122–33.

143. MGH Constitutiones vol. III, no. 644, pp. 627–31 (c. 1300).
144. MGH Constitutiones vol. II, no. 10, p. 12.
145. Arnoldi Chronica Slavorum, MGH Scriptores vol. XXI, p. 247 (1209).
146. Hucker, Kaiser Otto IV., pp. 90–4.
147. Explained by Bernhardt, Itinerant Kingship, pp. 60–8.
148. Weinfurter, Geschichte der Eichstätter Bischöfe, p. 83.
149. Fried, Der Weg in die Geschichte, p. 100.
150. P. Moraw, 'Versuch über die Entstehung des Reichstags' in H. Weber (ed.), Politische Ordnungen und soziale Kräfte im alten Reich, Veröffentlichungen des Instituts für Europäische Geschichte Mainz, Beiheft VIII (Wiesbaden, 1980) pp. 1–36.
151. Mommsen and Morrison, Imperial Lives and Letters, pp. 168–9 (1084 or 1097).
152. MGH Diplomata Frederick I, nos 501–3, pp. 429–35 (1166).
153. Mierow, Deeds of Frederick Barbarossa, p. 164; MGH Diplomata Frederick I, no. 151, pp. 255–60.
154. Mierow, Deeds of Frederick Barbarossa, p. 163; B. Schwenk, 'Das Hundetragen. Ein Rechtsbrauch im Mittelalter', Historisches Jahrbuch, CX (1990) 289–308.
155. MGH Diplomata Frederick I, nos 774, pp. 328–30 (1179) and 795, p. 362 (1180).
156. Mierow, Deeds of Frederick Barbarossa, p. 164; MGH Diplomata Frederick I, nos 143–5, pp. 240–4.
157. M. Lindner, 'Fest und Herrschaft unter Kaiser Friedrich Barbarossa' in Engel and Töpfer (ed.), Kaiser Friedrich Barbarossa, pp. 151–3.
158. MGH Diplomata Frederick I, no. 201, pp. 335–7.
159. Waitz, Chronica regia Coloniensis, p. 139; see J. Fleckenstein, 'Friedrich Barbarossa und das Rittertum. Zur Bedeutung der grossen Mainzer Hoftage von 1184 und 1188' in Festschrift für Hermann Heimpel zum 70. Geburtstag, vol. II, Veröffentlichungen des Max-Planck-Instituts für Geschichte, vol. XXXVI/2 (Göttingen, 1972) pp. 1023–41.
160. Trillmich, Quellen, pp. 334–6.
161. Reuter, Annals of Fulda, pp. 62–3.
162. For all the details, see E. Steindorff, Jahrbücher des deutschen Reiches unter Heinrich III., vol. I, new edn (Darmstadt, 1963) pp. 229–33.
163. G. Theuerkauf, 'Designation' in HRG vol. I, cols 682–5.

164. H. Bloch (ed.), *Annales Marbacenses qui dicuntur*, MGH Scriptores rerum Germanicarum in usum scholarum vol. IX (Hanover and Leipzig, 1907) p. 68.

165. C. C. Bayley, *The Formation of the German College of Electors in the Mid-Thirteenth Century* (Toronto, 1949). There is a colossal secondary literature in German.

166. W. D. Fritz (ed.), *Die Goldene Bulle Kaiser Karls IV. vom Jahre 1356*, MGH Fontes iuris in usum scholarum, vol. XI (Weimar, 1972).

167. G. Althoff and H. Keller, *Heinrich I. und Otto der Grosse. Neubeginn auf karolingischem Erbe*, Persönlichkeit und Geschichte, vols CXXII–III (Göttingen and Zurich, 1985) and the debates in H. Kämpf (ed.), *Die Entstehung des Deutschen Reiches (Deutschland um 900)* and in E. Hlawitschka (ed.), *Königswahl und Thronfolge in ottonisch-frühdeutscher Zeit*, Wege der Forschung, vols I and CLXXVIII (Darmstadt, 1971).

168. Bauer and Rau, *Quellen*, pp. 84–6.

169. Mommsen and Morrison, *Imperial Lives and Letters*, pp. 57–68.

170. Schmale and Schmale-Ott, *Quellen*, p. 334; W. Schlesinger, 'Die Wahl Rudolfs von Schwaben zum Gegenkönig 1077 in Forchheim' in Fleckenstein, *Investiturstreit und Reichsverfassung*, pp. 61–85.

171. Mierow, *Deeds of Frederick Barbarossa*, p, 115.

172. L. Vones, 'Der gescheiterte Königsmacher. Erzbischof Adalbert I. von Mainz und die Wahl von 1125', *Historisches Jahrbuch*, CXV (1995) 85–124.

173. Eckhardt, *Sachsenspiegel Landrecht*, p. 127.

174. For summaries of the arguments, see G. Theuerkauf, 'Königswahl' and E. Kaufmann, 'Kurfürsten' in HRG vol. II, cols 1061–5, 1277–90.

175. Albert of Stade, *Annales*, MGH Scriptores vol. XVI, p. 367.

176. Reported by E. Schubert in 'Kurfürsten' in LMA vol. V, cols 1581–3.

177. In English see Arnold, *Princes and Territories*, pp. 32–9.

178. MGH Constitutiones vol. II, no. 329, pp. 439–41.

179. Trillmich, *Quellen*, p. 536.

180. 'Elective Kingship and the Unity of Medieval Germany', *German History*, IX (1991) 124–35.

181. MGH Diplomata Henry II, no. 277, pp. 326–7 (1013–14) and Frederick I, no. 513, pp. 447–8 (1166); MGH Constitutiones vol. II, no. 193, pp. 236–8 (1235).

Conclusion: Tasks of Governance in Medieval Germany

1. MGH Constitutiones vol. II, no. 155, p. 190.
2. Trillmich, *Quellen*, p. 326; MGH Diplomata Henry IV, no. 283, pp. 366–7.
3. John of St Arnulf, *Vita Iohannis Abbatis Gorziensis*, MGH Scriptores vol. IV, pp. 376–7.
4. Mommsen and Morrison, *Imperial Lives and Letters*, p. 72; see now H. Hoffmann, *Mönchskönig und 'rex idiota'. Studien zur Kirchenpolitik Heinrichs II. und Konrads II.*, MGH Studien und Texte, vol. VIII (Hanover, 1993).
5. Pertinent remarks in J. B. Gillingham, *The Kingdom of Germany in the High Middle Ages, 900–1200*, Historical Association Pamphlets, no. LXXVII (London, 1971); Mommsen and Morrison, *Imperial Lives and Letters*, pp. 3–51; D. J. A. Matthew, 'Reflections on the Medieval Roman Empire', *History*, LXXVII (1992) 363–90; T. Reuter, 'The Medieval German *Sonderweg*? The Empire and its Rulers in the High Middle Ages' in Duggan, *Kings and Kingship*, pp. 179–211.
6. H. Dilcher, 'Authenticae' in HRG vol. I, cols 276–7.
7. A. Erler, 'Heiliges Römisches Reich' in HRG vol. II, cols 45–8; P. Moraw, 'Heiliges Reich' in LMA vol. IV, cols 2025–8.
8. A. Mayhew, *Rural Settlement and Farming in Germany* (London, 1973) pp. 37–90; Arnold, *Princes and Territories*, pp. 153–67.
9. MGH Constitutiones vol. II, no. 196 (ch. 28), pp. 246–7 (1235) and no. 270, p. 378 (1248).
10. For an account of them in English, Arnold, *Princes and Territories*, pp. 88–132, 186–210.
11. In English, see Bernhardt, *Itinerant Kingship*, pp. 60–8.
12. 'Die Pfalzen im dreizehnten Jahrhundert' in J. Fleckenstein (ed.), *Herrschaft und Stand. Untersuchungen zur Sozialgeschichte im 13. Jahrhundert*, Veröffentlichungen des Max-Planck-Instituts für Geschichte vol. LI (Göttingen, 1977) pp. 277–301.
13. *Ad Heinricum IV Imperatorem Libri VII*, MGH Scriptores vol. XI, pp. 597–681.
14. On the collision of these ideas and polemics, see now T. Struve, 'Die Stellung des Königtums in der politischen Theorie der Salierzeit' and H. Vollrath, 'Konfliktwahrnehmung und Konfliktdarstellung in erzählenden Quellen des 11. Jahrhunderts' in Weinfurter, *Die Salier und das Reich* iii, pp. 217–44, 279–96.

15. See Part II, note 70 above.

16. A. Wendehorst, 'Erlung' in LMA vol. III, col. 2155.

17. Mommsen and Morrison, *Imperial Lives and Letters*, pp. 102, 106, 121.

18. MGH Diplomata Lothar III, no. 80, pp. 124–6 (1136) and Frederick I, no. 568, p. 39 (1170).

19. MGH Diplomata Henry IV, no. 421, p. 563, adapting Romans 13, 4 and I Peter 2, 14.

20. H. Aubin, 'The Lands East of the Elbe and German Colonization Eastwards' in M. M. Postan (ed.), *The Cambridge Economic History of Europe*, vol. I, *The Agrarian Life of the Middle Ages*, 2nd edn (Cambridge, 1966) pp. 449–86; W. Schlesinger (ed.), *Die deutsche Ostsiedlung des Mittelalters als Problem der europäischen Geschichte*, Vorträge und Forschungen, vol. XVIII (Sigmaringen, 1975); F. L. Carsten, *The Origins of Prussia* (Oxford, 1954) pp. 1–88.

21. Arnold, *Count and Bishop*, pp. 1–43.

22. MGH Constitutiones vol. I, nos 426–7, pp. 608–10 (1084, 1094) and 430, pp. 613–15 (before 1108).

23. MGH Diplomata Frederick I, nos 25, pp. 39–44 (1152), 774, pp. 328–30 (1179) and 988, pp. 273–7 (1186/88).

24. Mierow, *Deeds of Frederick Barbarossa*, p. 109; MGH Diplomata Conrad III, no. 252, pp. 438–40 (1151) and Frederick I, no. 795, p. 363 (1180).

25. Arnold, *Princes and Territories*, pp. 100–2.

26. MGH Diplomata Frederick I, no. 546, pp. 3–7; F. Merzbacher, *Judicium Provinciale Ducatus Franconiae. Das kaiserliche Landgericht des Herzogtums Franken-Würzburg im Spätmittelalter*, Schriftenreihe zur bayerischen Landesgeschichte, vol. LIV (Munich, 1956).

27. W. Ebel, 'Lübisches Recht' and G. Buchda, 'Magdeburger Recht' in HRG vol. III, cols 77–84, 134–8: Engel, *Grosser Historischer Weltatlas* ii, p. 98.

28. G. Gudian, 'Die grundlegenden Institutionen der Länder', pp. 404–23, 447–9, 453–5 and A. Wolf, 'Die Gesetzgebung der entstehenden Territorien', pp. 586–626 in H. Coing (ed.), *Handbuch der Quellen und Literatur der neueren europäischen Privatrechtsgeschichte*, vol. I, *Mittelalter 1100–1500* (Munich, 1973).

29. MGH Constitutiones vol. II, no. 196, p. 241.

30. MGH Constitutiones vol. II, no. 305, p. 420.

31. 'Hochgerichtsbarkeit' in HRG vol. II, col. 173.

32. Arnold, *Princes and Territories*, pp. 186–210.
33. H. Helbig and L. Weinrich (eds), *Urkunden und erzählende Quellen zur deutschen Ostsiedlung im Mittelalter*, vol. I, AQ vol. XXVIA (Darmstadt, 1968) no. 48, pp. 206–8; *Herimanni Altahensis Annales*, MGH Scriptores vol. XVII, p. 397; *Annales Pegavienses et Bosovienses*, MGH Scriptores vol. XVI, p. 254.
34. Arnold, *Princes and Territories*, pp. 135–85.
35. MGH Constitutiones vol. III, no. 478, p. 466 (1292).
36. See J. Petersohn, ' "De ortu principum Thuringie". Eine Schrift über die Fürstenwürde der Landgrafen von Thüringen aus dem 12. Jahrhundert', *Deutsches Archiv*, XLVIII (1992) 585–608.
37. Helbig and Weinrich, *Ostsiedlung* i, no. 32, pp. 146–8 (*c.* 1160); H. Ludat, 'Albrecht der Bär' in LMA vol. I, cols 316–17.
38. P. Spiess, 'Pfalz (Kurpfalz)' in HRG vol. III, cols 1659–60.
39. MGH Diplomata Frederick I, no. 151, pp. 255–60; R. Hoke, 'Privilegium minus' in HRG vol. III, cols 2014–20.
40. Lechner, *Die Babenberger*, pp. 283–4.
41. MGH Constitutiones vol. II, no. 440, pp. 604–8 (now dated 1254); vol. III, no. 122, pp. 116–18 (1276) and no. 273, pp. 265–6 (1281).
42. MGH Diplomata Frederick I, no. 497, pp. 423–5 (1165).
43. MGH Constitutiones vol. II, no. 197, pp. 263–5 (1235); G. Pischke, 'Braunschweig–Lüneburg, Herzogtum' in LMA vol. II, cols 586–8.
44. Confirmed in MGH Diplomata Frederick I, no. 732, pp. 272–7 (1178).
45. MGH Constitutiones vol. III, no. 205, pp. 190–1; see H. Dopsch, 'Die Wittelsbacher und das Erzstift Salzburg' in Glaser, *Die Zeit der frühen Herzöge* i, pp. 268–84.
46. Weinrich, *Quellen*, no. 111, p. 426 and 126, pp. 508–10; L. Carlen, 'Eidgenossenschaft, Schweizerische' in HRG vol. I, cols 872–6.
47. C. J. Wells, *German: A Linguistic History to 1945* (Oxford, 1985) pp. 95–125, esp. p. 109.
48. W. König, *Atlas zur deutschen Sprache. Tafeln und Texte* (Munich, 1978) pp. 56–77; W. B. Lockwood, *An Informal History of the German Language*, The Language Library, 2nd edn (London, 1976) pp. 11–77.
49. Mommsen and Morrison, *Imperial Lives and Letters*, pp. 66–8.
50. MGH Constitutiones vol. II, no. 193, p. 237.

51. For example, MGH Diplomata Henry II, no. 283, pp. 334–5 (1014); Henry III, no. 294, pp. 399–400 (1052); Frederick I, no. 433, p. 328 (1164).
52. MGH Diplomata Frederick I, no. 616, pp. 106–7 (1174) and no. 886, p. 133 (1184).

Select Bibliography

D. Abulafia, *Frederick II. A Medieval Emperor* (London, 1988).

B. Arnold, *Princes and Territories in Medieval Germany* (Cambridge, 1991).

B. Arnold, *Count and Bishop in Medieval Germany* (Philadelphia, 1991).

B. S. Bachrach, *Merovingian Military Organization 481–751* (Minneapolis, 1972).

G. Barraclough, *Mediaeval Germany 911–1250*, 2 vols (Oxford, 1939 and 1961).

C. C. Bayley, *The Formation of the German College of Electors in the Mid-Thirteenth Century* (Toronto, 1949).

J. W. Bernhardt, *Itinerant Kingship and Royal Monasteries in Early Medieval Germany* (Cambridge, 1993).

U-R. Blumenthal, *The Investiture Controversy. Church and Monarchy from the Ninth to the Twelfth Century* (Philadelphia, 1988).

C. R. Bowlus, *Franks, Moravians, and Magyars. The Struggle for the Middle Danube, 788–907* (Philadelphia, 1995).

T. C. van Cleve, *The Emperor Frederick II of Hohenstaufen. Immutator Mundi* (Oxford, 1972).

K. F. Drew, *The Laws of the Salian Franks* (Philadelphia, 1991).

E. Emerton, *The Correspondence of Pope Gregory VII* (New York, 1932 and 1969).

G. P. Fehring, *The Archaeology of Medieval Germany. An Introduction*, transl. R. Samson (London and New York, 1991).

H. Fichtenau, *The Carolingian Empire*, transl. P. Munz (Oxford, 1957).

J. Fleckenstein, *Early Medieval Germany*, transl. B. S. Smith (Amsterdam, 1978).

R. Folz, *The Concept of Empire in Western Europe from the Fifth to the Fourteenth Century*, transl. S. A. Ogilvie (London, 1969).

H. Fuhrmann, *Germany in the High Middle Ages c. 1050–1200*, transl. T. Reuter (Cambridge, 1986).

F. L. Ganshof, *The Carolingians and the Frankish Monarchy. Studies in Carolingian History*, transl. J. Sondheimer (London, 1971).

P. J. Geary, *Before France and Germany. The Creation and Transformation of the Merovingian World* (New York and Oxford, 1988).

J. B. Gillingham, *The Kingdom of Germany in the High Middle Ages, 900–1200* (London, 1971).

P. Godman and R. Collins, *Charlemagne's Heir. New Perspectives on the Reign of Louis the Pious, 814–840* (Oxford, 1990).

A. Haverkamp, *Medieval Germany 1056–1273*, transl. H. Braun and R. Mortimer (Oxford, 1988).

B. H. Hill, *Medieval Monarchy in Action. The German Empire from Henry I to Henry IV* (London, 1972).

D. C. Jackman, *The Konradiner. A Study in Genealogical Methodology* (Frankfurt am Main, 1990).

C. S. Jaeger, *The Origins of Courtliness. Civilizing Trends and the Formation of Courtly Ideals 923–1210* (Philadelphia, 1985).

E. James, *The Franks* (Oxford and New York, 1988).

K. Jordan, *Henry the Lion. A Biography*, transl. P. S. Falla (Oxford, 1986).

P. D. King, *Charlemagne* (London, 1986).

K. J. Leyser, *Rule and Conflict in an Early Medieval Society. Ottonian Saxony* (London, 1979).

K. J. Leyser, *Medieval Germany and its Neighbours, 900–1250* (London, 1982).

K. J. Leyser, *Communications and Power in Medieval Europe*, 2 vols (London and Rio Grande, 1994).

P. Llewellyn, *Rome in the Dark Ages* (London, 1971 and 1993).

H. R. Loyn and J. Percival, *The Reign of Charlemagne. Documents on Carolingian Government and Administration* (London, 1975).

A. Mayhew, *Rural Settlement and Farming in Germany* (London, 1973).

H. Mayr-Harting, *Ottonian Book Illumination. An Historical Study*, 2 vols (London and New York, 1991).

C. C. Mierow, *The Deeds of Frederick Barbarossa by Otto of Freising and his Continuator, Rahewin* (New York, 1953).

T. E. Mommsen and K. F. Morrison, *Imperial Lives and Letters of the Eleventh Century* (New York and London, 1962).

P. Munz, *Frederick Barbarossa. A Study of Medieval Politics* (London, 1969).

T. Reuter, *Germany in the Early Middle Ages c. 800–1056* (London and New York, 1991).

T. Reuter, *The Annals of Fulda. Ninth-Century Histories Volume II* (Manchester and New York, 1992).

P. Riché, *The Carolingians. A Family who Forged Europe*, transl. M. I. Allen (Philadelphia, 1993).

I. S. Robinson, *Authority and Resistance in the Investiture Contest. The Polemical Literature of the late Eleventh Century* (Manchester and New York, 1978).

B. W. Scholz, *Carolingian Chronicles. Royal Frankish Annals and Nithard's Histories* (Ann Arbor, 1970).

G. Tabacco, *The Struggle for Power in Medieval Italy. Structures of Political Rule*, transl. R. B. Jensen (Cambridge, 1989).

L. Thorpe, *Einhard and Notker the Stammerer. Two Lives of Charlemagne* (Harmondsworth, 1969).

F. J. Tschan, *The Chronicle of the Slavs by Helmold, Priest of Bosau* (New York, 1935).

F. J. Tschan, *Saint Bernward of Hildesheim. His Life and Times*, 3 vols (Notre Dame, 1942–52).

J. M. Wallace-Hadrill, *The Fourth Book of the Chronicle of Fredegar with its Continuations* (London etc., 1960).

J. M. Wallace-Hadrill, *The Long-Haired Kings and Other Studies in Frankish History* (London, 1962).

H. Wolfram, *History of the Goths*, transl. T. J. Dunlap (Berkeley and London, 1988).

I. Wood, *The Merovingian Kingdoms 450–751* (London and New York, 1994).

F. A. Wright, *The Works of Liudprand of Cremona* (London, 1930).

Index

Anglo-Saxons, Angli, 25, 41, 46–7, 133
Annales regni Francorum, 2, 3, 18, 79
Annales Stadenses, 178
Annals of Fulda, 7, 8, 20, 129, 130, 132
Anno II, archbishop of Cologne, 11, 167
Annolied, 10–11, 12, 62–3
Anselm, Swabian count, 53–4
Antichrist, 116, 123–4
Apocalypse, 78, 121, 192
Apulia, 62, 113
Aquileia, patriarchate of, 61, 186
Aquitaine, 2, 18, 44
Archipoeta, 106
Arduin, margrave of Ivrea, 93, 175
Aribo, archbishop of Mainz, 161, 192
Armenia, 10, 107
Arn, bishop of Würzburg, 34
Arnaldus, son of Odalric, 146–7
Arnold, archbishop of Mainz, 172
Arnold of Lübeck, chronicler, 169
Arnulf of Carinthia, emperor, 20, 21, 22, 24, 28, 34, 36, 38, 83, 131, 132, 175
Arnulf, duke of Bavaria, 4, 21–2, 36, 49, 175
Ascanians, Saxon dynasty, 71, 189, 190
Augsburg, 53–4, 123, 131, 147, 153
Augustine of Hippo, bishop, 101, 184
Augustus Caesar, 115, 180
Austrasia, Frankish province, 17, 26, 31, 34, 37, 39, 128
Austria, 15, 20, 23, 109, 174, 177, 179, 189–90, 191
Avars, Avar khanate, 2, 15, 18, 19, 21, 24, 78
Azzo II, margrave of Este, 60

Babenbergs, Franconian dynasty, 35, 36
Babylon, Babylonia, 11, 40
Baden, margraves of, 179
Badenweiler, 165
Balderich of Florennes, biographer, 144

Balkans, 42
Bamberg, 35, 92, 114, 161, 163
foundation of bishopric in 1007, 57, 94, 121, 140–1, 149
bishops and see of, 58, 61, 67, 70, 72, 152, 179
bannus, judicial authority, 133, 137, 190
Basel, 67
Basil I, emperor, 82
Beatrice of Burgundy, empress, 173
Benedict V, pope, 98
Benedict VIII, pope, 93, 96, 124
Benedict IX, pope, 98
Benedict of Monte Soratte, chronicler, 87, 119
Benno II, bishop of Osnabrück, 143
Benzo, bishop of Alba, 123, 184
Berengar of Friuli, emperor, 83, 131
Berengar II of Ivrea, king, 84
Bernard, abbot of Clairvaux, 8, 101
Bernhard II, duke of Saxony, 173
Bernhard of Anhalt, duke of Saxony, 66, 71, 72, 169
Bernhardt, John, 159
Bernward, bishop of Hildesheim, 5, 91
Berthold, duke of Bavaria, 22
Berthold of Rheinfelden, duke of Swabia, 65
Berthold I of Zähringen, duke of Carinthia, 62, 63, 65
Berthold II, duke of Zähringen, 65, 154
Berthold V, duke of Zähringen, 169
Berthold, count of Schweinfurt, 147
Berthold of Reichenau, chronicler, 6
Besançon, 106, 109, 146, 176
Biberich, manor, 131
Billungs, Saxon dynasty, 45–6, 52–3, 60, 66, 71, 173
Birten, battle of (939), 136
Bitonto, cathedral, 114
Bogen, counts of, 72–3
Bohemia, 19, 50, 132, 173
kings of, 177–8, 179
Boleslav I Chrobry, duke of Poland, 90
Bologna, 103, 106

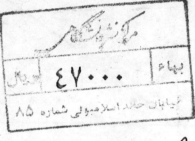